Other books in the Jossey-Bass Public Administration Series:

Reinventing
the Pentagon

Fred Thompson and L. R. Jones

Reinventing the Pentagon

How the New Public Management Can Bring Institutional Renewal

Jossey-Bass Publishers • San Francisco

Substantial discounts on bulk quantities of Jossey-Bass books are available to corporations, professional associations, and other organizations. For details and discount information, contact the special sales department at Jossey-Bass Inc., Publishers. (415) 433-1740; Fax (415) 433-0499.

For international orders, please contact your local Paramount Publishing International office.

Manufactured in the United States of America. Nearly all Jossey-Bass books and jackets are printed on recycled paper that contains at least 50 percent recycled waste, including 10 percent postconsumer waste. Many of our materials are also printed with vegetable-based ink; during the printing process these inks emit fewer volatile organic compounds (VOCs) than petroleum-based inks. VOCs contribute to the formation of smog.

Library of Congress Cataloging-in-Publication Data

Thompson, Frederick.
    Reinventing the Pentagon : how the new public management can bring institutional renewal / Fred Thompson, L. R. Jones. — 1st ed.
        p.   cm.—(The Jossey-Bass public administration series)
    Includes bibliographical references and index.
    ISBN 1-55542-710-3
    1. United States. Dept of Defense—Management—History.
    2. Government productivity—United States—History.   I. Jones, L. R.
    II. Title.   III. Series.
    UB153.T46   1994
    353.6—dc20   94-7515
                                                                            CIP

FIRST EDITION
HB Printing   10 9 8 7 6 5 4 3 2 1   *Code 9468*

The Jossey-Bass
Public Administration Series

Consulting Editor
Public Management and Administration

James L. Perry
Indiana University

Contents

Preface

BEFORE MILITARY FORCES can be used, they must be raised, equipped, and organized. Under the easiest of circumstances, this is a difficult, long-term, and highly complex managerial challenge. It calls for solutions to serious problems of organization and control, managing relationships with suppliers, and choosing between alternative institutional designs and governance arrangements. Under conditions of deep retrenchment, the challenge is doubly difficult. Although the Goldwater-Nichols Department of Defense Reorganization Act of 1986 corrected some of the more pathological administrative shortcomings of the Defense Department, we believe that it is still ill-equipped to meet this challenge.

The new public management provides some of the solutions the Department of Defense needs to deal with the problems it faces. The prominence of the new public management is due primarily to David Osborne, a journalist, and Ted Gaebler, a former city manager, and their extraordinary manifesto: *Reinventing Government: How the Entrepreneurial Spirit is Transforming the Public Sector from Schoolhouse to Statehouse, City Hall to the Pentagon* (1992). The recent publication of *The Gore Report on Reinventing Government: From Red Tape to Results, Creating a Government That Works Better and Costs Less* (1993) has further heightened interest in the new public management. The *Gore Report* calls for inventing "a government that puts people first" by creating a clear sense of mission, by steering more and rowing less, by delegating authority, by replacing rules and regulations with incentives, by developing budgets based on results, by exposing government operations to competition, by searching for market rather than administrative solutions, and, whenever possible, by measuring the success of government's actions in terms of customer satisfaction (p. 7).

Osborne and Gaebler freely admit that they did not originate the new public management. They acknowledge that their main contribution lies in "synthesizing the ideas and experiences of others." Rather, *Reinventing Government* is part of a much larger movement—one that is now worldwide. The new public management reformers are found in Argentina, Brazil, Britain, Canada, Denmark, Finland, Germany, the Netherlands, Singapore, Sweden, and especially New Zealand and Australia, as well as in governments at all three levels in the United States.

Background and Approach

What is new about the new public management? First of all, many of the core concepts of the new public management are new. Some reflect the dramatic restructuring that American business went through in the 1980s. Others—the critique of functional specialization, process reengineering, just-in-time inventory management, and activity-based costing and cycle-time burdening—are recent products of the information revolution. Second, while the presumption that managing in government is similar to and relies on many of the same skills and tools as managing in the private sector is not new, the enthusiasm with which it has been embraced by practicing public administrators is.

But the most important thing that is new about the new public management is its reliance on the new economics of institutions and organizations. The economics of institutions and organizations deals with issues of institutional design and administrative governance. It provides public managers with the tools they need to handle the complex design problems they face—problems that dwarf the simple make-or-buy decisions faced by their business counterparts. Consequently, it provides an analytical foundation for the new public management.

Furthermore, the economics of institutions and organizations has been put to the test and has been found to work. The design of regulatory instruments (ranging from effluent markets and bubbles to outright deregulation of the airlines and interstate motor carriage) in the United States and the privatization and securitization of an astonishing array of government-owned assets (and some liabilities) in Europe, Great Britain, Canada, and the antipodes are a few of its successes. If it were not for these accomplishments, we doubt that the ideas of the new public managers would command the attention they are now getting—nor would they deserve it.

Hence, we believe it is fair to say that the new public management owes as much to economists like Kenneth Arrow, David Baron, William Baumol, Albert Breton, Ronald Wintrobe, Harold Demsetz, Victor Goldberg, Michael Jensen, Paul Milgrom, William Niskanen, Roger Noll, Charles Schultze, and especially Ronald Coase and Oliver Williamson as it does to more popular management writers such as Peter Drucker, Theodore Levitt, Thomas Peters, Joseph Bower, or Robert Anthony.

Because they wish to appeal to a broad lay audience, however, many of the proponents of the new public management downplay its analytical roots in the economics of institutions and organizations. While the logic behind this approach is understandable, it has not been without cost. In the first place, the failure to acknowledge the analytical roots of the new public management has led many of our peers in the field of public administration to conclude that the new public management is mostly rhetoric without any real content. Consequently, they assert that it is neither new nor worthy of serious intellectual attention or study. In the second place, the failure to make explicit use of the economics of institutions and organizations often deprives the new public managers of the capacity to give concrete advice about the implementation of their constructive ideas.

In contrast, in *Reinventing the Pentagon* we explicitly acknowledge the relevance of the economics of institutions and organizations to the new public management and make use of its insights whenever possible. As a result, we are often able to be specific and concrete where more popular accounts are ambiguous or obscure. For example, like most of the advocates of the new public management, we talk about streamlining controls, transforming organizational structures, implementing performance budgeting, simplifying financial reporting, creating more flexible and responsive hiring systems, reinventing procurement, and reengineering administrative processes through the use of information technology. But we also show how to organize the Pentagon to make these reforms work—how to align the Department of Defense's organizational strategy with its structure, how to redesign governance relationships between its mission centers and their suppliers both within and outside the department, how to adjust individual and organizational self-interest to the objectives of national defense, how to choose between alternative program designs, how to implement responsibility budgets (the only sound approach to mission-driven, results-oriented budgeting), how to decentralize, when to replace rules and regulations with incentives, and when to use competition and market mechanisms rather than administrative solutions.

Our emphasis on organizational design and the choice of governance mechanisms also distinguishes this work from most of the literature on downsizing the Department of Defense, which focuses directly on the content of the defense budget and its formulation, preparation, and enactment. We focus on program and budget execution rather than formulation. We believe that the most important events of the spending cycle occur *after* the enactment of the budget. As a consequence, we stress the importance of well-designed and well-operated management controls to bringing about more efficient investment in weapons and support systems, maintenance of readiness and sustainability, and, ultimately, a better match between America's military force structure and logistical support capabilities and its foreign policy objectives and overseas commitments.

This book has a single subject but two intended audiences. Its subject is managing the U.S. Department of Defense. Its primary audience is made up of individuals who are concerned with applying the new public management to the Department of Defense, the world's largest and most complex organization. But we hope that it will also be of considerable interest to our colleagues in the field of public administration and policy who want to know more about the ideas that underlie the slogans and catch phrases used by the champions of the new public management and about the practical implementation of those ideas.

Outline of the Book

In the introduction to this volume, we show how much the Department of Defense will downsize during this decade and, by analogy to other demobilizations, demonstrate the increased importance of the efficiency with which military forces are raised, equipped, and organized.

Part One shows how the Pentagon got to be the way it is. Chapter One focuses on the consequences of the incomplete reorganization that followed World War II, the rise of pressures that led to administrative centralization, and the gradual emergence of a Cold War strategy.

Chapter Two addresses the failure of the Department of Defense to align its structure with its strategy, especially the failure of the administrative reform proposals of the Eisenhower administration and the unintended consequences of the well-intentioned but organizationally inept reforms carried out during the McNamara era.

Chapter Three concerns congressional attempts to make the Department of Defense more efficient and the Pentagon's response to congressional attention to the details of its administration. This response, as we show, ultimately embraced many of the tenets of the new public management—decentralizing decision-making powers; eliminating unneeded activities and administrative structures and investing in greater productivity; streamlining procurement, budgeting, and financial management; decentralizing personnel policy; eliminating regulatory overkill; and using market mechanisms to solve problems.

Part Two offers prescriptions for change. Chapter Four concerns the relationship between the Department of Defense and the industry that supplies it with the tools of war. It deals with the problem of modernizing the weapons industry and the weapons themselves.

Chapter Five looks at the problem of streamlining the acquisition process.

Chapter Six outlines the fundamental rules that should govern institutional design and show how they should be applied in the Department of Defense to redesign governance mechanisms and the Pentagon's relationships with its suppliers, both external and internal.

Chapter Seven is an extended case study of organizational reduction, focusing on the problem of base closure, which shows some of the causes as well the costs of administrative centralization and excessive congressional oversight and administrative control. This chapter demonstrates both the political feasibility of reinventing the Pentagon and the need for reformers to attend carefully to the propriety and the perceived fairness of the changes they make.

Chapter Eight presents our recommendations for reforming both the Department of Defense's internal architecture and its governance arrangements. It also outlines the changes in the Pentagon's personnel, accounting, and financial management practices and in the congressional appropriations, authorization, and oversight processes that are needed to make mission-driven, results-oriented budgeting a reality. At the end of this chapter, we assess the political and administrative feasibility of our recommendations.

Acknowledgments

We wish express our appreciation to the many men and women in the Department of Defense, Congress, the military commands, the defense agencies, and private industry that we interviewed for this volume. In particular, we would like to thank Robert Anthony and Donald Shycoff, former defense comptrollers; Sean O'Keefe, former Navy secretary; the military departments' assistant secretaries for financial management; Rear Admirals Richard Milligan and Stephen Loftus; and Charles Nemfakos, Robert Panek, and Peter Quinn, Navy budgeteers. Others to whom we owe thanks are Major General William McCall; Blair Ewing; Leonard Campbell; John Raines; Robert Shue; Colonel J. K. Stringer, Jr. (U.S.M.C., Ret.);

Rachel Kopperman, from the Office of the Defense Comptroller; Irving Buckstein, associate director of the Navy's Office of Programming; and Marvin Phaup and Roy Meyers of the Congressional Budget Office.

We also wish to express our appreciation for the help given us by Donald Atwood, who died as this volume went to press. Don Atwood was Secretary Dick Cheney's principal deputy and the driving force behind the management reforms initiated during that era. He was truly committed to reinventing the Pentagon; he will be missed.

We would like to thank the many academic colleagues who helped us with this research, including Michael Barzelay, Demetrios Caraley, Peter deLeon, Richard Doyle, Kenneth Euske, David Harr, William Kovacic, Pat Larkey, Earl Littrell, Jerry McCaffery, Steven Maser, Steven Mehay, James Perry, Tallman Trask, Aidan Vining, David Weimer, and especially Aaron Wildavsky. In addition, we would like to express our appreciation to our editorial team at Jossey-Bass: Alan R. Shrader, senior acquisitions editor, Public Administration Series; Susan R. Williams, editorial assistant; and Lasell Whipple, production editor. They gave us a lot of good advice. We appreciated it all and used it whenever we could.

We also thank our students at the Naval Postgraduate School, the Air War College, the Atkinson Graduate School of Management of Willamette University, and the School of International and Public Affairs, Columbia University, for listening to our ideas and questioning them.

Finally, we thank Mackendree Thompson, Donald Homuth, and, most of all, Ruth Crowley, for reading every word of various drafts of this book and advising us on its revision and for prodding us to finish it. This book is far clearer and shorter as a result of their efforts.

June 1994

Fred Thompson
Salem, Oregon

L. R. Jones
Monterey, California

To the memory of John J. Crowley, Sr., a model defense manager and analyst, as well as a devoted patriot, husband, father, grandfather, teacher, fisherman, and friend. Had he lived longer, this book would have been better. We miss his advice and counsel very much. We miss him very much.

Fred Thompson and L. R. Jones
June 1994

The Authors

FRED THOMPSON is the Grace and Elmer Goudy Professor of Public Management and Policy of the Atkinson Graduate School of Management, Willamette University, Salem, Oregon. He previously served on the faculty of the School of International and Public Affairs at Columbia University, has held visiting appointments at the Anderson Graduate School of Management at the University of California, Los Angeles, and the Faculty of Commerce of the University of British Columbia, and has lectured at the Air War College and the Industrial College of the Armed Forces. He was a senior economist with the Economic Council of Canada, where he participated in the production of its report, *Responsible Regulation*. He also worked for the California State Department of Finance and the California Postsecondary Education Commission and has been consulted by a number of organizations, including the Secretary of Defense's Commission on Base Closure and Realignment.

He received his B.A. degree (1964) from Pomona College in economics and history and his Ph.D. degree (1972) from Claremont Graduate School in government and economics. He was a Linhardt Traveling Fellow to Mexico and Central America, 1970–1971.

Thompson has authored or edited five books, including *Regulatory Reform in Canada* (with W. T. Stanbury, 1982), *Managing*

Public Enterprises (with W. T. Stanbury, 1982), and *Reforming Social Regulation* (with LeRoy Graymer, 1982), and he recently translated Fritz Scharph's *Crisis and Choice in European Social Democracy* (1991) with his wife, Ruth Crowley. His articles have appeared in a variety of journals, including the *Academy of Management Review*, the *California Management Review*, the *Journal of Economic Behavior and Organization*, the *Bell Journal of Economics, Public Choice*, the *American Political Science Review*, the *Political Science Quarterly*, the *Western Political Quarterly, Policy Sciences,* and *Policy Analysis,* as well as *Public Administration Review* and the *Journal of Policy Analysis and Management.* He is currently a member of the editorial boards of *Public Administration Review* and the *Municipal Finance Journal* and previously served on the boards of the *Policy Studies Journal* and the *Political Research Quarterly.*

LAWRENCE R. JONES is professor of financial management in the systems management department of the Naval Postgraduate School in Monterey, California, and a 1994 Fulbright Scholar. Previously he was a member of the faculties of the University of Oregon and the University of British Columbia and a visiting lecturer at East China University in Shanghai.

He received his B.A. degree (1967) from Stanford University in political science, his M.A.P.A. degree (1971) from the University of California, Berkeley, in public administration, and his Ph.D. degree (1977) from the University of California, Berkeley, in public policy and administration.

He is the author of more than fifty journal articles on a variety of subjects, including management and budget control, public financial management, and government regulation of business and financial markets. He has authored *Regulatory Policy and Practices: Regulating Better and Regulating Less* (with Fred Thompson, 1982), *University Budgeting for Critical Mass and Competition* (1985), *Government Response to Financial Constraints* (with Jerry McCafferey, 1989), *Mission Financing to Realign National Defense* (with Glenn Bixler, 1992), and *Corporate Environmental Policy and Government Regulation* (with John Baldwin, 1994). He is a member of the editorial boards of *Public Administration Review*,

Public Budgeting and Financial Management, and *Armed Forces Comptroller.*

His administrative appointments include the following: associate dean for faculty and graduate programs at the Naval Postgraduate School, graduate public affairs programs chair at the University of Oregon, and director of research for the California Student Aid Commission. He is currently chair of the Association for Budgeting and Financial Management (a section of the American Society for Public Administration).

Current Challenges
and Opportunities

THE COLD WAR is over. The military budget will now be cut, as it has been after every major conflict in American history. Yet several questions remain to be answered. Some have to do with the depth and speed of the cuts—how much and how fast? Others have to do with their economic consequences. Nearly two million defense jobs could disappear during this decade. Are the funds authorized for economic adjustment adequate to deal with a problem of this magnitude? What should government do, besides reducing military spending, to shift resources from military to civilian uses?

These are important questions, but perhaps the most important question to be answered has to do with the security concerns raised by the prospect of grand-scale demobilization. America's past wars have all been followed by substantial drops in military preparedness, proficiency, and vigor—declines that often went deeper than the postwar budget cuts themselves. The examples of the poorly trained and equipped GIs who were chewed to pieces by the North Koreans in 1950 or the hollow force of the 1970s created by reduced defense spending after Vietnam come readily to mind. Will this happen again?

This book is about the administrative changes that the Department of Defense must make if it is to meet the challenge of

1

shrinking to roughly half its former size. We believe that, if defense spending is to be reduced without enfeebling the military, the Pentagon must make massive changes in the way it does business—it must restructure, decentralize, and trim away the fat. Moreover, the changes in its organizational architecture and governance arrangements must be continuous, progressive, and enduring. This book is, therefore, also about institutional renewal, about obstacles to organizational change, and about overcoming those obstacles.

To say that this book is primarily about administrative reform and institutional renewal is not to say that it ignores completely the broader ramifications of peace. Nevertheless, we believe that questions of organizational architecture and governance are at least as important as the controversies about outlay levels and weapons systems that tend to preoccupy Congress, the media, and the public. Ultimately, questions of architecture and governance may even be as important as the question of economic conversion. After all, defense spending must fall and eventually the economy will adjust, but organizational muddle and administrative bloat can go on ad infinitum if not curbed by conscious acts of will.

How Much and How Fast?

Nowadays Congress and the Pentagon debate the budget piecemeal—item by item and title by title, on an annual basis, with items arrayed by object of expenditure class (personnel, operations and maintenance, procurement), by appropriation, and by military department. Most commentators follow this practice. Most also follow the federal government's practice of accounting for spending in terms of obligational authority (the legal authority to spend money for a specified purpose during a specified period) or annual outlays (cash disbursements) rather than resources consumed.

These budget battles preoccupy the players, and nearly everyone inside the Beltway wants to be counted as a player. They also generate a lot of sound and fury, but their significance overall may be more apparent than real. For example, when this was written, Congress had just concluded a vehement debate over whether to buy twenty B-2 bombers, which would equip two squadrons, or fourteen, which would equip only one. Does it matter that Congress decided to buy twenty? Probably not much. Viewed from the standpoint of present values, it costs something to add a B-2 to the Air Force's capital stock, but because the aircraft that will be replaced have higher operating and maintenance costs and are closer to the end of their operational life, the cost is not particularly great. Viewed from the standpoint of military capability, the B-2 provides a real increase in performance, but it is unlikely that the B-2's performance advantage delivers a corresponding military advantage in the current era. Paradoxically, intense controversy over the need for a particular weapons system is often evidence that the outcome really does not matter very much.

This conclusion holds a fortiori when we look beyond the trees of the individual items in the defense budget to the forest of annual outlays. Outlay levels appear to be almost entirely predictable using fairly simple models. Norman Augustine (1982, p. 123), for example, showed that, during the first thirty years of the Cold War, the following algorithm explained 90 percent of the annual change in the defense budget: "Congress will appropriate for defense the amount of funding approved the prior year plus three-fourths of whatever change the administration requests, less a 4 percent tax." J. Patrick Crecine (1975) also concluded that the process was nearly automatic and equally incremental: that the defense budget is equal to the previous year's nominal dollar budget plus 21 percent of the increase in the federal government's total spending (see also Kantor, 1979). More recently, others, using more sophisticated econometric techniques, have depreciated the inertial dimension of the defense budget somewhat and have assigned significant weight to certain macroeconomic variables, public opinion concerning defense spending, the level of perceived threat, and the actual level of armed conflict, as well as to institutional efforts aimed at controlling the defense top line (that is, total authorized outlays) (Hahm, Kamlet, and Mowery, 1992). Nevertheless, this research shows that the endless trench warfare over budget minutiae matters little to anyone but the participants themselves and the individuals who are directly affected by the battles.

Looking at defense spending piecemeal directs too much attention to marginal changes in personnel levels and the composition of the defense capital stock and too little to the fundamental concerns that should determine its size and rate of change. Instead, one should focus on the missions the military is called on to perform (such as defending Europe) and the capabilities needed to perform those missions. As with most productive entities, the Defense Department's capabilities have two dimensions: a stock dimension and a flow dimension. The stock dimension is largely captured by the term *force structure*. Force structure is Pentagonese for the organizations and equipment—the people and weapons—needed to perform the missions assigned to the military. The flow dimension is indicated by current spending levels. These, in turn, reflect the size of the force structure and determine its deployment, training levels, and equipment maintenance and replacement schedules.

Hence, to decide how much the United States should spend on defense, one must know what forces are needed and how ready they should be, how rapidly their equipment should be replaced, and what it will cost to make the transition to a smaller force structure. These transitional costs include liquidating obligations incurred during the Cold War and making investments to ensure that the resources freed up by demobilization are productively employed.

This is basically the approach taken by the Pentagon in 1990, when it outlined plans for the so-called *base force*. These plans reflected the changes taking place in what was then still the Soviet Union, the defection of its Eastern European allies, and new threats in the Middle East, as well as certain other changes in international affairs. The base force plan presumed the need for rapid deployment to regional conflicts—of the type executed in Desert Storm—and called for increased emphasis on airlift and sealift capacity, maritime and amphibious forces, and special operations forces. The plan was presented in terms of the following mission-related segments: strategic forces, Atlantic forces, Pacific forces, and contingency forces (see Jones, 1993).

When the Pentagon announced its base force plan, the Army had eighteen active and twelve reserve division; the Navy 560 ships, thirteen carrier groups, and three marine divisions; and the Air Force twenty-five active and twenty-four reserve wings. The net replacement value of the arms and equipment provided to this force was about $0.7 trillion, equal to about one-eighth of American business's total investment in plant and equipment. Based on wear and tear, wastage, and obsolescence, its average half-life was approximately ten years (Roll, 1978; Thompson, 1987). This meant that the Department of Defense had to buy about $80 billion worth of arms and equipment each year just to stay even. Sustaining a technological edge cost $40 billion for military research and development, and operating and maintaining the inventory at 1990 readiness levels cost $80 billion more. In 1990, the Pentagon actually purchased about $100 billion worth of equipment, which put it somewhat ahead of the game (that is, new investment exceeded depreciation, thereby increasing the military's fixed capital). Its operations, personnel, and overhead cost another $80 billion, for a grand total of nearly $300 billion.

The base force proposal called for cuts in the force structure of about one-third over five years: reducing the Army to twelve active and six reserve divisions; the Navy to 450 ships, including twelve carriers, eleven active and one reserve wings, and two and a half marine divisions; and the Air Force to fifteen active and eleven reserve wings. These reductions would permit the military's fixed capital to fall to about $0.55 trillion net. This implies a reduction in defense consumption from a steady-state level of $280 billion (in 1990 dollars) to about $220 billion (in 1990 dollars, or about $275 billion in 1996 dollars)—more than 20 percent.

This inference can be defended according to the following reasoning. Under the base force, depreciation of the remaining active military capital stock would cost roughly $60 billion in constant dollars. Operations and maintenance would cost $50 to $60 billion more, depending on the readiness levels sought—and the base force concept presumed continued high levels of readiness. Research and development spending is harder to estimate, but analysts often assume that for every $2 the United States spends on equipment, it must spend another $1 on research and development. According to this rule of thumb, the research and development budget could be cut from $37 billion a year to $30 billion, perhaps even more given the reductions in military research and development spending planned or already made by our erstwhile enemies and allies.

Another and more familiar way of looking at the reduction in defense consumption from steady-state levels is to estimate the direct budgetary consequences of reduced force structure. To begin with, it can be assumed that personnel levels, both military and civilian, should be reduced by about the same proportion as the force structure. The base force plan called for active-duty personnel levels to fall to 1.65 million (a reduction of nearly 24 percent from 1987 levels), reserves to 0.9 million (about 21 percent), and civilian employees to 0.94 million (about 9 percent).

Because the base force plan called for proportionate reductions in the military's fixed capital, it allowed for more than proportionate reductions in new investment—at least in the short run. It called for retirement of the Minuteman II missile system and Poseidon submarines, a reduction of the Trident submarine fleet to 18, a decrease in strategic bombers from 268 to 171, cutting 81 ships from the fleet, and deactivating older attack submarines and amphibious ships and the two remaining battleships. Among the programs it proposed for termination were the Trident submarine, the P-7A antisubmarine aircraft, the F-14D aircraft, the Navy Advanced Tactical Fighter, the Navy's A-12 attack fighter airplane, the Peacekeeper missile, the Mark XV aircraft identification system, the Boost Surveillance and Tracking System, the TACIT Rainbow cruise missile, the V-22 vertical takeoff and landing aircraft, the M-1 tank, the F-15E aircraft, the P-3A antisubmarine aircraft, the Apache helicopter, and the Army Helicopter Improvement Program.

The base force plan was designed to delay acquisition of a variety of systems, including the rail garrison missile system, the ASAT (antisatellite defense) system, the Milstar satellite program, and the Air Force's B-2 bomber. Plans to purchase the B-2 were scaled back from approximately 175 aircraft to four in fiscal year 1992 and seven in fiscal year 1993. The Strategic Defense Initiative (Star Wars) program was restructured to place greater emphasis on theater missile defense. Plans to procure the SSN-21 Seawolf attack submarine were reduced at this point from two per year to one. Similarly, the acquisition rate of the C-17 transport aircraft was scaled back, although not its total volume.

At the same time, the base force proposal clearly aimed to maintain readiness levels and in some areas to increase capacity. This goal was reflected in the Pentagon's cutback strategy, which emphasized maintenance of plant and equipment, selective modern-

ization, and continued high training levels; it targeted overheads—
management and support functions—for the heaviest cuts. Modernization in the Air Force, for example, was to continue with procurement of F-16 fighter aircraft and C-130 transports and additional buys
of the AMRAAM air-to-air missile system. Development of the Air
Force Advanced Tactical Fighter was continued. The C-17 transport
buy was reduced as noted but was continued to replace aging C-141s.
To improve mobility in the wake of Desert Storm, the base force plan
proposed to increase the size of the ready reserve fleet from 96 to 142
cargo ships.

The total collapse of the Soviet Union rendered the base force
plan obsolete. Even President Bush accepted the need for real budget cuts of 30 percent or more by 1997 and called for program cuts
that went far beyond base force levels: cancellation of the railroad car
basing for the Peacekeeper missile, the mobile version of the small
intercontinental ballistic missile (ICBM), and the SRAM-II short
range missile program, the Comanche helicopter program, Minuteman III long-range ballistic missile program, the air defense antitank system, the Block III tank program, the Advanced Air-to-Air
missile program, the Fixed Distribution underwater surveillance system, and the Line of Sight antitank program. He also stopped production of the Navy's advanced cruise missile, the Trident W-88
submarine warhead, and, eventually, the Seawolf submarine.

The Clinton administration took office committed to making even deeper cuts in defense spending. In September 1993 it
produced a plan for doing so, *National Security in the Post–Cold
War World* (Aspin, 1993), the so-called "bottom-up review," which
sought to identify the forces needed to conduct two Desert Storm–
sized operations simultaneously, while holding something in reserve, and to get there by 1997.

The bottom-up review calls for reducing the Army to ten
active and five reserve divisions, the Navy to 350 ships (although it
will not lose any aircraft carriers, air wings, or marine divisions),
and the Air Force to thirteen active and seven reserve wings. These
reductions should permit the military's fixed capital to fall to about
$0.50 trillion net, which implies steady-state defense consumption
levels of about $200 billion (in 1990 dollars, or about $250 billion
in 1997 dollars).

For the most part, Aspin's acquisition plans follow the blueprints outlined under his predecessor, although the bottom-up review adds three big procurement programs to the chopping block: $20 billion will be taken from the Strategic Defense Initiative, and both the Air Force's multirole fighter and the Navy's replacement for the aging A-6 Intruder (the AF-X attack bomber)—neither of which has started development—will be eliminated entirely. Under the bottom-up review, uniformed personnel levels will fall from about 1.7 million now to about 1.4 million and, in Europe, the base force level of 150,000 will be reduced by one-third. On the other hand, a third Seawolf-class attack submarine will be built, one more than had been planned, although the Navy's attack submarine fleet is slated to shrink from eighty-one to fifty-five (maybe forty-five later). This decision was made in order to keep two shipyards capable of building nuclear submarines (one in Connecticut, the other in Virginia) in business.

According to Paul Quinn-Judge (1993), the failure of the bottom-up review to call for deeper cuts in force structure and in defense spending disappointed some defense analysts, who had hoped for a complete reassessment of the defense force structure in the face of a changed world. Instead, many have dismissed the bottom-up review as a holding action, a warmed-over version of Bush-era defense proposals.

Of course, it is hard to say what America's force structure should look like in the year 2000 or beyond. However, some analysts outside of the Department of Defense, who have considered existing threats and the kind of capabilities needed to meet them, conclude that the United States can get by with a far smaller military establishment than that proposed by either the base force plan or the bottom-up review. William Kaufmann (1992), for example, argues that force structure and overheads can be cut in half: reducing the Army to seven active and ten reserve divisions; the Navy to 340 ships, six carrier groups, and two marine divisions; and the Air Force to thirteen active and twelve reserve wings. This would allow the active defense inventory to fall to about $0.4 trillion and, assuming prompt reductions in overheads, allow steady-state consumption to fall to about $180 billion per annum (in 1990 dollars).

Military spending amounted to nearly 5.7 percent of GNP in

1990. If force structure were, indeed, cut in half, spending could fall to less than 4 percent of GNP by fiscal 1995—in real terms about the same as 1980 levels—and to less than 3 percent of GNP by 2000. One reason why it will probably not be possible to reduce spending faster is that the buildup between 1980 and 1987 committed the Pentagon to many almost unbreakable long-run acquisition contracts. While most of these contracts contain the standard clause permitting cancellation "for the convenience of the government," many also call for the Department of Defense to pay substantial penalties in the case of premature cancellation. Another reason is that the Pentagon is committed to providing reasonable severance pay and help in finding new jobs and appropriate retraining programs to those who are put out of work by demobilization. A third reason is the cost of environmental cleanup on military bases. It has been estimated that it could cost as much as $50 billion to clean up the bases that will be closed before they can be transferred to the private sector (Jacob, 1992). Moreover, some costs (for example, health care) will continue to increase despite massive cuts in force structure. Recognition of these costs makes it clear that changes in force structure along the lines of those outlined in the previous paragraph will not permit real military spending to fall to $160 billion (in 1990 dollars) by the year 2001 (Church, 1990)—let alone sooner.

In any case, maintaining a truly ready military force, one that is capable of carrying out the missions it is assigned, is the most urgent challenge facing top managers in the Pentagon. Organizational reduction—reducing both force structure and overheads—is the second major challenge they face. Their third major challenge is the preservation of the defense industrial base.

Dismantling the Cold War Economy

Many claim that the defense industrial base is a tremendous drag on the American economy (Melman, 1988). They argue that defense spending has crowded out private investment in plant and equipment and in nonmilitary research and development and has thereby retarded the growth of the American economy and crippled its capacity to compete in world markets. They imply that, freed of this drag, the American economy could perhaps regain world leadership and would undoubtedly check its relative decline. Others argue the reverse: that the economy depends on military spending and that, if this prop were removed, it would fall into protracted recession (Cypher, 1987). We are inclined to deprecate both these benefits and costs of demobilization.

On the benefit side, we do not believe that military spending per se has "drained investment funds from the civilian economy." Robert Barro's analysis of the behavior of military purchases, GNP, and the components of GNP (Barro, 1990) is perhaps the best evidence on this point. Barro shows that wartime increases in military purchases primarily affect the investment portion of private spending. The change in private investment was 31 percent of the change in military spending during World War I, 25 percent of the change during World War II, and 42 percent of the change during the Korean War (private investment actually increased during the Vietnam War). Barro attributes decreased investment in wartime to the fact that increases in military spending were temporary. Because they did not significantly reduce permanent income, they did not substantially reduce current consumption levels.

We credit a more traditional explanation for reduced investment during wartime, stressing the effects of capacity constraints and bottlenecks in the machine tool, instrument engineering, and other mechanical and electrical engineering industries. At the start of World Wars I and II, the United States possessed insignificant inventories of war materials, a tiny armaments industry, and little or no military surge capacity. As a result, it was necessary to greatly expand production capacity to supply war materials for those conflicts. Therefore, the plant and equipment needed to open new military production lines had to come primarily at the expense of nonmilitary investment in plant and equipment, at least initially. Furthermore, insofar as military procurement consists of complex weapons systems and the like, it is also reasonable to assume that bottlenecks caused by rapid increases in military production primarily affected nonmilitary investment, since weapons system components are produced by industries whose nonmilitary output goes largely to investment.

Barro's inability to identify any significant crowding out of investment as a result of the Vietnam War tends to buttress our claims about capacity constraints, since the United States entered the Vietnam War with ample military stocks and military production capacity roughly sufficient to meet wartime requirements. In any case, Barro provides indisputable evidence that in peacetime, crowding out caused by increased military purchases affects primarily nonmilitary, primarily private, consumption. This conclusion is, of course, consistent with both the logic that holds that a permanent increase in government purchases is the economic equivalent of a reduction in permanent income and the logic that says that bottlenecks caused by rapid mobilization will be overcome in time.

Consequently, we doubt that reducing military spending will automatically increase private investment. Nevertheless, we are Keynesian enough to believe that the effect of government spending depends in part on how it is financed. This leads us to conclude that, if the peace dividend were applied to reducing corporate taxes or to reducing the deficit, private investment might increase.

On the cost side, we acknowledge that increases in military purchases have usually had a positive effect on GNP. If we exclude data from World War II, it appears that a $100 increase in military spending increases GNP by between $30 and $80. Turned around, these figures imply that cutting military spending by a trillion dollars will reduce GNP by at least $300 billion over the same period—about 1 percent of GNP if the cut were spread over five years. So long as the federal government pursues appropriate monetary and fiscal policies, the economy can easily accommodate a decrease in aggregate demand of this magnitude.

Easily is, of course, a matter of perspective. Markets, especially financial markets, readily adjust to circumstances. Asset values promptly change to reflect rational expectations about their future productivity. This means that the macroeconomic effects of changes in military spending start to be felt as soon as the change is reasonably likely. If we are right about the relationship between military spending and aggregate demand, by the time this volume appears in print, the postwar recession should be over. People and organizations do not adjust to changed circumstances quite so readily, however.

The process of economic conversion—absorbing displaced

workers, redeploying assets, and local adjustment—will continue for some time. Nevertheless, we believe that current federal and state programs are sufficient in size and scope to deal with most problems of economic adjustment. Murray Weidenbaum (1992, p. 15) would go even further. He argues that it is probably not necessary to treat displaced defense workers any more generously than "people who lose their jobs because of sluggish housing sales resulting from tight monetary policy or from reduced mining due to more stringent environmental regulations." Moreover, he reminds us that scientists, technicians, engineers, and accountants constitute a large fraction of the defense work force, that it should be easier for these individuals to find productive work than it was for the 1.7 million unskilled steel and autoworkers who lost their jobs during the 1980s, and that the Pentagon's separation incentives will help to ensure that the uniformed personnel who choose to leave the armed services are more confident of their ability to succeed in nonmilitary employment.

Weidenbaum would completely ignore the local consequences of economic adjustment. Like most economists, he prefers aiding households to aiding localities. Consequently, he would largely ignore the places hurt by reduced military spending. As a rule, aiding households rather than localities can be defended on grounds of both efficiency and vertical equity, although, given our political system, some would say that it smacks of naïveté. Ann Markusen and Joel Yudken, in a volume titled *Dismantling the Cold War Economy* (1992), show that in this case concern with local consequences is not only good politics, it may also be good economics. They point out that defense activities are site specific—that they are carried out in research centers, manufacturing plants, and on military bases—and that these sites have an opportunity cost, which consists of their value to the local economy in an alternative use. Markusen and Yudken show that not all of these sites have the same opportunity costs: some defense uses make significant net contributions to local economies, others make little or none, and a few are actually nuisances. They imply that most of the sites used for military bases and defense plants in the urbanized part of California, for example, would make much larger contributions to the local economy if they were allocated instead to their best alternative uses. They conclude that the Pentagon should take this opportunity cost into account in deciding which centers, plants, and bases to close.

Markusen and Yudken also call for a coherent program of organizational triage to decide promptly and surely which major defense contractors will survive. This, they argue, will minimize the cost of transition to a demilitarized economy, while preserving essential military industrial capacity. Besides, as they explain, in the absence of a coherent program, these decisions will not be made by an impartial and impersonal market but will be administered through a series of uncoordinated government procurement actions. They believe that these decisions should be made explicit and clear-cut rather than left to chance.

It is hard to disagree with this argument. American defense production relies on some of the oldest manufacturing plants in the world, most of them dating back to World War II. With many plants designed for volume assembly of single designs over long periods, defense manufacturing in the United States is almost as inflexible today as it was then. As domestic demand decreases, either weapons systems unit costs will have to be far higher than they are now to redress unused capacity or the industry will have to be drastically rationalized. Even Weidenbaum might have endorsed the need for a coherent program of organizational triage if he had anticipated the depth of the coming cuts in military spending.

Administrative Reform

We would like to be able to claim that organizational and institutional renewal will produce substantial savings as well as help to ensure that our defense dollars are well spent. But by themselves, they will not do so. There is no painless way to cut hundreds of billions of dollars from the defense budget. The only way to save significant amounts of money is to trim away whole departments, programs, and activities. As we have seen, this means firing employees, canceling contracts, and closing offices, schools, military bases, and defense plants. The administrative reforms discussed here can improve mission performance and facilitate and expedite the delivery of military services. They can help public officials save money by providing them with better managerial equipment to increase the efficiency of the department's routine operations. They can help public officials trim programs and activities by helping them distinguish between activities that add value and those that do not. But they will help only if top managers in the Pentagon are authorized to carry out the kind of administrative triage that is needed to save essential programs and activities—and are motivated to do so. As the report of the President's Committee on Administrative Management explained in 1937 (p. 2): "It has been demonstrated over and over again in large organizations of every type in business and government that genuine savings in operation and true economics are achieved only by the provision of adequate managerial machinery which will afford an opportunity for central executive direction to pursue day after day and year after year, in season and out of season, the task of cutting costs, of improving service, and of raising standards of performance." These reasons are valid and sufficient. Only disappointment and public disaffection can result from claims that organizational renewal cannot fulfill and was never designed to fulfill. Those who claim that administrative reforms will result in extravagant saving are in reality its worst enemies.

Challenge Versus Opportunity

The real significance of administrative reform is suggested by what happened in France and Germany after World War I. Both demobilized; both made huge cuts in defense spending. Because of the Treaty of Versailles, Germany made far deeper cuts than France. The victorious allies forced Germany to reduce its officer corps to 4,000—one-fifteenth of prewar levels—to cut the size of its army to 200,000 men, and to scrap its weapons. During the next twenty years, 1920 to 1940, France outspent Germany three to one on defense (see Doughty, 1988; Messerschmidt, 1988).

In 1940, Germany utterly defeated France in a campaign lasting only six weeks. The difference between the two military establishments is that the French tried to preserve everything. The French maintained an army of over one million men, with a corps of professional officers appropriate to an army five times that size, and a high command that was top heavy with the victors of 1918.

In the end, France preserved nothing. In contrast, the Germans looked to the future and emphasized the essentials of combat success: excellent leaders at all levels, modern weapons and tactics, and highly trained personnel.

German success was in no small measure due to the conditions imposed on Germany by the Treaty of Versailles. Size limits meant that the German army had to be highly selective. This ensured an officer corps of the highest quality, as well as superior enlisted personnel. According to James Corum (1992, p. 47; see also Dupuy, 1977, and Van Creveld, 1982), the German army was by no means crippled by a shortage of officers. On the contrary, he argues that the German army was actually better off, because it had to develop a lean and efficient administrative structure that was free of the bureaucratic nonessentials that so preoccupy officers in other armies and that inhibit their combat effectiveness. Size limits also meant that the German army could rely on long-service volunteers and could afford to provide them with the best of training, weapons, and equipment.

Because they had to scrap their existing weapons and were prohibited from acquiring new ones, the Germans stressed research and development rather than the production and deployment of weapons. Their aim was to stay abreast of technological developments and to ensure that the tactical ideas they adopted matched the capabilities of the weapons they would use and those that could be used against them. This meant that they were free to develop new weapons and the tactics to go along with them.

Because they did not have to use resources to support personnel or to acquire equipment, the Germans were also free to emphasize operations, training, and field maneuvers. According to Corum (1992, p. 205), "Thanks to the Reichswehr's excellent training program and the German Army's unrelenting emphasis on multidivisional maneuvers, a typical German Army captain or major would have participated in more multidivisional maneuvers than the average British or French general. The quality of German training would also account for the consistent battlefield superiority demonstrated by the German Army throughout World War II." While the Germans noticeably improved in training and in handling large bodies of troops using modern weapons and tactics, the French stagnated. Because of the size of their army and because they were saddled with large stockpiles of weapons left over from the Great War, the French could neither afford new equipment nor achieve high levels of training and operating tempos. Their officer corps was large, mediocre, bureaucratic, and old. Consequently, their tactics were frozen in the year 1918, and their troops were ill-trained, ill-equipped, and ill-led.

The Germans were forced to make hard choices that ensured military preparedness, proficiency, and vigor, and the French were not. If the United States is to meet the military challenges of the coming decades, mechanisms must be established that will ensure that hard choices are made and implemented effectively.

PART ONE

Lessons from
the Postwar Era

CHAPTER ONE

Creating the
Department of Defense

The Management Challenge

ACCORDING TO Peter F. Drucker (1953, pp. 343-344), "A manager, in the first place, *sets objectives.* . . . Secondly, a manager *organizes.* . . . Next a manager *motivates.* . . . The fourth basic element in the work of the manager is *the job of measurement.* . . . Finally, a manager *develops* people." These are the key functions of top management in any organization. The top managers in the Department of Defense have not always satisfactorily performed them, in part because they have been distracted by lower-level tasks (operating, controlling, and budgeting), and in part because they have been preoccupied by struggles with the military departments and Congress over the scope of their authority. We believe this state of affairs is due largely to the incomplete implementation of organizational and budgetary reforms initiated over thirty years ago. As S. E. Huntington (1984, p. 21) has observed,

> Criticism has been directed at many aspects of defense department organization, including, for instance, procedures for weapon system procurement. Varied as the criticisms have been, however, they have tended to focus on the strategic side of the defense establishment—how decisions are made on overall policy, on the development of military forces, programs,

and weapons, and on the use of military force. These criticisms tend to articulate in a variety of ways a single underlying
theme: that there is a gap between defense organization and
strategic purpose. This gap is the result of the failure to
achieve the purpose of organizational reforms instituted [at
the end of the Eisenhower era].

In this and the following chapters, we will explain and seek to
defend these claims. But first we must explain what we mean by
organizational structure and organizational strategy.

Organizational Structure and Organizational Strategy

By organizational structure, we mean three distinct but related
things (Galbraith and Nathanson, 1978, pp. 1-75; Andrews, 1971,
esp. p. 41; Anthony, 1965; Belkaoui, 1986, pp. 3-12; see also Huntington, 1961, pp. 3-4). In the first place, we mean the division of
labor in the organization: dividing work into tasks or roles such as
operations, logistics and transportation, and training, and recom-
bining them into administrative units, such as branches, departments, bureaus, or divisions according to mission, function, and/
or region. This is the organization's administrative structure—the
structure depicted in organizational charts, including tables of organization and equipment. In the second place, we mean the distribution of authority and responsibility to individuals within the
organization. This is the organization's responsibility structure. In
the third place, we mean the organization's system of measuring
and evaluating performance—how it organizes information on inputs, costs, activities, and outputs. This is the organization's account or control structure. An account structure should be oriented
to administrative units or responsibility centers—optimally to both,
since the information provided by these accounts can be used both
to coordinate unit activities and to control the behavior of responsibility center managers—or to some analytically relevant construct.
     The management literature tells us that two basic rules gov-
ern organizational design. First, strategy should determine structure. Strategy means the pattern of purposes and policies that
defines the organization and its missions and that positions it rel-

ative to its environment. Single-mission organizations should be organized along functional lines; multimission organizations should be organized along mission lines; multimission, multifunction organizations should be organized along matrix lines. Where a matrix organization is large enough to justify an extensive division of labor, responsibility centers ought to be designated as either mission or support centers, with the latter linked to the former by a system of internal markets and prices.

The second basic rule is that the organization should be as decentralized as possible (Zald, 1964, pp. 19–26; Becker and Neuhauser, 1975; Vancil, 1979). Most students of management believe that the effectiveness of large, complex organizations improves when authority and responsibility are delegated down into the organization.[1] Of course, authority should not be arbitrarily or capriciously delegated. Decentralization requires prior clarification of the purpose or function of each administrative unit and responsibility center, procedures for setting objectives and for monitoring and rewarding performance, and a control structure that links each responsibility center to the goals of the organization as a whole.

Military analysts and students of public administration often confuse centralization with unity of command—that is, policy direction from the top, hierarchically established goals, and central control procedures (see, for example, Cohen and Gooch, 1990, pp. 84–93, 216–224). Unity of command characterizes all well-managed organizations. Centralization is characterized by the use of before-the-fact controls, by rules and regulations that specify what must be done as well as how, when, where, and by whom. Decentralization is characterized by after-the-fact controls, by rewards and performance targets that are high enough to elicit the best efforts from an organization's personnel.[2]

Mission attributes constrain the degree of decentralization possible within an organization (Thompson, 1967, chaps. 3 to 6). Some missions require precise orchestration and coordination of complex bundles of tasks if they are to be carried out successfully. Missions that have this attribute—for instance, performing Beethoven's Ninth Symphony or invading Europe—must be coordinated by a single authority responsible for both the allocation of assignments specifying who must do what and the ultimate success of the mission. The existence of reciprocal interdependence (that is, activities that must be carried out simultaneously to be successful) severely limits the degree to which the responsibility structure of an organization can be decentralized. Goal ambiguity (that is, ambiguous administrative boundaries and roles and mission responsibilities) also constrains decentralization. Unlike reciprocal interdependence, however, goal ambiguity is usually self-inflicted.

At the other extreme, where organizational missions or activities do not directly impinge on each other, decentralization is not at all constrained. For instance, the performance of General Motors' truck division does not depend on the performance of the Cadillac division or on any of General Motors' other operating divisions; hence General Motors' top management delegates full operational authority to the managers of its truck division. This same pattern characterized the authority given theater commanders in World War II.

Nevertheless, as long as the missions or activities in question are performed within the bounds of a single organization, even where decentralization is complete or very nearly so, mission performance may be constrained by the total pool of resources available to the organization—top-management attention, production capacity, or access to capital. Hence, even in a decentralized organization, it may be necessary for top management to evaluate the organization's missions and ration the limited resources among them.

The significance of common pool or common property resources is in part a function of the organization's time horizon. In the short run, nearly every resource is constrained. In the long run, there are no real resource constraints. As Eliot Cohen and John Gooch (1990) explain, aligning military organization with defense strategy is especially difficult, because military strategy has two aspects, each with a fundamentally different time horizon: (1) raising, equipping, and organizing armed forces, and (2) using the armed forces in support of political objectives. Where combat is concerned, short-run considerations obviously predominate, since the exigencies of combat compel the use of existing forces. Furthermore, successful conduct of combat operations frequently requires centralization of authority to overcome the problem of reciprocal interdependence (see, for example, Cohen and Gooch, 1990, p. 51).

Nowadays, information processing and communications equipment permits real-time distribution of intelligence data and coordination of combined-arms operations at multiple levels. By accelerating the orientation-observation-adaption cycle, the use of this equipment has had the paradoxical effect of simultaneously increasing both the value of individual initiative on the part of the units taking part in operations and the importance of vesting mission commanders with comprehensive authority to govern by fiat (Coakley, 1992).

In contrast, preparing forces for combat, the main topic of this volume, is governed primarily by longer-run considerations. One implication is that in peacetime, at least, there may be few if any common pool resources, aside from top-management attention, that have to be rationed from the top. Another is that raising, equipping, and organizing armed forces can and therefore should be as decentralized as possible.

For the most part, the activities associated with preparing forces for combat fall into an intermediate range between reciprocal and pooled interdependence called *sequential interdependence*. In this range, mission performance depends on the sequential performance of a series of tasks or functions. That is, work goes one way, from one administrative unit to the next. For example, the sale of aluminum ingots depends on the following sequence of activities: mining, transporting the ore to a processing site, smelting and fabricating it into ingots, and finally distributing the finished product to end users. Or to take another example, mail service involves pickup, sorting, transportation, and finally delivery. Supplying trained and equipped formations for combat relies on a similar sequence of activities.

Sequential interdependence should not constrain decentralization. The relationship between sequentially dependent administrative units is essentially bilateral in nature. Where bilateral relationships are concerned, it is usually possible to set up some kind of transactional arrangement to eliminate or internalize spillovers. In many cases, these relationships can be governed satisfactorily via buyer-seller arrangements and, where they occur within the organization, by appropriate transfer prices (Bailey, 1967; Hitch and McKean, 1960, pp. 396–402; see also Hirschleifer, 1964).

The failure to think these structural relationships through, to clarify administrative boundaries, functional roles, and mission responsibilities, and to develop a control structure that links each administrative unit and responsibility center to the goals of the organization as a whole is highly inimical to decentralization. This failure produces an organization that is rife with externalities and common property resources, one in which everything depends on everything else—in other words, an organization in which effective decentralization is impossible.

Complex organizations that fail to sort out the relationships between their component units—i.e., that fail to align their administrative structure with their responsibility and control structures—must choose between centralization at the top and organizational chaos. Given that choice, centralization at the top is often the preferable alternative.

Our basic criticism of the Department of Defense in general and the Office of the Secretary of Defense in particular is that it has failed to clarify administrative boundaries and roles and mission responsibilities and to delegate authority accordingly. Instead, it has alternated between delegating authority to the military departments and centralizing authority in the hands of the Secretary of Defense. Each swing of this pendulum has produced failures and excesses, in some cases arising out of the pursuit of parochial interests on the part of the military departments; it has then led to renewed centralization, to a further proliferation of rules and regulations aimed at preventing error, to auditors and inspectors general charged with monitoring compliance with the rules, to overstaffing, and ultimately to incrustation, inflexibility, and immobility. Of course, we do not believe that anyone in the Office of the Secretary of Defense ever consciously chose the extreme centralization that characterizes the Pentagon. No one ever consciously chooses obesity; it is acquired, one bite at a time, over an extended period.

Most managers within the Department of Defense would have probably agreed with Charles Hitch and Roland McKean's (1960, pp. 236–238) observation:

Decentralization of the decision-making function is an extremely attractive administrative objective—in the military as elsewhere. The man on the spot can act quickly and flexibly. He has intimate first-hand knowledge of many factors relevant to his decision. Large hierarchical organizations, by contrast, tend to be sluggish and hidebound by rules and regulations. Much of the time and energies [of the organization's top management] are consumed in attempting to assemble at the center, the information so readily available "on the firing line"; and since these efforts are never successful, their decisions have to be made on the basis of information both incomplete and stale. Decentralization of decision-making responsibility has the further advantage of providing training, experience, and a testing ground for junior officers. The best way to develop qualities of responsibility, ingenuity, judgment, and so on, and to identify them is to provide genuine opportunities for their exercise. . . . Unfortunately the superficial illogicalities of decentralization are more strikingly obvious than the deadening consequences of extreme centralization.

Hitch, for example, continued to stress his absolute dedication to decentralization and the ultimate goal of empowing subordinates throughout his tenure as Defense Comptroller during the McNamara era, when at the same time he was the driving force behind the installation of the most comprehensive central planning apparatus this side of Moscow.

Decision Making for Defense, 1945–1960

We have three reasons for beginning this discussion with the postwar era. First, the gap between America's defense organization and its defense strategy is a legacy of that era, as are its inefficient defense industries and its sprawling military base structure. Both the industries and the base structure were established during World War II and preserved largely intact into the present, despite their size and increasing obsolescence. Second, the United States enjoyed an abundance of military power in that period, especially at the beginning, just as it does now. Because of this similarity, the example of defense policy in the postwar era speaks to the present with special eloquence and urgency. Finally, we will argue, reasons one and two were not unrelated.

The failure of the Pentagon's top management to clarify administrative boundaries and roles and mission responsibilities and to delegate authority accordingly reflected a propensity to adopt short-run piecemeal solutions to the pressing fiscal, organizational, and political problem they faced. How do we account for this disturbing propensity? Frankly, we believe that the abundance of military power enjoyed by the United States in the immediate postwar period was crucial to management's failure to make farsighted choices about defense organization or to understand the need for those choices.

The fact is that, in the short run, America could easily afford inefficient defense organization. Historians tend to stress American postwar weakness. They remind us that the Army was reduced from over 8,000,000 to 1,070,000 men and women in 1947, the Navy and Marine Corps from over 3,400,000 to fewer than a million, and the Air Force from 218 groups to 45 (Weigley, 1983). Furthermore, the United States had only a handful of assembled cores for atomic bombs and a single wing of specially modified B-29 bombers to deliver them (Bracken, 1980).

Samuel Huntington (1961, p. 59) summarizes the conventional wisdom: "In June 1950, American armed forces included only 10 understrength Army divisions and 11 regimental combat teams, 671 ships in the Navy, 2 very under strength Marine Divisions, 48 Air Force wings (including 18 in SAC), and a total personnel strength of about 1,461,000 men. If war broke out in Europe, . . . American capabilities would be limited to air-atomic strikes at the Soviet Union."

What this summary ignores is the overwhelming residual military capacity of the United States, the weakness of potential enemies, and the absence of any serious overseas commitments that would call for the use of military forces short of general war. In the first place, the United States had just demonstrated the capacity to mobilize and equip fifteen million men and women for war. Furthermore, this remarkable accomplishment by no means pressed the country to the limit of its resources. In 1942, Army planners estimated that more than twenty million soldiers could be armed, given

civilian consumption levels comparable to those of the British in
World War II. By 1945, GNP was 50 percent higher than in 1942.
America also possessed a large reservoir of trained personnel, experienced commanders, a huge inventory of modern weapons—
planes, tanks, and especially ships—and a substantial lead in military technology.

In contrast, the other victorious powers were exhausted by
their efforts. Having made a superhuman effort to defeat Nazi Germany, the Soviet Union was particularly depleted. Indeed, the magnitude of the Soviet Union's effort in World War II would have been
inconceivable if the Nazis had been less vile or if the Soviet Union
had been denied the material and logistical support provided by the
United States. Because the Soviet Union maintained a very large
standing army after the war, it was possible to imagine a scenario
in which American occupation forces in Germany were driven out
of Europe. But that would have led to a full-scale war. In the immediate postwar era, the only plausible outcome of a full-scale war
with the Soviet Union would have been its defeat and the total
destruction of the Red Army.[3]

Even if one were to take into account the huge increase in its
commitments that occurred during the 1940s, one would still conclude that the United States possessed a surplus of power. In the
absence of scarcity, there is no need for choice. Weaknesses in defense organization could be overlooked, as they were by the framers
of the National Security Act, or in extremis overcome, as they often
had been during World War II, by virtue of sheer weight of resources. Putting up with a little administrative fat or procedural
incoherence probably seemed a tolerable price to pay to pacify stake-
holders in the military departments, the defense industry, and
Congress.

Historical Basis

It should also be acknowledged that the organizational problems
confronting the Pentagon's top management in the postwar era
were both novel and exceedingly complex. It is hard to be farsighted
when long-term problems have no easy or obvious solutions. As
William A. Niskanen (1967, p. 6) explains, before World War II, the
administrative structure of the American defense establishment was

for the most part aligned with its responsibility and control structures. Up to that time, each of the military departments had a single primary mission and each defined its mission in functional terms: land combat was the primary mission/function of the Army, sea combat was the primary mission/function of the Navy, and tactical air support of land combat was the primary mission/function of the Army Air Force.

We do not mean to imply that there were no controversies over missions and roles before the end of World War II; on the contrary, intraorganizational competition is common within most large, complex organizations and to a degree healthy. One of the more difficult and divisive issues of the interwar period involved the competition between the Army Air Force, the Coast Artillery, and the Navy for the coastal defense mission/function. The American defeat at Pearl Harbor and shortly thereafter in the Philippines has been attributed to the failure to resolve the organizational problems inherent in this dispute (Millis, 1956, pp. 222–232, 256). Moreover, during the war, the Army found it necessary to operate troopships and the marines to acquire their own air support and so on. Nevertheless, because each of the military departments had a single primary mission as well as a single primary function, it was possible for most decisions about using military forces, as well as about raising, equipping, and organizing them, to be made successfully along service lines.

The rapid development of military technology and the worldwide proliferation of American commitments after World War II irreversibly sundered the relationship between the armed services and their traditional functions and missions and created new combat missions and roles for them to perform. Rivalry between the military departments over the allocation of mission and functional responsibility and, therefore, resources was the most visible organizational symptom of the changes wrought by the new military technologies. The allocation of missions and roles was the most prominent administrative policy issue of the postwar period.

Rivals for a Mission

Nuclear explosives created a singular, even extraordinary, new defense mission—preparing for, coping with, and avoiding the consequences of strategic nuclear exchange.

The main postwar policy debate inspired by the A-bomb had to do with organizational structure. There was little serious debate at that time as to whether nuclear weapons should be used in a general war. Indeed, few if any military commentators questioned the now-alien notion that their use would be decisive in combat. Instead, the postwar debate reflected the efforts of the military departments to provide distinctive, valued services that would win for them the support needed to grow or, at least, to survive. Each justified its role in terms of delivering these weapons. The Air Force wanted to drop them from land-based bombers, the Navy from carrier-based bombers, and all three of the services ultimately invested resources in the development and deployment of nuclear-tipped ballistic rockets and cruise missiles.

The Army program called for a standing army of two million troops and universal military training, together with the investment in industrial capacity needed to equip a modern mass army. Its justification for universal military training was that B-29 bombers and their immediate successors would need advanced bases to reach potential targets and that a large army would be required to take and secure suitably located bases.

Universal military training was a nonstarter from the word go, however. It was obvious that it would take less time to train a mass army than to equip one, and there was no chance that weapons would be stocked to supply a mass army. Stocking and maintaining an up-to-date weapons inventory sufficient to arm fifteen million members of the armed services would have required roughly 20 percent of America's postwar GNP. Congress did, however, reauthorize the draft after the war.

In the battle for the bomb and, therefore, institutional support, the fiercest rivals were the Air Force and the Navy (Hammond, 1963; see also Huntington, 1961, pp. 155–169). This organizational battle came to public attention with the so-called Admirals' Revolt of 1948. At that time, the Navy argued, with considerable merit, that carrier-based aircraft were more reliable and less vulnerable than land-based aircraft as platforms for the delivery of atomic weapons. Of course, this argument was not employed on behalf of existing delivery systems, but in support of the construction of larger carriers (the Forrestal Class) and the development of an advanced carrier-based bomber, the A3D, or B-66 in its Air Force version (Davis, 1973). The Air Force rebutted Navy claims by reference to aircraft then in development that would give the Strategic Air Command (SAC), the A-bomb delivering component of the Air Force, the means to reach potential targets, thus guaranteeing the reliability of the American nuclear deterrent.

Although the so-called Admirals' Revolt and the consequent debate over the allocation of the strategic mission failed to wrest the delivery of nuclear weapons from the Air Force's grasp, the revolt succeeded in denying the Air Force a monopoly over the delivery of atomic weapons. Navy competition also probably stimulated the Air Force to improve its competence to penetrate Soviet air space and to reach potential targets from secure bases.

Testimony delivered at congressional hearings held as a result of the Admirals' Revolt made it clear that SAC lacked the capacity to perform its assigned mission in 1948. At that time, the Air Force's chief weapon was the B-36 bomber, a large, slow aircraft that flew at high altitude—high enough to be visible at a great distance, but not high enough to avoid antiaircraft fire, let alone modern jet interceptors. The vulnerability of the B-36 was amply demonstrated in practice exercises run against the North American Air Defense Command (NORAD). In these exercises, less than 5 percent of B-36s were judged to have reached their assigned targets.

This record was especially embarrassing when it was contrasted with available carrier-based aircraft such as the A-1 Skyraider. According to James Fallows (1981, p. 159), "In the first few years after WWII, the U.S. Navy had a force of propeller driven single-engine aircraft known as A-1Es. In those years, A-1 pilots would fly practice raids from carriers in the Pacific to inland targets. . . . The planes were extraordinarily slow; they cruised at about 140 knots. . . . But because they were so maneuverable . . . they could . . . conceal themselves in 'ground clutter' on radar screens. In the entire history of these exercises . . . the radars from the Air Defense Command never tracked the A-1s and the interceptors never caught one." During the Vietnam War, the A-1 repeated its performance, demonstrating greater utility in the close support role than F-4 Phantoms, F-105 Thunderchiefs, or A-7 Corsairs, according to reports "of forward air controllers, pilot after-action reports, and numerous articles in the open literature" (Merritt and Sprey, 1973, p. 487). It should be noted, however, that the A-1 was not nuclear capable.

Several other technologies—surface-to-air missiles, helicopters, and so on—were also significant to military organization, since their use did not fit neatly within the functional boundaries of the existing military departments.

Defense Budgeting During
the Eisenhower Administration

The Eisenhower administration (1953–1960) officially adopted the doctrine of massive retaliation. To an extent, this decision was the result of the administration's fiscal priorities, which stressed a balanced budget and control of military spending. As Secretary of Defense Charles Wilson supposedly explained at the time, "The U.S. can't afford anything but a big war." Massive retaliation was intended to deter a big war.

The Eisenhower military budgets reflected two priorities: to hold military outlays to less than 10 percent of GNP and to provide an adequate nuclear deterrent. Military outlays were, in fact, held to approximately 10 percent of GNP during most of this period, with the Air Force, Navy, and Army receiving shares of 45 percent, 33 percent, and 22 percent of total outlays.

Because "massive retaliation" was what the president and Congress would buy, that is what the services tried to provide. Strategic deterrence had three aspects: the ability to strike the Soviet Union in time of war, the ability to defend against Soviet air strikes directed at the United States, and the ability to mitigate damages from a successful Soviet air strike. SAC and the Navy's carriers provided the capacity to strike the Soviet Union with nuclear weapons. At the same time, each of the military departments mounted frantic ballistic and guided missile programs, hoping to win or maintain this mission for themselves. Consequently, the 1950s produced an astonishing array of delivery systems, including the B-47, B-52, B-58, and B-66 bombers, the Snark cruise missile, and the Thor, Jupiter, Polaris, Atlas, Titan, and Minuteman ballistic missiles. While these developments afforded civilian authorities ample opportunities to choose between alternative systems and deployment options, those opportunities were seldom fully exploited.

When, for example, both the Army and the Air Force developed more or less satisfactory intermediate-range ballistic missiles, the Jupiter and the Thor, both were permitted to deploy them (Armacost, 1969). The Navy was also encouraged to proceed with its own intermediate-range, submarine-launched ballistic missile program, the Polaris (Beard, 1976).

Much the same thing occurred with air defense, the responsibility of NORAD. At NORAD's peak, the United States and Canada maintained an elaborate inventory of continental defenses: 400 radars, 2,600 interceptor planes, and 70 early-warning aircraft, staffed by more than 200,000 American and Canadian personnel. Here, too, technological development permitted the other services to claim a piece of the action. All three services developed effective radar-guided ground-to-air missiles: the Air Force's Bomarc, the Navy's Talos, and the Army's Nike series. Again, all three systems were ultimately deployed. NORAD installed over 400 Bomarc launchers across Canada, and every important urban-industrial area of the United States was defended by Army Nike surface-to-air missiles. The Russian bomber threat failed to materialize, however. Instead, the Soviets invested their resources in big, land-based ballistic missiles. Consequently, after 1958, efforts to defend against Soviet air strikes were deemphasized and allowed to decline (Yanarella, 1969).

Because the United States could not actively defend against ICBMs, attention turned to passive and civil defense—to hardening and hiding potential targets and to mitigating damages to the population from a Soviet strike through construction of blast and fallout shelters and stockpiling of food, water, and medical supplies.

The failure of civil defense clearly signaled that the doctrine of massive retaliation was on its way out. After 1960, there was increasing doubt about the American ability to meet a Soviet invasion of Western Europe with nuclear weapons, although the United States probably retained the capacity to "ride out" a surprise attack well into the 1960s and to launch a successful preemptive nuclear strike into the early 1970s. Nevertheless, as Herman Kahn inadvertently demonstrated in his polemic on the merits of passive defense,

On Thermonuclear War (1960), the game was increasingly not worth the ante.

The budgetary corollary to the U.S. commitment to massive deterrence and strategic defense was the deprivation of conventional forces. Arguably, strategic missions consumed as much as three-fourths of the Air Force's resources during the 1953–1960 period, roughly half of the Navy's, and nearly a fifth of the Army's. According to this accounting, strategic forces represented over half of total defense spending during the Eisenhower era. The remainder had to be stretched to cover all of the conventional missions assigned to the three military departments (Office of the Assistant Secretary of Defense [Comptroller], 1984, p. 80).

A second corollary of the commitment to massive deterrence was inattention on the part of the Pentagon's top management to planning and organizing for conventional war. As a consequence, inertia took over. Rather than buying a lean, mean military force that could actually fight and that relied as much as possible on the civilian industrial base, the defense establishment occupied itself with maintaining the infrastructure of World War II. The substitution of military fat for muscle that took place during the Eisenhower era is illustrated by the reduction that took place in the size of the Army's infantry and mechanized divisions from three brigades to five regiments. Conventional force structure was weakened in a variety of less visible ways as well. Readiness, maintenance, and operating tempo levels suffered. Training was rarely realistic or demanding enough to ensure combat readiness. The training exercises and programs that were carried out seldom featured combined operations or tested the ability of active and reserve forces to work together.

It is not surprising that the military departments were ill-prepared to perform many conventional missions, functions, or activities during this era. Inadequacies were particularly evident with respect to functions that were assigned to one military department but that were intended to support a mission assigned to one of its rivals. The supplying services gained nothing from providing services to their rivals, thereby diverting resources to purposes that were not valued from those that were. Therefore, they often didn't supply their rivals. The Air Force deemphasized both airlift and close-ground support. These functions were entirely designed to facilitate the performance of missions assigned to the Army. The Navy slighted antisubmarine patrol and sealift for much the same reasons. The Army sought to compensate by developing the capacity to perform some of these activities for itself, but its resources were limited (Bergerson, 1980).

In the short run, preservation of the training and logistical facilities, the cadres, and the development commands and the military industrial base needed to fight a full-scale war undoubtedly made a contribution to conventional deterrence. Their survival meant that the United States could be fully mobilized for war in eighteen to twenty-four months—half the time it had taken in World War II.

Over time, however, this infrastructure grew increasingly obsolete and, given existing technological and military realities, irrelevant. Even more harmful, the human component of this infrastructure was frequently underemployed. Many officers had no real mission to perform or function to discharge. Because the Department of Defense is obligated to keep its personnel busy, however, work was made for them, primarily performing overhead activities. Make-work ultimately enfeebles organizations. As Drucker (1982, pp. 422–423) explains, "The third deadly sin of the public administrator is to believe that 'fat is beautiful' despite the obvious fact that mass does not do work; brains and muscles do. In fact, overweight inhibits work, and gross overweight totally immobilizes. . . . Overstaffing is not only much harder to correct than understaffing, it makes nonperformance practically certain. For overstaffing always focuses energies on the inside, on 'administration' rather than 'results,' on the machinery rather than its purpose. It always leads to meetings and memoranda becoming ends in themselves. It immobilizes behind a facade of furious busyness."

Administrative overstaffing is the particular bane of the armed forces in peacetime, perhaps because desks are so much cheaper to buy, operate, and maintain than planes, tanks, and ships (the main subject of Parkinson's law was after all the British Admiralty). Administrative overstaffing leads to immobility, which in turn leads to higher staffing levels, as managers try to overcome immobility by sheer weight of numbers. Not only is overstaffing of overhead activities self-defeating, it encourages the bureaucratization of the whole organization.

One invidious manifestation of this pathology is personnel rotation, as the organization attempts to give everyone a shot at performing real work. As Huntington (1961, p. 311) explains, "Rotation conflicts with innovation. When . . . senior personnel change every few years, no one individual has the incentive or the time to make major changes. Routine and formalized procedures are employed because they can be known to all and because they minimize the disruptive impact of continuously changing personnel. . . . Discontinuity in personnel reflects institutional rigidities, on the one hand, and creates additional obstacles to change on the other."

Another manifestation of this pathology is the centralized system of personnel evaluation that overstaffing promotes. Since most employees do not perform value-adding activities, it is both unfair and administratively inconvenient to base individual evaluations on unit performance. Instead, personnel evaluation in bureaucratic organizations tends to be based on educational attainments and career experiences. (Uniformed personnel in the armed forces refer to this as *ticket punching.*) As a result, the system is largely incapable of motivating high levels of performance or of identifying qualified candidates for higher responsibilities (see Bassford, 1988; note the contrast with the selection and evaluation mechanisms described by Van Creveld, 1982, or Murray, 1992).

A third pathology inspired by overstaffing is increased bureaucratic politics. Organizations that are fully and productively occupied have few resources left over for defending their budgets, their autonomy, and their influence. Nor is it usually necessary for them to mount such a defense. Their performance speaks for itself. In contrast, turgid organizations are sluggish organizations. They are burdened with redundant offices, departments, and installations. Since their managers have no vital responsibilities, they expend their energies bickering and bargaining over who should do what.

All three of these pathologies infected large parts of the American military establishment in the 1945–1960 period. The increasingly top-heavy and bureaucratic character of much of the De-

partment of Defense is especially evident when it is contrasted with
SAC during this era.

Development of the Strategic Air Command

Under the doctrine of massive retaliation, delivering A-bombs was
the military's overriding mission. The Pentagon's top management
took the ability to perform this mission seriously and gave it their
full support and attention. They were especially careful that the
military units entrusted with this vital mission not become en-
crusted with the layers of bureaucracy that weakened so much of the
rest of the defense establishment.

SAC was the chosen instrument through which this mission
was to be carried out. In 1948, it lacked bombs, planes, bases, and
trained personnel. Five years later, these deficiencies had been corrected. SAC had become a combat-ready force, fully prepared for
employment. This remarkable organizational turnaround is the
story of an exceptional leader, General Curtis LeMay, and of the
exceptional latitude he was given to carry it out. As Huntington
(1961, p. 308) acknowledges, "The creation of the bombs, the
planes, and the bases for strategic deterrence became meaningful as
they were integrated into an organization clearly devoted to strategic
deterrence. Only in 1949 did such an organization begin to emerge."

Problem of Administrative Reform

Organizational leadership—the capacity to infuse an organization
with value, to create and successfully maintain an organization's
distinctive competence in the face of changing technology and competitive pressures—is everywhere the exception rather than the rule,
but it is especially rare in the public sector. There are at least two
reasons for this. First, the examples that come to mind—Gifford
Pinchot, Robert Moses, Hyman Rickover, and LeMay—suggest that
it is not enough to be a program innovator or entrepreneur to be
an exceptional leader in the public sector. One must be an exceptional organizer or manager as well. Such qualities are rare.

In his classic study of business organizations, *Strategy and
Structure* (1962), Alfred Chandler observed that successful entrepre-

neurs rarely establish the organizational structures needed to carry out their product-market strategies. According to Chandler, most product innovators are not trained to design an effective organization or psychologically inclined to do the rigorous, logical thinking necessary for management analysis. The psychological distance between the entrepreneur (for example, General Motors' William Durant) and the organizer (for instance, W. P. Sloan) typically means that the formulation of a firm's product-market strategy precedes the implementation of an appropriate organizational structure by several years and usually requires at least one leadership change at the top of the organization. Furthermore, this transition is often a painful one. Only when structural deficiencies threaten the survival of the firm and the strategy formulator or entrepreneur leaves the firm (or is forced out) will the new structure be created and put into place.

The second reason that organizational leadership is not the rule is that, in the public sector, political and economic pressures rarely induce this transition, nor are they usually severe enough in peacetime to stimulate attention to the kind of continuous quality improvement that organizations must have if they are to maintain high performance levels. Therefore, if the program innovator fails to align organizational structure with organizational purpose, product, or mission, the appropriate match may never be achieved.

As we have seen, the first task of organizational design (Galbraith and Nathanson, 1978, pp. 1-25; Hofer and Schendel, 1976) is combining roles into administrative entities or units; the second is arranging the units in relation to one another.

The key to successful performance of the first task is specialization—that is, grouping workers performing similar tasks together into organizational units. Specialization is constrained by the rate and volume of activity performed at a specific location and the span of control, or limit of effective supervision. Effective supervision is always a function of the ease or difficulty of monitoring the performance of subordinates.

The key to successful performance of the second task is integration: positioning units relative to each other according to the kind and direction of their dependence on each other (Thompson, 1967, pp. 114-136). Integration is realized through the responsibility structure of the organization. The allocation of responsibility and authority within an organization should aim to minimize spillovers between administrative units and the transaction costs associated with the coordination of interdependency. This aim reflects the assumption that the attention of top management is a scarce and valuable asset that must be carefully husbanded, and also the belief that proximity to operational problems facilitates problem solutions.

Of course, the belief that the responsibility center manager best situated to deal with a problem is the one closest to the problem presupposes adequate input and output measurement for each responsibility center. It also presupposes that the responsibility center manager has adequate information for purposes of capital budgeting (that is, cost-benefit analysis of asset acquisitions and other related problems such as make-or-buy and maintenance policy decisions).

Hence it follows that the design of organizational structure is more than arranging boxes next to one another on an organizational chart. It involves matching structure and information systems as well as organizational processes to achieve a fit or congruency between all of these dimensions. Information must be available to control or coordinate activities, to measure performance effectively, and to forecast and plan. Reward systems must provide incentives to motivate managers to work productively and in conformance with organizational policies. And the organization must be designed to facilitate the selection, training, and development of its personnel, so that they can carry out their assigned responsibilities.

LeMay's Contribution

LeMay defined the purpose or mission of SAC clearly and succinctly: it was to maintain the capacity to "bomb the Soviet Union back to the Stone Age." Everyone, including SAC's sponsors and personnel, could understand the significance and content of that mission. Because LeMay's SAC had a single, clearly defined purpose (or, to use the jargon of organization theory, because it was a single-product, single-mission organization), it was possible for LeMay and his subordinates to organize SAC along functional lines and to establish unambiguous quantitative standards for unit performance and clear-cut criteria for the evaluation of alternative delivery systems, readiness options, or basing configurations. Satisfactory performance standards permitted the evaluation of subordinate commanders and, together with appropriate rewards for exceptional performance, served to motivate them to perform to the best of their abilities. In turn, this meant that LeMay could delegate considerable operational authority, along with responsibility, to his subordinate commanders. According to Huntington (1961, p. 312),

> LeMay's achievement was a military organization in which all else was ruthlessly subordinated to combat readiness and effectiveness justified in terms of the mission which the organization served. This identification required the differentiation of the organization from other groups, symbolized perhaps by LeMay's transfer of SAC headquarters from Bolling Field near Washington to Offut Air Force Base in Nebraska a month after assuming command. It was further emphasized by creating the expectations that special demands would be made on SAC personnel, that special standards of readiness were required of SAC units, that special measures of security were required for SAC bases, that special standards of performance were required of SAC crews, and that special benefits and rewards were available when those standards were exceeded.

Time and Authority

Despite LeMay's leadership qualities, his accomplishments probably would not have been possible had he not been afforded exceptional latitude and time to make his reforms felt. After all, his predecessor as SAC commander, General George Kennedy, had shown himself to be a brilliant innovator and organizational leader during World War II but was unable to turn SAC into an effective fighting force (Borowski, 1986).

In the first place, LeMay was given full authority to define SAC's organizational strategy or mission, including the authority to reject peripheral missions not consistent with SAC's distinctive competence, and to align SAC's structure to its strategy. Second, LeMay was given command of all the resources required to carry out

SAC's mission. He had the authority to decide who and what SAC needed and who and what it did not. This effectively subordinated both the training and the procurement functions to SAC. In addition, SAC adopted the military "buyer-seller" system—that is, the use of working capital and enterprise funds to acquire materials and supplies, transportation services, and some maintenance activities. Third, and perhaps most important, he was given time. It takes time to turn an existing organization around, often more time than it takes to create the same organization from scratch. Again, Huntington (1961, pp. 311–312) tells us,

> LeMay was able to work his transformation of SAC because he commanded it for over eight years. This was "the longest tenure of major command in the history of the Air Force," and it was a significant departure from the normal military practice of rotating officers through three- to four-year tours of duty. Rotation was introduced by Elihu Root to break the political power of the Army's long-entrenched Washington bureau chiefs. By preventing any single individual from becoming identified with a particular office or organizational unit and from building up continuing sources of support for that office or unit, it strengthens civilian control and stimulates identification with the service as a whole. . . . LeMay's eight-year tenure at SAC gave him a unique opportunity both to make fundamental changes in his organization and to develop substantial public support for its program.[4]

Equipping SAC

Time was also required to implement the capital investment program that SAC needed to perform its mission—and to figure out those needs. Because LeMay was assured that he would be around to see the results of his efforts, he could afford to take the long view, to strive for the kind of continuous, long-term improvements that are needed to make organizations efficient and effective and to keep them that way. The significance of this factor, and the contribution it makes to organizational learning and development, is reflected in the process of equipping SAC with aircraft.

In response to criticisms of SAC in 1948–1949, the Air Force decided to equip it with the B-47 bomber. This plane had none of the inadequacies of the B-36. Indeed, it was an exceptional aircraft and appeared—initially—to meet all of SAC's requirements. For example, T. A. Marschak (1965, p. 105) claims in reference to the B-47 that "since WWII no other advance (except perhaps thermonuclear weapons) has given the United States a comparable strategic advantage." Furthermore, the B-47 is still cited as a model for the procurement and acquisition of advanced weapons systems (Marschak, Glennen, and Summers, 1967). The construction of the first prototype took only two years, from fall 1945 to December 1947, the prototyping cost less than $30 million (a low figure compared to contemporary bomber programs), and the first production version was delivered to the Air Force only two years after the flight of the first prototype.

Following World War II, jet bombers were a brand-new, highly risky technology. The B-47 started out as a high-risk, low-cost experiment. The YB-47 prototype was intended to test the feasibility of employing the swept-back wing on large aircraft. Much of the rest of the technology employed in the YB-47 was "off the shelf" or had already been tested. For example, prototype B-47s employed the Allison J-35 jet engine, which was already in use. Furthermore, the prototype was not designed to meet strict performance specifications based on mission requirements. The exploratory nature of the YB-47 is demonstrated by the simultaneous development of three other bomber prototypes, all featuring the same engine: two more conventional and, therefore, less risky designs (the XB-46 and the XB-48), and the even more aerodynamically advanced flying wing (the YB-49). In this case, the developers got lucky; the swept-wing experiment worked.

All four of these prototypes appeared within a six-month period and were, therefore, available to be simultaneously tested and evaluated. As it happened, the YB-47 not only equaled or outperformed its competitors on all relevant criteria (range, speed, ceiling, bomb load, and stability); it also ran away from currently operational jet fighters (Marschak, 1965, p. 103). This outcome not only ensured that the B-47 concept was superior to more conventional designs, it also meant that engineering development could be undertaken without running the risk that an available but untested concept would shortly render it obsolete.

In other words, the Air Force carefully hedged its bets in its management of jet bomber development in the immediate postwar years. It was a winner both in terms of development time, which was guaranteed by a strategy of parallel development, and in terms of product quality, which was not. In this case, savings in development time may have been worth the cost of simultaneous exploration of the full array of attractive options, not to mention any additional benefits that might have derived from the real competition between rival private contractors: Boeing, Martin, Convair, and Northop.

The B-47 appeared to be so good that it was reengined and rushed into production before all the bugs were out of it and also before it was determined that it could satisfactorily meet the mission requirements of SAC. Perhaps for the Air Force the important thing was that the introduction of the B-47 served to squash the Admirals' Revolt and to justify support of SAC at the expense of nearly everything else—with the exception of the Navy's supercarrier program. Forty B-47s were on order in March 1949. By April 1951, that number had grown to 1,500, although the last of these was not delivered until 1957, when the B-47 equipped thirty-two SAC wings.

Within the Air Force, however, questions about the B-47's capabilities were raised as early as 1952. For example, the Operational Engineering Section at MacDill Air Force Base (Fox, 1974, p. 382) reported to Air Development Center in June 1952 that "we will soon have hundreds of efficient flying machines that can . . . cope with almost any emergency . . . and host every feature of modern science. . . . There is only one thing wrong with these B-47s—they can't fly far enough to reach the target." Fully loaded (that is, carrying a nuclear device), the maximum operational radius of the B-47 was no more than 1,300 miles. This was not sufficient to reach many potential targets from SAC forward bases in England, Spain, North Africa, Okinawa, or Alaska.

LeMay dealt with this problem by planning some combat missions as one-way trips. This nearly doubled the striking range of the B-47, bringing it to about 2,500 miles, which was sufficient to reach almost all potential targets in the Soviet Union without refueling. Consequently, attention shifted from the B-47's range to the vulnerability of its overseas bases (Smith, 1964). To evaluate this issue, SAC asked the RAND Corporation to prepare a study of the overseas basing problem. The RAND report, prepared by Albert Wohlsetter and others and presented to the Air Force in 1953, concluded that a surprise attack could eliminate SAC's overseas bases and that the Soviet Union had or would soon have the capability to execute such an attack. The implication of this report was that SAC's B-47s could not deter a Soviet attack on Europe. If the Soviets actually meant to invade Europe, SAC's overseas bases merely invited a preemptive strike prior to invasion.

These results were not made public until 1958, but they were highly influential within SAC. They caused LeMay to give SAC's highest priority to air-to-air refueling, a satisfactory quick fix to the problem, and apparently triggered the 1954 decision to acquire and deploy nearly 400 Boeing B-52 bombers with intercontinental range—five times the number that had been contemplated only four years earlier. Fortunately, the B-52, which had been in development since 1945, was available for acquisition. The B-52 had the B-47's speed and ceiling and could carry a far larger bomb load. Furthermore, owing to the care with which its development had been managed, the B-52 experienced few of the postprototype difficulties of other bomber programs (Marschak, 1965).

The first deliveries of the B-52 were made to the Air Force in 1955. In that same year, the Department of Defense scheduled the retirement of the B-47. The oldest units were retired in 1958, and retirement was complete by 1962, only five years after the last B-47s were delivered. In short, the B-47 consumed nearly 25 percent of America's defense budget for nearly ten years, and then it was dropped because it no longer provided adequate deterrent capability.

In this case, the acquiring organization was dedicated to performance of its mission. It took criticism seriously enough to pursue its implications to an objective conclusion and acted on them, speedily adapting to new information and changed circumstances. SAC showed the same willingness to sacrifice assets and organizational units to perform its mission in a more effective fashion a few years later, when it sought responsibility for ICBM delivery, at the cost of three-fourths of its bomber fleet. In both instances,

SAC responded to a changing environment with long-term solutions rather than depending on Band-Aids or sweeping the problem under the table.

And, finally, when in 1990 its mission was completed, it quietly and efficiently prepared to stand down—closed its headquarters, folded its tents, and like an old soldier, faded away.

One moral of this story is that, where the stakes are high enough, the Department of Defense is fully capable of high levels of performance—if the Office of the Secretary of Defense properly performs its top-management function, if mission commanders are given the authority they need to carry out their assigned responsibilities, and if Congress lets them get on with the job.

CHAPTER TWO

Controlling the
Military Departments

The Strategy/Structure Mismatch

As a single-mission, single-function organization, SAC faced design problems that were fairly simple, especially when compared with those posed to the Department of Defense by America's postwar commitments to diverse, far-flung allies. Arguably these commitments posed a far greater structural challenge to the American military establishment than did even the new technologies. These commitments required the pattern of purposes that defined America's defense strategy to be reformulated in terms of regional defense objectives. They also required deployment of substantial conventional forces and logistical capabilities overseas, although this requirement was not fully recognized until after it became evident that the United States could not rely on the use of tactical nuclear weapons and the threat of massive retaliation to achieve its foreign policy objectives.

In nearly every case, America's regional defense plans called for operations involving a combination of ground, sea, and air forces. Not only did this subordinate combat functions to regional mission objectives, it also implied that the three military departments would have to prepare their forces for a variety of missions in different theaters, since most regional defense plans contemplated the use of units from more than one of the military departments. Depending on how their units were earmarked for various regional contingencies, each of the military departments now had several missions, the majority of which were to be achieved in collaboration with other services. This often meant that the performance of units supplied by the Air Force, say, had important spillover effects on the performance of units from the Army or the Navy.

Not surprisingly, each of the military departments sought to internalize these externalities by assuming functional roles that had traditionally been the sole responsibility of one of the other services. Of the services, the Navy carried this process the furthest, as Niskanen (1967, p. 7) explains:

> Each of the services developed forces in new . . . areas as a hedge against changes in strategic concepts and military technology. An attempt to limit interservice competition was made in the Key West agreement of 1947, but this agreement was rapidly—and understandably—undermined. . . . The Navy, whose position was threatened by the absence of a significant Soviet surface navy, was most successful in broadening its mission base. They developed an effective contribution to the strategic offensive forces, first with the carrier air forces and subsequently with the Polaris missile submarines; they also developed substantial antisubmarine forces to defend coastal waters and to protect sealift to the theaters where the large Soviet submarine force would be a threat. The Marines have been partly transformed from a navy-supported assault force to a more independent, sustained land-combat force. The carrier air forces have been reoriented to provide tactical air support for land combat in all theaters.

Unification of the Military Departments

In 1945, it was obvious that combat operations called for unified command of ground, air, and sea forces at the theater level. This lesson had been amply demonstrated by the American experience in World War II, when operations had been placed under joint commanders whose authority cut across traditional departmental lines. On balance, this system worked fairly well. Nevertheless, interservice rivalry and doctrinal rigidity caused enough problems for defense analysts to hope that the organizational apparatus for facilitating joint operations could be improved. Veterans of the war in the Pacific were especially critical of the impediments to effective combined operations caused by interservice rivalry (see, for example, Spector, 1984).

Furthermore, because joint operations require joint strategy, many—among them, President Harry S. Truman—concluded that budgeting and administration should also be unified. Most defense analysts evidently believed that this could be accomplished by unifying the military departments under a single civilian head (Stockfisch, 1973, pp. 132–133; see Huzar, 1946).

Unification was nominally achieved by the National Security Act of 1947, which established the Office of the Secretary of Defense to head the new Department of Defense and the Joint Chiefs of Staff to coordinate the raising, equipping, and organizing of military forces and the planning for their use in the pursuit of political objectives. The act also created the National Security Council to assist the president in the formulation of foreign policy objectives.

As a practical matter, however, neither the Office of the Secretary of Defense nor the Joint Chiefs were granted the authority they needed to execute their responsibilities. The Office of the Secretary of Defense lacked appointment, reorganization, and budget authority, and the Joint Chiefs lacked command authority. Consequently, aside from adding an additional layer of bureaucracy to the American defense establishment, the National Security Act did little more than ratify the status quo. The Key West Agreement of the Service Chiefs of March 1948 formally recognized this fact.

Arguably, the aim of the Key West Agreement was to suppress interservice competition, not to increase strategic cooperation or operational coordination (Niskanen, 1967, p. 6; Halperin and Halperin, 1983–84). In any case, the Key West Agreement endorsed the traditional functional boundaries of the military departments, stating that the primary function of the Air Force was to control the air, that of the Navy to control the sea, and that of the Army to defeat enemy ground forces. In addition to these primary functions, it acknowledged, "Each service is charged with collateral functions, wherein its forces are to be employed to support and supplement the other services. . . . As an illustration of this principle, strategic air warfare has been assigned as a primary function of the Air Force, and the Navy is assigned as a primary function the conduct of air operations necessary for the accomplishment of objectives in a naval campaign. . . . The Navy will not be prohibited from attacking any targets, inland or otherwise, which are necessary for the accomplishment of its mission" (quoted in Halperin and Halperin, 1983–84, p. 116).

There were perhaps three reasons for the failure to do more to correct the acknowledged deficiencies in U.S. defense organizations just after the end of World War II. First, no one really knew how to organize to meet the military contingencies of the second half of the twentieth century. Military analysts endorsed the concept of unified command headed by a single civilian authority, with a strong chief of staff reporting directly to the president, but beyond that basic point there was little agreement about what should be done. Moreover, it appears that even the more thoroughgoing unification proposals of that era were incomplete, as well as bureaucratically and politically naive. They focused entirely on the administrative structure of what is now the Department of Defense and usually ignored its responsibility and control structures.

Second, thoroughgoing unification threatened the interests of the existing military departments. As Demetrios Caraley (1966; see also Stockfisch, 1973, p. 133) explains, the Navy was particularly loathe to grant the Office of the Secretary of Defense the authority to organize it, if not out of existence, then at least into the backwaters of defense policy. Nor was this an unrealistic concern. The Air Force had designs on the Navy's planes and carriers, and the Army wanted control of the Marine Corps. If the Air Force and the Army had been successful in achieving these aims—and these aims had a long history in the interwar era (Shiner, 1981; Hone, 1982)—the only significant combat mission retained by the Navy would have been submarine patrol. Not only would it have been hard to justify a five-ocean navy in the face of no-ocean opponents; the Army and particularly the Air Force were organizationally and politically ascendant in the immediate postwar era.

In addition, rivalries between the military departments often served congressional prerogatives.

From this perspective, it seems almost as if the postwar reformers were more concerned about the symptoms of the gap between the nation's defense strategy and the structure of its military establishment, especially interservice rivalry, than they were about the gap itself. The organizational reform proposal that had the broadest support within the defense policy community at that time was aimed directly at the elimination of service competition. It proposed to reestablish unity of organizational structure by creating a single uniformed service and thoroughly restructuring its component branches on strictly functional lines (see Huzar, 1946; Hammond, 1961; Huntington, 1961, pp. 369–425; in contrast, see Ries, 1964). This is, incidentally, how the Soviet military establishment was organized. And advocates of this approach still exist (Byron, 1983; see, however, Halperin and Halperin, 1983–84). Obviously this proposal was not adopted—primarily because it threatened the prerogatives of the military departments and perhaps those of Congress as well.

But even if this proposal had been bureaucratically and politically acceptable, it made little sense in its original form. As Edward Luttwak (1984) has observed, military leadership and tradition are critical to the capacity of the Department of Defense to protect and defend the United States. It is axiomatic that the performance of any organization depends on its culture. Organizational culture is, of course, merely a shorthand way of referring to a bundle of values, traits, and norms shared by members of an organization, including mutual trust, personal and group loyalty, and individual attributes such as self-control or intrinsic motivation. It is what pushes people to perform adequately in difficult or highly demanding circumstances, even when it is not in their interest to do so. The traditions of the military departments and their component elements are an irreplaceable reservoir of institutional culture and values. It would be foolish indeed to discard or even threaten so valuable an organizational asset. This fact necessarily constrains reorganization and personnel options within the defense establishment and, insofar as unification threatens military tradition, it should rule out that option entirely.

Perhaps even more important, this proposal would have reestablished the unity of organizational structure at the cost of divorcing it from organizational strategy. As we have seen, America's post-war defense strategy was formulated in terms of missions that called for combined operations: strategic nuclear exchange and regional defense. The preparation and conduct of combined operations requires unity of command at the mission level. Making function and role central to military organization would have denied mission commanders the authority needed to orchestrate the actions of various military units supplied by different services to achieve a common objective.

Instead, coordination would have depended on the voluntary cooperation of the functional elements assigned to accomplish the mission objective, perhaps enforced by the Joint Chiefs of Staff, where they could reach consensus, or, where they could not, by the president or his deputy, the Secretary of Defense. This prospect may have seemed less disheartening when these offices were occupied by Eisenhower and George C. Marshall than subsequently. But it must have seemed rather far-fetched even then. During World War II, theater commanders were given absolute authority over the units assigned to them. When the Korean War broke out, one of the first acts of the Truman administration was to give General Douglas MacArthur full command of all American forces in Asia, although that authority was subsequently withdrawn after his defeat by the Chinese Peoples' Liberation Army and MacArthur was eventually dismissed (Manchester, 1978, p. 549; Luttwak, 1984, p. 27).

Furthermore, this proposal misinterpreted the real significance of the interdepartmental rivalry that broke out over roles and missions in the postwar period. The logic of creating a single uniformed service and restructuring its component branches on strictly functional lines seems to be that, if authority is sufficiently concentrated, fiat will suffice to suppress interdepartmental rivalry—in which case everything will be fine. What this ignores is that interdepartmental squabbles over roles and missions are really struggles for resources, which is ultimately to say that they are over organizational boundaries and proprietorship; but since property rights are lacking, they can only be resolved by fiat or bargaining between the interested parties, usually at someone else's expense. The solution, however, does not lie in suppressing conflict but in establishing appropriate organizational boundaries and property rights.

For example, for over forty years the Army has criticized the Air Force for its neglect of close air support and tactical airlift (see Bergerson, 1980; also Head, 1973). This dispute arises because the Air Force does not materially benefit from supplying air support and tactical airlift services to the Army and because it provides them at no cost to the Army. Consequently, the Air Force has no incentive to bolster its contributions to these functions and the Army has no incentive to economize on them. Several defense secretaries have tried to resolve this dispute by fiat, but imposed solutions that run counter to institutional self-interest seldom last and, in this case, they have not. The most recent manifestation of this conflict is seen in the fact that, despite the Army's emphasis on night attack, Air Force close air support aircraft still cannot see in the dark (Ropelewski, 1990). The clear meaning of this story is that there is a problem because the benefits (costs) from air support and tactical airlift services spill over the boundaries of the Air Force (Army). Most organizational theorists would say that the solution to this problem lies in the internalization of these externalities, either by assigning responsibility for them to the Army or by charging the user for services rendered.

Defense Reorganization Act of 1958

The next major organizational reform of the American military establishment came about ten years after the National Security Act of 1947. Recognizing the need for unity of operational command at the mission level, the Eisenhower administration proposed and the Congress passed the Defense Reorganization Act of 1958 (Huntington, 1984, p. 24; see also Hobkirk, 1983; Kinnard, 1977). This act increased the authority of the Office of the Secretary of Defense and provided for the reorganization of combat command along regional lines, which could have gone a long way toward reconciling America's defense structure with its strategy. The combatant (or "unified" and "specified") commands created by the Eisenhower administration were intended to be the principal instruments of American defense policy, each using forces supplied by the military departments. Eisenhower wanted to decentralize operational authority and responsibility to mission and theater commanders, because he believed

that the combatant commanders (CINCs in contempory defense terminology) were best situated and motivated to plan operations and
to determine the size and composition of the forces required to accomplish their assigned combat missions as well as to carry them
out. Eisenhower's commitment to decentralization was evidently
based on his experience as a theater commander during World War
II, but it may have been reinforced by the performance levels
achieved by the Air Force under decentralization in the period following the Korean War, especially that of the SAC under General
Curtis LeMay.

The Eisenhower reforms implicitly *assigned the military departments a distinctly subordinate or supporting role vis-à-vis the
combatant commands.* The military departments were to recruit,
train, and equip forces (units) to perform combat and support roles.
As we will explain shortly, if combatant commanders had also been
given the freedom to select the units they wanted from among those
supplied by the military departments, the Eisenhower reforms
might have transformed interdepartmental rivalry from a liability
into an asset. However, such a transformation would have required
financial or budgetary resources to flow to the military departments
through the combatant commands, and Eisenhower did not propose this system. Instead, combatant commanders had to take the
forces the military departments supplied and the military departments retained full administrative control over those forces: "The
combat forces of each service are supposedly controlled by 'unified'
or 'specified' joint service commands, but they still respond first and
last to their own service fiefdoms, which train, equip, and maintain
them with their own supporting commands, under the supervision
of their own service chiefs, who alone decide the fate of each officer's
career" (Luttwak, 1984, p. 91). In other words, the Eisenhower reforms sought to align America's defense structure with its strategy,
but what they accomplished was to divorce the military's responsibility structure from its administrative structure and its system of
measuring and evaluating performance.

Consequently, instead of clarifying administrative boundaries and mission responsibilities and developing a control structure that linked each responsibility center and administrative unit
to a coherent set of mission objectives, the Eisenhower reforms made

a vastly complicated bureaucracy even more complicated and created additional spillovers and common property resources where none had existed before. Because the cooperation of the supplying military department remained voluntary, combatant commanders found it necessary to make concessions to "buy" their cooperation, using the only currency available to them. And because it is easier for bureaucracies to add than to subtract, these concessions often took the form of long-term treaties guaranteeing the cooperating military department an enhanced role in the implementation of the combatant command's plans and activities. It is possible that these kinds of concessions may have cost some commands the capacity to achieve their assigned objectives. It is certain that they reinforced the propensity of the military departments to develop forces to perform a variety of functions and roles, even where others could supply equivalent forces or close substitutes in a more cost-effective fashion.

Centralization Under McNamara

During the 1950s and even later, most analysts were far more concerned about the problem of allocating resources to and within the Department of Defense than they were with its organizational structure or management controls. From here, it is easy to recognize their shortsightedness and to criticize them for it. But hindsight is always clearer than foresight, and in this instance their myopia was understandable. Thirty years ago, there was little real evidence of a gap between defense organization and strategic purpose, let alone of its seriousness. The visible symptoms of this gap—failure at the operational level and terminal bloat at the administrative level—still lay in the future. At the same time, it was obvious that the proliferation of overseas commitments, rapid technological change, and the subsequent transition from massive retaliation to flexible response required urgent changes in the shape and size of the U.S. military force structure and its logistical support capabilities.

Because the problem was defined in terms of making choices about the allocation of resources, the solution was equally obvious as well as equally shortsighted: have the Office of the Secretary of Defense figure out what to do and order the military departments to do it. This solution, however, carried with it two additional problems. The first was that the Office of the Secretary of Defense believed that it lacked the information needed to figure out what to do. The second was that the Office of the Secretary of Defense could not simply tell the military departments what to do. The Office of the Secretary of Defense does not supply resources to the military departments; Congress does. And Congress is not called on to fund the capability to do things (that is, perform missions, functions, or tasks). Congress provides funds to buy things. In the 1950s, the military departments requested and Congress provided funds in terms of the following object-of-expenditure classes: research, development, testing, and evaluation; procurement; construction; personnel; and operations and maintenance. The distinction between funding by administrative component and by object-of-expenditure class, function, or mission is illustrated in Table 2.1.

To get the military departments to do what it wanted them to do, the Office of the Secretary of Defense believed that first it had to figure out what the military departments needed. Then the military departments had to be told to ask Congress for funds to buy the things they needed—to carry out the Office of the Secretary of Defense's wishes. Finally, Congress had to give the military departments the funds they requested. This last was not seen as a serious hurdle, however, since congressional acquiescence could be assumed (Schlesinger, 1982, pp. 395–396).

The Planning, Programming, and Budgeting System— or Mr. Hitch's Marvelous Budgeting Machine

To help the Office of the Secretary of Defense tell the military departments what to do, a group of economists led by Charles Hitch at the RAND Corporation developed a comprehensive set of accounting and budgeting procedures. Together with wholesale changes in the Department of Defense's control structure, away from one oriented to administrative units to one oriented to functional constructs, these concepts and procedures comprised the planning, programming, and budgeting system—the PPBS process (Novick, 1954, 1956; Smithies, 1955, pp. 257–277; Hitch and McKean, 1960, pp. 44–65; see also Seligman, 1965; Baldwin, 1965; Korb, 1977; Hobkirk, 1983).

**Table 2.1. Principal Defense Budget Formats, Fiscal Year 1987
(in billions of fiscal year 1989 dollars).**

Items	Budget authority
Appropriation title (object-of-expenditure class)	
Military personnel	79
Operation and maintenance	88
Procurement	86
Research, development, testing, and evaluation	38
Military construction	5
Military family housing	3
Other	2
Total	302
Components (branch of service)	
Army	80
Navy and Marine Corps	101
Air Force	99
Defense agencies, Office of the Secretary of Defense, Joint Chiefs of Staff	21
Defensewide	1
Total	302
Program	
Strategic forces	22
General-purpose forces	122
Intelligence and communications	29
Airlift and sealift	7
National Guard and Reserve	17
Research and development	29
Central supply and maintenance	23
Training, medical, and other general personnel activities	38
Administration and associated activities	7
Support of other nations	8
Total	302
Mission	
Strategic nuclear retaliation	53

**Table 2.1. Principal Defense Budget Formats, Fiscal Year 1987
(in billions of fiscal year 1989 dollars), Cont'd.**

Items	Budget authority
Theater nuclear retaliation	3
Conventional defense of:	
Central Europe	82
Northern Europe	17
Greece and Turkey	10
Persian Gulf States	22
Republic of Korea	13
Pacific and Indian Oceans	22
Continental United States, plus	43
Hawaii, Alaska, Panama, Atlantic, and Caribbean	
Intelligence and communications	37
Total	302

Source: Office of Management and Budget, 1989; Office of the Assistant Secretary of Defense (Comptroller), 1988; Kaufmann, 1986.

The PPBS process installed in the Pentagon by Hitch under Robert S. McNamara remains in effect to this day, although it has been modified in various respects. It starts with the Joint Strategic Objectives Plan (JSOP), written annually by the Joint Chiefs and the service chiefs. The JSOP is then broken down by function into broad programs (for example, strategic retaliatory forces); these are further subdivided into hundreds of subprograms or program elements (for instance, the Midgetman system).

The Office of the Secretary of Defense then issues the Defense Guidance, which steers the military departments' budgeting and programming. The next step in the PPBS process is the production of the Future Year Defense Plan (FYDP). The FYDP details both the Department of Defense's continuing programmatic commitments (its base) and its new commitments (increments or decrements) in terms of force structure (including sizes and types of forces) and readiness levels, inventories and logistical capabilities, and the development of new weapons and support systems.

Next comes programming. In the context of PPBS, programming comprises the identification of program alternatives, forecasting and evaluating the consequences of program alternatives, and deciding which program alternatives to carry out. The consequences of the Pentagon's programming decisions are estimated in terms of the amount, character, and timing of inputs, including all acquisitions and construction, to be funded for each program package (assuming no change in commitments) during the next six-year (originally five-year) period, although in practice only the estimates for the first two years are used by the Department of Defense.

This process generates an array of Program Objective Memoranda. The Program Objective Memoranda are expressed in terms of current dollars and arrayed by military department, object of expenditure, and function. The first two years of the Program Objective Memoranda provide the basis for the military departments' budget requests to Congress.

In the context of PPBS, budgeting means preparing an annual spending plan. The Pentagon's budget requests set forth the Department of Defense's policies and spending proposals in monetary terms for the next fiscal year and provides a revised estimate of the current year's spending (in the fiscal 1991 budget, the current year is fiscal 1990). The Pentagon's spending plan is arrayed by program. It is also arrayed by military department, by object of expenditure, by federal budget classification code to meet the needs of the president's Office of Management and Budget, and by appropriation categories, with most research and development programs, major acquisitions, and construction projects individually scheduled to meet the needs of Congress.

Note that legislative budgets are formulated in terms of budget authority, while the executive budget, including that of the Department of Defense, is expressed in terms of expenditures or outlays. Budget authority is the authority to incur obligations on behalf of the U.S. government, which means signing contracts, placing orders, or hiring employees; outlays involve the liquidation of obligations, which means making payments or disbursing cash.

PPBS Versus Capital Budgeting

PPBS has many of the aims and some of attributes of the capital budgets and management control systems used by well-run organizations in the private sector, but the differences are great and in several respects decisive. In the first place, most well-managed businesses employ multiple budgets: capital budgets, operating budgets, and cash budgets. In this context, capital budgeting is concerned with all policy decisions—that is, all decisions that have long-term consequences for the organization, including those governing operations and not just those involving the acquisition of plant and equipment. The time horizon of a capital budget is the life of the decision; its focus is the discounted present value of the alternative in question. Operating budgeting is concerned with the behavior of responsibility center managers. It seeks to ensure that they carry out the organization's policies as efficiently and effectively as possible. Consequently, it comprehends both responsibility and outlay budgeting (see Chapter Five). Its time horizon is the operating cycle of the responsibility center in question, perhaps a month or even a week in the case of cost and revenue centers, usually longer where investment and profit centers are concerned. Its focus is on the performance of the responsibility center, outputs produced and resources consumed—where possible, these are measured in current dollars. The cash budget is concerned with providing liquidity when needed at a minimum cost. Its time horizon is the cash flow cycle, the temporal pattern of receipts and outlays experienced by the entity.

In contrast, the U.S. government has a single "budget." The only problem the federal budget and financial control system is well designed to solve is the liquidity problem, since the U.S. government's cash flow cycle has a period of one year and its accounts are maintained on cash as well as an obligation and a purchases basis. Paradoxically, however, liquidity is not a serious problem for the U.S. government.

Furthermore, private sector capital budgeting is selective, usually concerned only with new initiatives, and then only with changes in policy that are expected to yield benefits for longer than a year. In the language of public administration, one might even say that private sector capital budgeting is radically incremental (see

Wildavsky, 1966b, pp. 96–98). In contrast, the Pentagon's requests for budget authority are absolutely comprehensive. They reflect all planned asset acquisitions, including current assets—assets that are acquired and consumed during the fiscal year in support of continuing policies—as well as all long-term assets that will be consumed over an extended period, including those that replace existing assets that have been lost or have worn out.

In the second place, private sector capital budgeting tends to be a continuous process. Most well-managed firms always have an array of policy proposals under development. The decision to go ahead with a proposal is usually made only once, when the proposal is ripe, and is usually reconsidered only if the investment turns sour. In most cases, the proposal's champion within the organization is given the authority and the responsibility for implementing it (Bower, 1970). In contrast, budgeting in the Pentagon tends to be repetitive; all programs are reconsidered annually on the basis of a rigid schedule. New initiatives in the Pentagon must be supported by elaborate analytical justifications and reviewed and approved by hundreds of people all along the line from the lowest to the highest echelon, including the Joint Chiefs and the Secretary of Defense. The purpose of this repetitious review is evidently that, if one keeps hammering away at them, bad decisions will be defeated by attrition. The reality is that this process leads either to paralysis by analysis or to endless logrolling among the interested parties at every level. Moreover, the new initiative's principal advocate is seldom assigned responsibility for its implementation, although according to Vincent Davis (1973), this is precisely how most effective military innovations are carried out. Instead, responsibility is usually given to someone else, often in an entirely different administrative unit.

Another difference is that the objective of capital budgeting in the private sector is the identification of all policy options with positive net-present values, since in the absence of real limits on the availability of cash or managerial attention, the welfare of a firm's shareholders will be maximized by the implementation of all projects offering positive net-present values. The five-year defense program mimics private sector capital budgeting in that it shows the future implications of current decisions, albeit in a somewhat truncated manner. Moreover, many of these decisions are informed by cost-benefit and cost-effectiveness analysis. But nothing in the Pentagon's requests for budget authority depicts the future implications of current decisions in present-value terms. Otherwise Congress would not routinely stretch out weapons systems acquisition programs, often thereby increasing program cost by as much as 60 percent, to reduce the deficit and to avoid borrowing at interest rates of 10 percent or less. In content, the budget requests transmitted by the president to Congress are more like pro forma cash budgets than anything else found in the private sector.

The biggest difference, however, between the budget authority given to the Pentagon and the capital budgets approved by top management in the private sector lies in its relationship to the Department of Defense's management-control structure.

PPBS Versus Operational Budgeting

Management control is supposed to be a process for motivating and inspiring people, especially subordinate managers, to serve the policies and purposes of the organizations to which they belong. It is only secondarily a process for detecting and correcting unintentional performance errors and intentional irregularities, such as theft or misuse of resources. In most well-managed businesses, the primary instrument of management control is operational budgeting, which embraces both the formulation of operating budgets and their execution. In operating-budget formulation, an organization's policies, the results of all past capital budgeting decisions, are converted into terms that correspond to the domains of administrative units and their managers (Anthony and Young, 1988, p. 19). In budget execution, operations are monitored and subordinate managers evaluated and rewarded.

The Pentagon's budgeting system does this, of course. But there are critical differences between programming and budgeting in the Department of Defense and standard practices in well-run firms. The federal appropriations process produces a detailed spending or resource-acquisition plan that must be scrupulously executed just as it was approved. In contrast, operating budgets in the private sector are remarkably sparing of detail, often consisting of no more than a handful of quantitative performance standards.

This difference reflects the efforts made by firms to decentralize authority and responsibility down into their organizations. Decentralization means giving departmental managers the maximum feasible authority—or, in the alternative, subjecting them to a minimum of constraints. Hence, decentralization requires operating budgets to be stripped to the minimum needed to motivate and inspire subordinates to maximize their contribution to the organization as a whole. Most large decentralized firms produce fairly comprehensive operating reports describing many relevant aspects of the performance of their component departments and managers, but only a few of these are used to evaluate operations and to motivate subordinates. Ideally, the operating budget of a decentralized organization would contain a single number, goal, or performance target (for example, a sales quota, a unit-cost standard, or a profit or return-on-investment target) for each administrative unit.

Responsibility budgeting is the most common approach to operational budgeting used by decentralized organizations (see Chapter Six). The fundamental construct of responsibility budgeting is an account or control structure oriented toward responsibility centers. According to Robert N. Anthony and David Young (1988, pp. 8–9; see also Belkaoui, 1986, pp. 86–94; Demski and Feltham, 1976, pp. 143–144,152–159), a responsibility center is an administrative unit headed by a manager who is responsible for its actions. Responsibility centers have purposes or objectives, and they use inputs (resources) to produce outputs (goods or services). The outputs of a well-designed responsibility center will be closely related to its objectives.

Responsibility centers can be classified along two dimensions: (1) The integration dimension—that is, the relationship between the responsibility center's objectives and the overall purposes and policies of the organization; and (2) the decentralization dimension—that is, the amount of authority delegated to the responsibility manager, measured in terms of her discretion to acquire and use assets.

On the first dimension, a responsibility center can be either a mission center or a support center (Anthony and Young, 1988,

pp. 365–386). The output of a mission center contributes directly to
the organization's objectives. The output of a support center is an
input to another responsibility center in the organization, another
support center, or a mission center.

On the second dimension, revenue and expense centers are
found at one extreme and profit and investment centers at the other
(Anthony and Young, 1988, pp. 365–386). Expense is a monetary
measure of resources consumed, revenue is a monetary measure of
services delivered, and profit is simply the difference between the
two. A support center may be either an expense center or a profit
or investment center. If the latter, it "sells" its services to other
responsibility centers and its "profit" is the difference between its
expenses and the "revenue" it gets from the "sale" of its services.

In the context of decentralization, budget execution means
monitoring a responsibility center's performance in terms of the
target specified and rewarding its manager accordingly. It might be
noted that, if a target is high enough to elicit the manager's best
efforts, it cannot be achieved 100 percent of the time. As Andrew
Stedry (1960) has observed, a target that can be achieved with cer-
tainty is necessarily too low (see also Hofstede, 1967; Hopwood,
1976; Thompson, 1984).

How Capital Budgets Should Relate to Operating Budgets

Effective decentralization is possible in the private sector in part
because capital budgeting and operational budgeting are treated as
related but distinct processes. An organization's responsibility
budget should reflect its commitments. Thus, a decision to invest
resources in a new initiative should be reflected in the operating
budgets of all the responsibility centers affected. The controller
should revise operating budgets to reflect the increases in organizational performance that justified the decision to go ahead with the
initiative. She should specify the increases in performance expected
of each administrative unit or responsibility center, revise evaluative
standards to take account of anticipated improvements, and assign
responsibility for realizing them. But the purpose and the content

of capital and operating budgets—deciding and doing—are supposed to be kept distinct.

The Pentagon makes no such distinction, however. For the most part, operating managers within the Department of Defense may do only what their budget says they can do; they may not do what they are not authorized to do. Their budgets tell them they may incur obligations to buy things—and that is it. Their budgets focus exclusively on resources to be acquired by individual administrative units and on the timing of those acquisitions—on objects of expenditure rather than performance targets, on many inputs rather than a few critical outputs or results. In other words, operating managers have no real discretion to acquire or use assets; without that discretion, they cannot be held responsible for the performance of the administrative units they nominally head (Belkaoui, 1986, pp. 295–301).

Of course, PPBS did not cause a shift away from responsibility budgets to outlay budgets or from incentives and targets to fiscal rules and constraints within the Department of Defense. The military has long relied on before-the-fact controls. If Mr. Hitch's budget machine had any effect on the distribution of power and authority within the Department of Defense, it was merely to shift the locus of central authority out of the hands of the service and branch chiefs and into the hands of Robert S. McNamara (see Kaufmann, 1964, pp. 126–45; see also Art, 1968; Coulam, 1977).

In an important book on defense budgeting, Frederick C. Mosher (1954, pp. 237–243) advanced a proposal for a program budget that would have permitted the Office of the Secretary of Defense to make essential policy decisions but that would at the same time have permitted considerable decentralization of operations. Like his counterparts at RAND, Mosher proposed program packaging to help the Office of the Secretary of Defense establish strategic priorities and ration capital between major programs. He also proposed a functional account structure to force alternatives to the surface and to help the Office of the Secretary of Defense identify the most cost-effective service supplier. Mosher, however, envisioned this upward-oriented program budget operating in synchronization with a results-oriented operating budget, structured along administrative lines, that would have provided the primary vehicle for internal planning and control.

In retrospect, it seems unfortunate that the RAND version of program budgeting was adopted instead of Mosher's. Not that all of Mosher's proposals were up to the mark: like his RAND counterparts, Mosher overlooked the significance of the distinction between mission and function and between responsibility and administrative structure. Moreover, his solution to the problem of reconciling the exigencies of management control with the congressional budgetary process—lagging the operating budget behind the program budget by a year and having it start only after programs had been authorized—was somewhat awkward. But, unlike his RAND counterparts, Mosher clearly recognized that different kinds of budgets are needed for different purposes, for which different arrangements and timing are appropriate, and understood the importance of aligning administrative, responsibility, and account structures. These insights are the keys to effective management in any large and complex organization. During the 1950s or shortly thereafter, Congress might have willingly provided budget authority in terms of function or mission rather than object-of-expenditure categories and delegated to the Office of the Secretary of Defense the flexibility needed to implement a results-oriented operating budget. This was not the case during the 1970s and 1980s; it may not be the case now.

Aborted Reforms

Effective decentralization of Department of Defense would have required more than the installation of a results-oriented operating budget, however. At a minimum, responsibility budgeting and decentralization would have required prior clarification of the purpose of the major administrative units and responsibility centers in the Department of Defense and of their relationships to each other. Thinking organizational purpose through and reorganizing to bring the Department of Defense's structure into line with U.S. defense strategy was the singular challenge facing its top management in the postwar era. For one reason or another, the Office of the Secretary of Defense consistently failed to recognize the significance of this challenge or to meet it.

It can be argued that Eisenhower's and McNamara's organizational and budgeting reforms provided a necessary foundation for a rebuilt Department of Defense—that they failed only because their efforts did not go far enough. Building an organization is a lot like building a bridge. In both cases, one must often tear down in order to build up. In the jargon of organizational theorists, the working parts of an organization must be both differentiated—the process of dividing work into tasks or roles—and integrated—recombined into administrative units. Differentiation necessarily precedes integration (Connor, 1984, pp. 30–38; see also Lorsch, 1974).

Eisenhower's and McNamara's reforms effectively carried out the process of differentiation by reducing the Department of Defense to its basic constituent elements. Eisenhower divorced the Department of Defense's responsibility structure from its administrative structure. And by reorienting the focus of its control structure away from administrative units to functional constructs, McNamara divorced the Department of Defense's control structure from both.

Moreover, one must often centralize in order to decentralize (Perrow, 1977). Unity of command, policy direction from the top, and central control procedures are preconditions of effective intraorganizational decentralization. Eisenhower provided the Office of the Secretary of Defense with the authority needed to make organizational policy and strategy and McNamara used that authority to the fullest to shape the U.S. military force structure and its logistical support capabilities to the requirements of the doctrine of flexible response.

Unfortunately, neither Eisenhower nor McNamara carried his reforms through to completion. Like a bridge under construction, Eisenhower's and McNamara's organizational and budgeting reforms increased congestion and slowed movement to a standstill but did not shorten the trip one bit and will not until the project is finished.

This outcome cannot be blamed on ignorance. McNamara particularly appreciated the significance of organizational design and development. According to Daniel Seligman (1965, pp. 119–120),

McNamara's organizational changes began with a demand for an office in charge of organizational planning. He had set up an office for organization in his early days at Ford, and had briefly headed it himself; he was dismayed to discover that there was no such office then in existence at the Pentagon. Any such problems in this area—e.g., about who had jurisdiction over any new management function—were likely to be addressed by creating an ad hoc committee to look into the matter; there were scores of these committees roaming the corridors of the Pentagon during certain periods in the 1950s. McNamara announced immediately that he had to have a permanent office in charge of organizational matters. The importance he attaches to it is evidenced in the fact that he has made its head . . . an Assistant Secretary of Defense.

McNamara also claimed that he wanted to push all decisions to the lowest appropriate level and recognized the need to make organizational changes to implement his management philosophy.

Project Prime was the most promising of the organizational design and development efforts initiated under McNamara. Project Prime was developed by Robert N. Anthony (Juola, 1993, pp. 43–44), who succeeded Hitch as defense comptroller in September 1965. Like Mosher, Anthony recognized the significance of the distinction between making policy and executing it, between planning and operating. This distinction was reflected in the comprehensive resource management system he proposed for the Department of Defense, with a separate results-oriented operational budgeting component. Moreover, Anthony saw the need for prior clarification of organizational purpose, boundaries, and relationships, and for an account structure that would tie the organization together. The account structure he proposed was firmly grounded in the principles of responsibility budgeting and accounting. Anthony (1962) proposed that the Department of Defense should:

1. Classify all administrative units as either mission or support centers.
2. Charge all costs accrued by support centers—including charges

for the use of capital assets and inventory depletion—to the mission centers they serve.[1]

3. Fund mission centers to cover their expected expenses—including support center charges.
4. Establish a working capital fund to provide short-term financing for support units.
5. Establish a capital asset fund to provide long-term financing of capital assets and to encourage efficient management of their acquisition, use, and disposition.

The only significant conceptual difference between Anthony's system and standard practice in the private sector is that he proposed to establish separate funds to manage the acquisition, use, and disposition of fixed assets and some inventories, but this too is now standard practice in many not-for-profit organizations, including the Department of Defense.

The principal formal device by which a measure of intraorganizational decentralization is accomplished within the Department of Defense is the revolving fund. These funds involve buyer-seller arrangements internal to the Department of Defense. They have actually been in use for some time. The Navy had a revolving fund as early as 1878. Modern-day revolving funds date to the 1947 National Security Act, which authorized the defense secretary to use them to manage support activities within the Department of Defense.

Two kinds of funds have been established under this authority: stock and industrial funds. Stock funds are used to purchase supplies in bulk from commercial sources and hold them in inventory until they are supplied to the customer—usually a military unit or facility. Industrial funds are used to purchase industrial or commercial services (for example, depot maintenance, transportation, and so on) from production units within the Department of Defense. Both kinds of funds are supposed to be financed by reimbursements from customers' appropriations (Juola, 1993, p. 43).

Anthony's proposal would have merely expanded the scope of this device and enhanced its effectiveness by establishing rules for setting transfer prices prospectively rather than retrospectively and by making support center managers responsible for meeting explicit financial targets. Revolving funds encourage efficient choice on the part of support centers, as well as the units that use their services, only if prices are set ahead of time and support centers nominally charge all of their expenses against revenues earned delivering services. Furthermore, support centers must be treated as responsibility centers—their managers must be fully authorized to incur expenses to deliver services, and held responsible for meeting the stated financial goals of their centers (Bailey, 1967, p. 343).

Consequences of Centralization Under McNamara

Anthony's system was supposed to be operational by July 1967. But like many of the organizational design and development efforts initiated under McNamara, Anthony's proposals never really got off the ground. This failure can probably be attributed to the press of operating problems. By 1965, it was clear that nothing important could happen in Office of the Secretary of Defense without McNamara's attention and support and that McNamara was preoccupied with other, more immediate concerns, first with the pacification of the Dominican Republic and then with the agonies of Vietnam. It is hard after all to remember that you are there to drain the swamp when you are up to your waist in alligators. Besides, reorganization probably did not seem critical. To most independent observers, centralization appeared to work under McNamara. Indeed, it appeared to work brilliantly.

In his first four years as Secretary of Defense, with only a 13 percent increase in budget authority, McNamara greatly enhanced both the survivability of America's strategic forces and the adequacy and mobility of its tactical forces. He tripled the number of nuclear warheads in the strategic alert forces and made massive investments in the Minuteman and Polaris missile systems. He increased the number of combat-ready Army divisions from eleven to sixteen and Air Force tactical wings from sixteen to twenty-one. He strengthened Marine Corps manpower from 175,000 to 190,000 and increased the special forces tenfold. He doubled airlift capability and quadrupled sealift, giving the United States the capability to deploy an extraordinary array of military forces at points all over the world, rapidly and efficiently (Seligman, 1965, p. 117). The purpose of this buildup was to increase the number of options available in a crisis, especially the capability to wage conventional war (Kaufmann, 1964, p. 36).

Of course, McNamara's accomplishments were only partly—if at all—attributable to improved management systems. Of far greater importance were a series of tough-nosed decisions involving offsetting reductions in existing force structure (for example, Air Force interceptor squadrons were reduced from 65 to 27 and strategic bomber squadrons from 140 to 40), the availability of a variety of weapons systems to choose from, and considerable luck (see Schlesinger, 1967). These decisions were so adroit that the basic force structure established under McNamara lasted through the Cold War essentially unchanged (Jones and Doyle, 1992).

Since the important changes in doctrine and force structure made under McNamara reflected policy decisions that were made in early 1961, before the implementation of the new program format or the formal programming system (Niskanen, 1967, p. 9), this meant that nearly thirty years would go by before Mr. Hitch's budgeting machine would be used to help the Office of the Secretary of Defense establish its strategic priorities or to ration capital between major programs. According to remarks made in April 1992 by then-Secretary Dick Cheney and Comptroller Sean O'Keefe, PPBS played a key role in the first comprehensive alteration in the force structure of the United States made since 1961, the base force proposal outlined in the 1991 FYDP. This means that the elaborate mechanisms of the PPBS process were used throughout the entire Cold War merely to grind out updated tables of organization and equipment and to fill them with new weaponry and trained personnel—rarely has process so completely triumphed over purpose.

The organizational costs of McNamara's successes were not at first evident. Subsequent events have shown, however, that his accomplishments were largely Pyrrhic victories. He provided the material means to project U.S. power worldwide and to respond flexibly to a variety of contingencies. But, according to Benjamin Schemmer, where our military once had clear missions, a clear-cut chain of command, McNamara left the Department of Defense with a structure that was administratively bloated and organizationally incapable. Instead of crisp decision making and clear-cut control of military strategy and operations, his organizational legacy was log-rolling at every level up to and including the Joint Chiefs, a fragmented control structure, and a murky, committeelike chain of command (Schemmer, 1990, p. 5).

Schemmer (1990, p. 5) further alleges that "the fragmentation and logrolling, the complex, multi-layered, multi-departmental chains of command so characteristic of later American military actions and the consequent need for planning and close supervision at the Joint Chiefs level or higher" were the root cause of the Pentagon's uninterrupted succession of military, administrative, and political failures between the 1960s and the 1980s—the loss of the Vietnam War, the Pueblo and Mayaguez incidents, the failed attempts to rescue prisoners at Son Tay and Iran, especially the Desert One fiasco, the bombing of the Marine barracks in Lebanon, and the successful but sloppy intervention in Grenada, botched weapons (such as the version of the M-16 rifle initially issued to troops in Vietnam), and aborted weapons systems development programs (such as the MBT-70 tank or the DIVAD antiaircraft artillery system).

Whether Schemmer is correct about the root cause of these failures (we are of course inclined to agree with his evaluation), the simple fact is that McNamara carried to the extreme the process that began when MacArthur was relieved of his command during the Korean War. He strictly subordinated the military to his authority and centralized authority over both aspects of military strategy—using the armed forces of the United States in support of political objectives, including the authority to conduct military operations, and raising, equipping, and organizing the armed forces—in his hands.

This was costly for two reasons. First, it violated the rule that authority should be centralized as close to the job as possible. Centralization of authority over military operations at the top of the Pentagon obviates the need to give mission commanders full operational authority over nominally subordinate units, especially those assigned from other military departments. As we have seen, however, successful conduct of military operations requires precise orchestration and coordination of complex bundles of tasks. Centralization of this authority in McNamara's hands denied nominal mission commanders the authority they needed to carry out their missions.

Second, because he failed to clarify administrative boundaries, roles, and mission responsibilities and to delegate authority accordingly, he centralized things at the top that never needed to be centralized at all. As we have seen, preparing forces for combat is governed primarily by long-run considerations and should be governed by other kinds of transactional arrangements. Given this failure, when administrative failures occurred, as is inevitable under any governance arrangement, top management responded by creating another mechanism, process, or unit to prevent future recurrences and overlaying it onto the existing organization. Gradually, but inexorably, bureaucracy thickened, costs rose, and administrative performance declined. This phenomenon is especially evident in the acquisition of major weapons systems. Its consequences are suggested by the time it now takes to develop and deploy them. In the early postwar period, the trend was consistently downward. Development time continued to fall throughout the decade of the 1950s but increased in the 1960s and continued to increase through the early 1980s (Smith and others, 1988).

CHAPTER THREE

Reengineering
the Pentagon

Organizational Change After McNamara

THE AUTHORITY OF the Office of the Secretary of Defense ebbed and flowed in the 1970s and early 1980s. Melvin Laird and especially Caspar Weinberger largely deferred to the military departments. James Schlesinger and Harold Brown sought to achieve the semblance of unity of command and tried to regain for the Office of the Secretary of Defense some of the authority and responsibility that Laird returned to the military departments (see Stubbing, 1986, pp. 259–398). The consequences of strengthening the military departments at the expense of the Office of the Secretary of Defense might have been predicted. In organizations that lack direction and discipline, decentralization of authority provides an ideal environment for the pursuit of parochial self-interest to the detriment of the organization as a whole. Nevertheless, at the time these consequences seemed surprising.

Under the austere defense budgets that followed the Vietnam War, undisciplined decentralization led to the poorly trained, poorly led "hollow force" of the mid 1970s. It also encourged the further proliferation of the bureaucratic layers that enfeebles so much of the defense establishment. During the prosperity that followed, American military capability increased significantly, although many observers would agree with Daniel Wirls's (1992,

p. 224) conclusion that the $760 buildup that started in the late 1970s "was wasteful and inefficient, often fraudulently so [that] . . . there was a yawning disparity between how much was paid and what was obtained," and that it "was irrelevant to many of our most important security concerns."

About the only effective managerial innovation that emerged during the 1970s and early 1980s was due to Secretary Laird's deputy, David Packard, who tried to replace the paper competitions installed under McNamara with prototype competitions. This approach ("fly before you buy") had once been standard practice in the Department of Defense. It required contractors to be selected based on the performance of working prototypes. Both the F-16 and the A-10 programs used this approach (Stubbing, 1986, pp. 304–305).

With the breakup of the Soviet empire, things began to change, in part due to congressional pressure. Under Secretary Dick Cheney, the Department of Defense made a remarkable commitment to the new public management. Under the rubric of reinventing government, these reforms continued under his successor, Les Aspin.

Congress Gets into the Act

During the 1970s and 1980, at the same time that the Office of the Secretary of Defense was struggling with the military departments to define the scope of its authority, Congress was withdrawing much of the authority it had delegated to the military establishment. During the 1930–1960 period, Congress deferred to the executive with regard to most issues of substantive military policy and their implementation through the budget, although it drew the line short of waiving its right to prior review of executive action and balked at some of the more radical reforms of defense organization proposed by the executive, such as the elimination of the military departments' secretariats (Hitch, 1965, pp. 14–16). In particular, it provided standing, open-ended authorizations covering the military departments' personnel levels, formations and deployment, and investment. For example, in fiscal year 1957 the Air Force was authorized an end strength of one million officers and enlisted personnel and 24,000 aircraft, deployed to 200 wings (Dawson, 1963; Dexter, 1963).

Of course, the military departments were rarely if ever provided the budget authority they needed to attain authorized operating and investment levels. Furthermore, their annual appropriations bills continued to be painstakingly itemized and qualified by special interest language (although not by pre-World War II standards or today's). However, once the appropriations committees had a hard estimate of the sum of the individual spending items included in a department's appropriation, they often struck a deal with the department, granting it almost complete discretion to transfer funds between items and time periods in return for holding actual spending under that sum (Macmahon, 1963, pp. 370-376). Members of the appropriations committees—especially the House Appropriations Committee—were willing to trade latitude in budget execution for lower spending levels because they saw themselves primarily as guardians of the public purse rather than as managers (Wildavsky, 1966a).

Consequently, Huntington (1961, pp. 132-133) could claim in 1961 that "at times in the past Congress formally legislated and limited military programs through unit and personnel authorization, appropriations, and the authorization of weapons development. As instruments of control and elimination, these [have] fallen into disuse. . . . Congress never vetoes directly a major strategic program, a force level recommendation, or a major weapons system proposed by the Administration in power." Huntington (pp. 139-140) concluded that the only real issue remaining was whether Congress could compel the Pentagon to spend money to maintain forces or acquire assets that the executive did not want.

Despite the deference given the executive by Congress during this period, the Pentagon was careful to observe the forms and usages of congressional supremacy, to respect its prerogatives, and to respond to congressional concerns about the effect of military policy at the constituency level, especially those having to do with the size and composition of guard and reserve forces and military base locations and operations. In addition, the Pentagon may have initiated some weapons and support systems projects because they were the pets of influential senators or representatives. It maintained a few projects for that reason long after they would have otherwise been canceled—for example, Senator Henry Jackson's nuclear-powered bomber (Baldwin, 1965, p. 250).

Moreover, during this period the Pentagon was committed to maintaining a large number of military prime contractors in business and to ensuring relatively stable production levels. The primary purpose behind these policies was the maintenance of production capacity that could be called on in time of war (Kaldor, 1981, pp. 61–74; Markusen and Yudken, 1992, 33–47; see also Kurth, 1973). This commitment also had the effect of keeping a number of firms busy, of spreading contracts around from firm to firm, and of stabilizing employment levels. The evidence is compelling that Congress did not often influence the source selection process and generally exercised relatively little influence over the size of contract awards or their duration (Fox, 1974, pp. 280–283; see also Mayer, 1990). Nevertheless, the military departments were careful to notify senators and representatives prior to awarding contracts so that they could announce them to their constituents and claim credit for the local consequences of the Pentagon's acquisition actions.

Both of these patterns started to change around 1960. First, the Office of the Secretary of Defense overstepped itself by willfully ignoring congressional prerogatives and constituency concerns. Secretary McNamara was especially insensitive to congressional prerogatives and concerns. He unilaterally canceled pet projects. He stopped warning Congress of impending acquisitions and base closure and realignment actions. And he refused to go along with the willingness of the appropriations committees to trade latitude in budget execution for lower spending levels, insisting that his budget was precisely what was needed for defense, not one penny more—and not one penny less (Seligman, 1965; Baldwin, 1965).

Later, Congress lost confidence in the Pentagon's competence and perhaps in the integrity of many of its leaders and employees. This gradual loss of confidence in the military establishment not only reflected an unbroken succession of operational failures and habitual fiascos in weapons systems development. It also resulted from fabulous tales of waste, fraud, and abuse in the procurement process (hammers, coffee makers, and toilet seats). Other factors included the failure of some Pentagon officials to

show proper deference to the sensibilities of their political masters
and their ill-advised attempts to play political hardball with
Congress (for example, using the discretion to shift spending from
one location to another to reward legislative supporters or to punish
opponents, hoping to extort congressional support for various in-
stitutionally favored programs).

In any case, Congress subsequently withdrew much of the
authority over defense strategy and its implementation that it had
delegated to the executive. In 1959, Congress enacted Public Law 86-
149, which required annual congressional authorization of appropriations for the procurement of aircraft, naval vessels, and missiles.
In 1962, it enacted Public Law 87-436, which required annual congressional authorization for research, development, testing, and
evaluation projects associated with aircraft, naval vessels, and missiles. In 1964, Public Law 88-174 extended the requirement of annual authorization to all Department of Defense research and
development projects. In 1965, Public Law 89-37 required annual
authorization for the acquisition of all tracked vehicles. Subsequent
laws enacted in 1969, 1970, and 1981 extended this requirement to
all other ammunition-firing weapons, torpedoes and related support equipment, and ammunition.

In 1967, Public Law 90-168 required annual congressional
authorization of the personnel levels of the special reserve forces. In
1970, Public Law 91-441 extended this requirement to all active-
duty personnel in each component of the Armed Forces. In 1973,
Public Law 93-155 further extended this requirement to cover the
civilian employees of the Department of Defense. In 1972, Public
Law 92-436 required annual congressional authorization for recruit
training and advanced individual training levels, officer training
levels, and enrollments at military and civilian institutions. In 1980,
Public Law 96-342 required annual congressional authorization for
operations and maintenance funding in support of the Department
of Defense and its components. In 1983, Public Law 98-94 required
annual congressional authorization for working-capital funds (Committee on Armed Services, U.S. Senate, 1986, Appendix B).

In addition to telling the Department of Defense what to buy,
Congress has also used its authority to guide the acquisition process. Congress often acts as if corruption and favoritism were the

root causes of the acquisition system's failures, including cost overruns, schedule slippages, and weapons systems that do not work or are simply too expensive (see Brian-Bland and Rasor, 1986, p. 106). The complement to the belief that the acquisition system is riddled with fraud and abuse on the part of both contractors and acquisition personnel is that greatly increased regulation and oversight are needed to fix the system. As a result, Congress has added to the existing 1,150 feet of legislation and case law governing procurement an assortment of new laws aimed at further disciplining Pentagon acquisitions (Kovacic, 1990b; Blum and Lobaco, 1987; Smith and Beck, 1987). In 1988 alone, Congress added eight new laws with over fifty provisions governing defense acquisitions (Kovacic, 1990b, p. 105).

Some of this legislation has addressed overcharging and double-charging for materials and services, payroll padding (FAR 31 & 52 [cost mischarging]; 10 U.S.C. §2306 [inaccurate cost or pricing data submitted to government]; 18 U.S.C. §287 [submission of false claims to a government agency], §371 [conspiracy], §1001 [submission of false statements to a government agency]; §1341, §1343 [mail fraud]), misappropriation of government property, bribery, kickbacks (18 U.S.C. §201; 41 U.S.C. §§51-54 [bribery, kickbacks, influence peddling]), and conflicts of interest (18 U.S.C. §207; 18 U.S.C. §281).

Perhaps the most far-reaching of the new laws is the 1986 qui tam section of the False Claims Act (31 U.S.C. §§3729-3731) (see France, 1990; Thompson, 1988). The term *qui tam* comes from the medieval Latin expression "Qui tam pro domino rege quam pro se in hoc parte sequitur," which means "who brings action for the king as well as for himself." The qui tam provisions reflect suspicion of both private defense contractors and acquisition managers in government. They were designed to lure whistleblowers out of the woodwork by handsomely rewarding them (and their lawyers) for taking private action against contracting abuses. They empower anyone who discovers someone defrauding the government to sue the wrongdoer on its behalf. Plaintiffs who win in court can pocket 15 to 25 percent (30 percent if the government chooses not to join the case) of total penalties (which include triple damages and fines of up to $10,000 per false claim), plus attorney fees and costs. This law also subjects employers that punish or fire whistleblowers to heavy penalties. It is particularly far reaching because almost every failure to acknowledge or report a violation of federal regulations constitutes statutory fraud. Furthermore, "knowingly" making a false claim also comprehends "should have known." Proof of actual knowledge or specific intent to defraud is not required.

Other recent acquisition "reforms" include the Competition in Contracting Act of 1984, which called for contracts—and subcontracts—to be let on the basis of "technically acceptable, low bid" auctions, small-business set-asides, spare parts breakout, labor cost and work breakdown estimates, random drug testing, and more rigorous product testing (Public Law 98-369; Public Law 99-145, 10 U.S.C. §2438[b][1]; Public Law 99-591, 10 U.S.C. §2365[a]; Public Law 100-456). To the list of recent reforms should be added revolving-door legislation, which prohibits senior Pentagon acquisition personnel, including political appointees, from taking positions with defense firms for two years after they leave government (Public Law 99-145, 10 U.S.C. §2438). In all, there are now 853 separate laws governing defense acquisition, according to the Pentagon's Acquisition Law Advisory Panel (Roos, 1992).[1]

As Congress has gained familiarity with the Pentagon and its workings, it has increasingly used its legislative powers to influence substantive military policy and to implement policy through the budget and the acquisition process, and to take responsibility for some of the high-level management functions that top managers in the Department of Defense have too often failed to perform satisfactorily. While we are generally skeptical of congressional abilities to manage the Department of Defense, we acknowledge that Congress can claim responsibility for at least one outstanding achievement during this era: the enactment of the Goldwater-Nichols Department of Defense Reorganization Act of 1986 over the opposition of Secretary Weinberger (see Boo, 1991). By passing into law some of the proposals that had initially been put forth under the Eisenhower administration, the Goldwater-Nichols Act corrected some of the more pathological administrative shortcomings of the defense department. This law clarified the role of the Joint Chiefs of Staff and strengthened the position of its chair in the chain of command and in the actual employment of combatant forces. The Goldwater-

Nichols Act also gave the combatant commanders an indirect role in peacetime resource allocation and specified that the commanders of all the military units assigned to a combatant command would be under their exclusive authority, direction, and control. Perhaps most important, it gave them a voice in the assignment and evaluation of component commanders and the power to fire subordinates and made successful joint duty assignment a prerequisite for promotion to general or flag rank (Coakley, 1992, pp. 120–121). Thus, the Goldwater-Nichols Act unambiguously reestablished the principle of unity of combat command, thereby greatly enhancing the ability of the United States to use its military forces in support of political objectives—although not necessarily to prepare them for that use.

Blue Ribbon Commissions

The Goldwater-Nichols Act was inspired in part by the findings of two blue ribbon commissions established by Reagan administration to investigate government operations: the Grace Commission and the Packard Commission. Both were narrowly charged. The Grace Commission was addressed to cost control, the Packard Commission to waste and inefficiency in the acquisition process. Both, however, came to believe that the problems they found were largely manifestations of more basic organizational flaws and both strongly urged the kinds of reforms that have come to be associated with the new public management—downsizing, rightsizing, and deregulating the Pentagon and making it more centered on outputs and results.

Grace Commission

The Grace Commission's diagnosis of the Pentagon's organizational problems was straightforward (and absolutely consistent with the thesis advanced in this volume): the Office of the Secretary of Defense had failed to deal with fundamental questions of architecture and governance. Because its managers had neglected the functions of top management—planning, organizing, staffing, and organizational development—they had by default been forced to assume lower-level management functions—operating, controlling, and budgeting. Overwhelmed by administrative detail, they had had little time to perform their proper functions. As a result, the Pentagon had become turgid, sluggish, and burdened with offices, departments, and installations that were no longer vital and with managers who had no clear idea of their responsibilities and who constantly bickered over who should do what.

The Grace Commission report further noted:

> Government, and DOD in particular, does not delegate authority well. The impact of holding authority at the top of the organization . . . is to weaken the entire organization. The lower levels do not create or innovate. They respond to the hierarchy rather than propose and initiate; they . . . avoid risks. . . . The upper levels of the organization become overloaded. They respond quite naturally by adding deputies and assistants . . . [and] layers to the organization, and this diffuses authority and responsibility even further. This is in direct contrast to private sector experience which has clearly demonstrated that the effectiveness of a large, complex organization improves when authority is delegated down into the organization along with responsibility. Decisions then are made by those with either the most pertinent knowledge of the situation or with the highest stake in the outcome of the decisions [President's Private Sector Survey on Cost Control (Grace Commission), 1983, pp. 47–48].

The Grace Commission was also critical of certain excuses given for the failure of the Pentagon's top managers to perform their most important function: "If the top managers do not have time to plan ahead, and to set goals and manage by objectives, how can they possibly expect their subordinate managers to do so? We were told repeatedly that goal setting was more difficult in government because the profit motive was absent. Our conclusion is that, because there is no profit motive and because there is such a high turnover in top management, there is far greater need for long-term goal setting in government than in the private sector" (President's

Private Sector Survey on Cost Control [Grace Commission], 1983, p. 49).

In keeping with its diagnosis, the Grace Commission report prescribed a radical redesign of the Department of Defense. Its recommendations included:

1. Reorganization of the civilian management functions of the Office of the Secretary of Defense, perhaps along the lines of the Department of Defense program budget categories, with separate deputy secretaries for production and research and development acquisitions
2. Careful delineation of organizational units performing line and staff functions
3. Wholesale pruning of decision-making and review committees
4. Elimination of the civilian secretariats of the military departments: Air Force, Army, and Navy
5. Reorganization and redefinition of the role of the Joint Chiefs of Staff
6. Assumption of responsibility for the delivery of civilian support services by the Office of the Secretary of Defense: base support operations, wholesale warehousing, traffic management, contract administration, audit, direct health care, and overseas military sales

This last recommendation would have consolidated many of the functions currently performed by the military departments under the direct authority of the Office of the Secretary of Defense. This recommendation is not inconsistent with the commission's endorsement of decentralization. Rather, the report concludes that, so far as civilian support services are concerned, decentralization along service lines makes little sense—it would be better to organize them on regional or geographic lines.

Packard Commission

In a sense, the Packard Commission took up where the Grace Commission left off. Recurring stories about acquisition fraud, waste, and abuse prompted President Reagan to create the Blue Ribbon

Commission on Defense Management—called the Packard Commission after its head, David Packard, chair of the board of the
Hewlett-Packard corporation and former Undersecretary of Defense. The commission was established in 1985 and composed of
prominent leaders from industry and government who were asked
to evaluate the effectiveness of defense acquisition organization and
procedures, to determine how they might be improved, and to recommend changes that would lead to improved performance.

The commission reported the following year, with a preliminary report in January, an interim report in April, and a final report
in June. Most of the commission's recommendations were narrowly
addressed to acquisition issues (we will examine these in greater
detail in the next two chapters). However, the commission quickly
concluded that it would not be possible to make significant improvements in acquisition management without fundamental
changes in the architecture of the Department of Defense.

Like the Grace Commission, the Packard Commission observed that the Pentagon did a poor job of delegating authority. It
further observed that authority could not be effectively delegated
within the Pentagon because its exercise was not linked to a system
of performance measurement or to the organization's internal system of rewards and sanctions. Consequently, the Packard Commission called for a major overhaul of the way the Pentagon does
business.

Matrix management is the crux of the organizational approach advocated by the Packard Commission report. Under matrix
management, mission responsibility would be differentiated from
the management of support services. That is, combat responsibility
would be independent of direct responsibility for provisioning,
training, and equipping military units. According to the Packard
Commission, combat should be the responsibility of the joint and
specified commands and, ultimately, the chair of the Joint Chiefs
of Staff. Training, equipping, and provisioning military units
should continue to be the responsibility of the military departments
and the consolidated support agencies.

One important difference between the system proposed by
the Packard Commission and the system it criticized is that the
Packard Commission called for line managers in the military de-

partments and the central support agencies to be evaluated in part in terms of their ability to persuade mission commanders to pay for and use the services they supplied. In turn, their component divisions would be held strictly accountable for realizing a return on their investment in plant and equipment (Blue Ribbon Commission on Defense Management [Packard Commission], 1986a).

In other words, the Packard Commission implied that the combat commands should be linked to the military department via a system of transfer prices, as should military formations and their suppliers within the Department of Defense, and that the whole system should be tied together by a common system of accounts and an integrated responsibility structure.

Pentagon Response

Shortly after Secretary Dick Cheney was confirmed by the Senate in the spring of 1989, President Bush asked him to report on the Department of Defense's implementation of the Goldwater-Nichols Act and of the recommendations made by the Grace and Packard commissions.[2] His response to this request is contained in the *Defense Management Report* (Cheney, 1989), published in June 1989. The *Defense Management Report* called for sweeping changes in organizational process and structure designed to increase the efficiency of the Department of Defense and to compel it to operate in a businesslike fashion (Office of the Secretary of Defense, 1991b). As Secretary Cheney explained,

> We are changing the way that we do business. We're cutting out redundant operations and streamlining management. We're instituting common business practices throughout the department and the benefits are tangible. We estimate that the Department of Defense will save over $70 billion between now and the end of [fiscal year] 97 as a result of these changes. Every dollar we save by cutting out the cost of doing business is a dollar that we do not have to cut out of force structure, out of weapon systems, out of readiness, or out of the quality of life for our men and women in uniform [Office of the Assistant Secretary of Defense (Public Affairs), 1991b, p. 2].

These changes included streamlining and disciplining the weapons systems acquisition process and consolidating all communications, data processing, and financial and accounting systems, contract management services, maintenance and supply activities, research and development, and intelligence operations, as well as the elaboration of a comprehensive cost-accounting and managerial control structure. The broader administrative control system contemplated under this set of initiatives comprehended a matrix structure for the Department of Defense, with its combat units and military bases linked to support centers by transfer prices and accrual accounts.

Consolidation

The *Defense Management Report* proposed to consolidate the logistics functions (purchasing, warehousing, depot maintenance, and so on) of the individual services under the direct authority of the Office of the Secretary of Defense—through the Defense Logistics Agency and the Defense Depot Maintenance Council. This has been interpreted to mean reducing 34 separate supply depots and approximately 3,500 separate parts and equipment warehouses to 26 regional centers. The aim of this initiative was reducing operating outlays, but it has also been argued that consolidation of the logistics function will reduce overheads and inventory carrying and transportation costs and improve management control and customer service, in part through greater competition (see Harr and Godfrey, 1991a).

Secretary Cheney subsequently carried out Department of Defense-wide consolidations of commissaries, printing operations, correctional facilities, engineering services, and health care administration, along with corresponding reductions in the administrative staffs of the military department secretariats, and called for greater competition in science and technology development between the various defense research laboratories, in addition to their reorganization and consolidation (Office of the Assistant Secretary of Defense [Comptroller], 1992a).

Corporate Information Management

The *Defense Management Report* also led to efforts designed to consolidate a multiplicity of information, data processing, and telecommunications systems into a single Department of Defense system and to standardize its computer procedures and software. This effort comprehended the intelligence systems and was supposed to result in consolidation and elimination of redundant functional units in the military departments and the unified commands.

Again, the aim of the Corporate Information Management system was to strengthen the defense department's ability to use its data processing, communications, and information management resources, while reducing their cost. It also played a key role in the consolidation of finance and accounting centers in each of the services into a single Defense-wide service.

Payroll and Accounting Systems

Consolidation of information systems started with payroll and accounting systems. At one time, there were nearly 30 different payroll systems and at least 250 accounting systems in use throughout the Department of Defense. The Defense Finance and Accounting Service sought to consolidate accounting, payroll, travel, and other financial management systems and to eliminate redundant finance and accounting centers and staff. On October 1, 1992, 14,000 employees were reassigned to the Defense Finance and Accounting Service from the military departments and defense agencies, initially reducing total finance and accounting positions by about 1,000. As its first director, Albert Conte, observed, "The Defense Finance and Accounting Service was charged to be an agent of change. We have initiated more change in the fifteen months of our existence than most Department of Defense organizations have in two decades. . . . When this process is completed over the next few years, we will have changed a great deal of the Department of Defense finance and accounting culture, eliminating unnecessary and duplicative accounting and payroll systems and cutting total financial management systems to a handful. This is the DFAS mandate."

Business Operations Fund

In our opinion, the most important management reform initiated during the Cheney era was the establishment of the Department of Defense–wide Business Operations Fund (see Jones, 1992b). This $80 billion revolving fund was designed to consolidate management and accounting for business-type activities throughout the Department of Defense. These operations range from repairing aircraft to delivering medical supplies to front-line troops—in short, all the activities that have both customers and suppliers in the Department of Defense.

The Business Operations Fund was approved by Congress in 1991 and was managed personally by deputy defense comptroller Donald Shycoff and a small staff of unit-cost experts at the Pentagon. The fund includes nine industrial and stock funds, the Defense Finance and Accounting Service, the Defense Industrial Plant Equipment Service, the Defense Logistics Agency, the Defense Commissary Agency, and other agencies. As we have observed, the Department of Defense has a long history of revolving-fund use, but previously these funds were operated under the authority of the military departments and defense agencies rather than the Office of the Secretary of Defense.

A key component of the Business Operations Fund was its use of historical costs to establish prices for service provided to users within the Department of Defense. Under the "unit-costing initiative," transfer prices were supposed to reflect fully distributed average total costs, rather than direct costs as was previously the case, computed on an accrual rather than an outlay basis. When an aircraft was overhauled, for example, parts, labor, depreciation of equipment, rents, and all other cost factors were to be included in the price of the job. According to the Pentagon, unit costing would "improve cost visibility and accountability to enhance business management and improve the decision making process; [help to establish] financial and performance standards for operational managers, [and clarify or identify] the relationship between providers and customers of commercial-type services, . . . the full cost of business area activities, . . . mobilization and surge costs, as well as military personnel costs" (Office of the Assistant Secretary of Defense [Comptroller], 1992b, p. 1).

The Pentagon actually planned to use the Business Operations Fund to finance a sizable portion of its business and support functions on a unit-cost basis in fiscal year 1993. The units performing these functions were to be given budgets expressed in terms of costs per unit of output, rather than in the traditional manner using "control numbers" or spending targets and ceilings. According to Donald Shycoff, this new approach to budgeting "says [to military departments and defense agencies] here is the output and performance level that we expect you to produce and here is the price that we will pay for that output." Shycoff indicated that entities would be entitled to their full budget only if they met the performance targets set by the Office of the Secretary.

Implementation of Management Initiatives

The ideas underlying the Business Operations Fund are sound. The model on which it is based rests on extensive business practice and a well-developed intellectual foundation in the public management literature (see, for example, Barzelay, 1992). Moreover, these ideas have been successfully implemented by the Naval Supply Systems Command (Harr, 1989, 1990) and the Defense Logistics Agency (Harr and Godfrey, 1991a, 1991b). Harr also clearly explains the operating logic of the Business Operations Fund and unit costing and shows the importance of finding mission and service costs, using a meaningful form of accrual accounting.

The implementation of these ideas on a Department of Defense–wide basis has not been smooth. Interviews with key participants in this process have made us aware of the special political and organizational obstacles these reforms faced. In the first place, its size, complexity, and organizational incoherence predispose the Department of Defense to bureaucratic inertia. Under the best of circumstances, implementing changes in the Department of Defense can be immensely difficult, and these were major changes.

The secretariats of the military departments were particularly unenthusiastic about these reforms and in some instances actively hostile. Many individuals in the military departments understandably doubted that unit costing would serve their department's interests; more opposed consolidation; and nearly everyone was outraged that projected savings from the proposed reforms had been summarily deducted from their budgets—although this is fairly standard business practice. Not only did the military departments lose personnel and administrative authority as a result of consolidation, they also lost control over the timing of cash flows. And, to add injury to insult, they were required to reimburse the Business Operations Fund for services they had previously provided for themselves, at what they considered exorbitant prices.

Nevertheless, the military departments' biggest objection to the Business Operations Fund was that, by uncovering their internal finances to external critics in Congress and the General Accounting Office, they would be exposed to further budgetary penalties. They also feared that the information generated by the Business Operations Fund was open to misuse by external observers, especially those in Congress, most of whom remain unfamiliar with the use of working capital or its place in the system of expense accounting used by the Business Operations Fund.

This was not an idle concern. When Navy Industrial and Stock Funds were consolidated into the Business Operations Fund, the General Accounting Office "discovered" $2 billion in surplus cash. Congress pulled this amount from the Business Operations Fund, despite the insistence of both the Navy and the Defense Comptroller that the positive cash balance of the Navy components of the Business Operations Fund was an accounting artifact produced by the timing of transactions and that from the standpoint of the Department of Defense as a whole, there was no surplus—net current assets were entirely offset by assets and liabilities elsewhere in the system.

For the most part, the reformers effectively grappled with these and other obstacles: seeking the support of the uniformed personnel of the military departments as well as their civilian secretariats, using reimbursement to motivate cost measurement, and so forth. For example, when Shycoff failed to persuade Congress to restore the amount it pulled from the Navy's portion of the Business Operations Fund, he made the Navy whole using surplus accumulated from the sale of excess property to the public and other transactions. Moreover, Shycoff and his staff exerted great personal effort to try to explain what they were doing and how the principles supporting the Business Operations Fund should be implemented. If the reformers had had more time, they might have triumphed over these obstacles and others.

Even so, we are inclined to believe that some of the obstacles the reformers encountered were of their own construction. Despite their commitment to making a success of the Business Operations Fund and unit costing, they failed to communicate a satisfactory understanding of what had to be done, who was going to do it, or why it should be done throughout the Department of Defense. Moreover, the cost-finding principles promulgated by the Defense Comptroller's office (for example, see Shycoff, 1990; Defense Finance and Accounting Service, 1990) were confusing to the managers and line controllers in the military departments and the defense agencies who were responsible for their implementation. The cost-finding principles were confusing in part because full-cost accounting was new to the Department of Defense and in part because of the wrong-headed way depreciation and working capital were handled, but mostly because they were manifestly incomprehensible. Of course, if producers of unit-cost information did not understand what was wanted of them, they could not possibly produce it. Consequently, cost-accounting systems remained a hodgepodge to the end of the Cheney era. Many were exceedingly primitive—even rudimentary standard costs and direct labor-hour measurements were frequently lacking. To top it all off, the Defense Finance and Accounting Service failed to produce a consolidated accounting system in time to support the unit-cost concept (Chapin, 1993, p. 2).

Few of the participants knew exactly what they were supposed to be doing, especially those charged with the implementation of the Business Operations Fund and unit costing in the military departments. Most also lacked the expertise in cost accounting and transfer pricing needed to figure it out. For example, almost nobody outside of the Defense Comptroller's immediate circle seemed to appreciate the need for changes in responsibility structure and management philosophy to go along with the changes being made in the account structure of the Department of Defense (see Barzelay, 1992). Yet, as Harr (1990) shows, reorganization of supply depots on a mission (he uses the term *product*) basis rather than a functional basis was central to the success of the activity accounting system implemented by the Naval Supply Systems Command—as was an orientation to customer satisfaction. We also had trouble finding anyone in the Department of Defense, the General Accounting Office (see Chapin, 1993), or even the Congressional Budget Office (see Blum, 1993, pp. 19–20) who really understood the difference between arm's-length transactions and the use of transfer prices. And nobody in the Department of Defense but Shycoff and his immediate staff seemed to know what the finished product would look like when it was done.

Stop Paving the Cow Paths

Finally, as ambitious as these management reforms of the Cheney era were, they were probably not ambitious enough. The Cheney-era reformers aimed for reductions in overheads of 10 to 20 percent to be achieved through consolidation and computerization. Some of these planned savings never materialized, owing to increased average salaries and transition costs that were higher than anticipated. Consequently, the Pentagon's work force actually increased 12 percent between 1985 and 1993.

Instead, the reformers should have recognized that many of the Pentagon's work flows, job designs, control mechanisms, and organizational structures are either superfluous or obsolete, and started over. Reengineering processes—restructuring as well as downsizing and defatting—would probably improve administrative performance and, by slimming the Pentagon bureaucracy, save a lot of money. As Michael Hammer (1990, pp. 104, 107) explained in an article in the *Harvard Business Review,* "It is time to stop paving the cow paths. Instead of embedding outdated processes in silicon and software, we should obliterate them and start over. We should reengineer our [organizations]; use the power of modern information processing technology to radically redesign our . . . processes in order achieve dramatic improvements in their performance. . . . We cannot achieve breakthroughs in performance merely by cutting fat or automating existing processes. Rather we must challenge the old assumptions and shed old rules."

Hammer illustrates reengineering with the revolution that took place in Ford's system of accounts payable. In the early 1980s, Ford's auditors carefully studied accounts-payable activities and concluded that, by consolidating, by rationalizing processes, and by installing new computer systems, payroll staff could be cut 20 percent—from 500 employees to 400. Ford was pleased with its plan to slim the accounts-payable payroll—until it looked at Mazda, whose entire accounts-payable organization consisted of five clerks. Consequently, Ford did not "settle for the modest changes it first envisioned. It opted for radical change—and achieved dramatic improvement." Through reengineering, Ford cut the required number of manual accounting transactions and reconciliations associated with processing and paying for the goods it used from nine to three, thereby producing "a 75 percent reduction in head count, not the twenty percent it would have gotten with a conventional program." Hammer notes that the changes Ford made in its accounts-payable operation also resulted in improved materials management and more accurate financial information.

The principles of reengineering are fairly simple. First, whenever possible, design jobs around an objective or outcome instead of a single function—functional specialization and sequential execution are inherently inimical to expeditious processing. Second, whenever possible, have those who use the output of activity perform the activity and have the people who produce information process it, since they have the greatest need for information and the greatest interest in its accuracy. The use of modern data bases, expert systems, and telecommunications networks provides many, if not all, of the benefits that once made administrative centralization and specialization of administrative functions such as reporting, accounting, purchasing, or quality assurance (economies of scale, high levels of coordination, and standardization) attractive, without sacrificing any of the benefits of decentralization. Third, capture information once and at the source. Fourth, coordinate parallel activities during their performance, not after they are completed. And last, give the people who do the work responsibility for making decisions and build control into job design (Hammer, 1990, pp. 108–112).

The contrast between how Ford handles its accounts payable and standard operating procedures in the Department of Defense could not be more striking. In the Navy, for example, it takes twenty-six manual accounting transactions and nine reconciliations—thirty-five steps in all—for a user to obtain authorized supplies from a qualified vendor (Hemingway, 1993, pp. 8–12). This system is not only cumbersome, it often leads to bad service and excessive investment in inventories. According to the *Gore Report*, the system also causes frequent delays in obtaining repair parts. And, these delays keep a large proportion of the Navy's cars and trucks out of commission, which forces the Navy to buy 10 percent more vehicles than it really needs (Gore, 1993, p. 12).

Lt. Commander Anne Wilson Hemingway shows that computerization could eliminate over half of the steps in the Navy's accounts-payable process (Hemingway, 1993, p. 25). But why are fourteen, let alone thirty-five, accounting records needed where Ford gets by with three? One answer is that the Navy fails to capture information once and at the source. Instead, each step in the supply process—requisition, receipt, certification of invoice, reconciliation, and revision—is repeated on up the chain of command. Moreover, the people who produce information do not process it. Processing is handled by financial management specialists at every level from the cost center to the Financial Information Processing Center of the Defense Accounting Office.

But the most important reason is that the Navy does not build financial control into job designs. Captains of naval vessels, for example, are not held responsible for controlling costs and have little discretion as to the mix or quantity of resources used by their commands. Even in peacetime, their effectiveness in managing resources has no bearing on the evaluation of their performance. Indeed, their budget is determined at a higher level. The system of ordering and processing supplies is primarily intended to ensure that neither they nor higher-level authorities exceed their obligational authority, which is divided into 50 separate accounts, 557 management codes, and 1,769 accounting lines. In other words, the Navy relies on what we refer to in Chapter Six as before-the-fact controls, where after-the-fact controls would be more appropriate.

The principles of process reengineering imply that the Navy's 400 ship commanders should instead be responsible for their purchases and that they should be supported by a standardized information system. Under this approach the Defense Accounting Office would be responsible only for maintaining a data base on vendors, which it would share with ship commanders, and for using the data base to negotiate contracts with vendors on behalf of the Department of Defense as a whole and to monitor purchases made by responsibility center commanders. Instead of rules preventing them from incurring excess obligations, ship commanders could be evaluated during peacetime at least in part on the basis of their success in managing costs. The adoption of this approach or something like it would permit the number of manual accounting entries needed to make a purchase to be reduced from thirty-five to three: order, receipt, and payment. At Hewlett-Packard, its adoption resulted in substantial cost savings and a better than 100 percent improvement in service (Hammer, 1990, p. 110).

The New Administration

The new administration under President Clinton came into office committed to creating a new fighting force for the twenty-first century—smaller and leaner, but faster and high-tech—capable of facing the new challenges of the post–Cold War world.[3] The Clinton administration also took office with a strong desire to save money on defense, although without a plan for precisely how to do it. Nevertheless, it was assumed that it would try to do more to implement the new public management than had its predecessor—or, to use the now-fashionable language, that the new administration would reinvent and reengineer the Pentagon. Those who made this assumption clearly underestimated the amount of time it would take for a management team to be installed and take charge of the Department of Defense. Besides, the crises in Somalia and Bosnia, the bottom-up review of force structure and requirements discussed in the introduction to this volume, and the replacement of Secretary of Defense Les Aspin absorbed much of the time and attention of the new management team. Thirteen months into the Clinton administration, its promise remains glittering; its practical accomplishments elusive.

Like those of his immediate predecessors, Clinton's administrative reform efforts were announced by a report, *The Gore Report*

*on Reinventing Government: From Red Tape to Results, Creating
a Government That Works Better and Costs Less* (Gore, 1993). So
far as the Department of Defense is concerned, the Gore report cov-
ers roughly the same ground as the Grace Commission and the
Packard Commission reports, although its rhetoric and the vision
of government are different. Some of its recommendations (Gore,
1993, pp. 136, 160–167) are:

- Improve government performance through strategic and quality
  management, by strengthening the corps of senior leaders, and
  by improved program design.
- Develop mission-driven, results-oriented budgets; incorporate
  performance objectives and results as key elements in budget and
  management reviews; reduce overitemization and excessive subdi-
  vision of funds in financial operating plans and remove overly
  detailed restrictions and earmarks from appropriations; measure
  direct costs; simplify the apportionment process, expedite reprogramming of funds, permit rollovers of unobligated balances; increase the use of multiyear and no-year appropriations.
- Reinvent procurement by reducing administrative burdens and
  unnecessary regulatory controls; take advantage of the technological advances and efficient procurement practices of the commercial marketplace; encourage "best-value" procurement and
  promote excellence in vendor performance.
- Create a flexible, decentralized, and responsive hiring system.
- Improve financial management by fully integrating budget, financial, and program information; use technology to streamline
  financial services; reduce financial regulations and requirements; simplify financial reporting; and "franchise" internal
  services.
- Establish a long-term fixed-asset planning process and incorporate it into federal budgeting to ensure that choices are not biased
  against long-term investments; expand the capital investment
  fund and manage its operations in a more businesslike fashion.
- Reengineer programs to cut cost and improve performance.
- Improve distribution systems to reduce costly inventories and

provide incentives to dispose of excess property; allow managers
and commanders to purchase the best-value common supplies
and services from public or private sources; outsource noncore
functions.

- Implement a systems design approach to management control:
  streamline the internal controls program; reduce internal regulations and management control positions at least 50 percent;
  and expand the use of waivers to encourage innovation.
- Improve relations between the legislative and executive branches;
  negotiate reductions in the reports provided to Congress and
  seek enhanced rescission authority from Congress and the authority to reorganize agencies.

Unfortunately, when it comes to laying out specifics, the
Gore Report all too often reads like a parody of the behavior it
criticizes: it is precise and specific when talking about what it is
against—rules, regulations, detailed budget language, stifling red
tape; it is often frustratingly vague when it talks about what it is
for. It rightly emphasizes the importance of improving government
performance through strategic management, rethinking program
design, and mission-driven, results-oriented budgets. But when it
talks about implementing these ideas, its recommendations are
often either superficial or inconsequential. The *Gore Report* calls
for executive branch employees to "attend appropriate educational
sessions on strategic and quality management" (p. 160), for the
President's Management Council to "commission the development
of a handbook to help federal managers understand the strengths
and weaknesses of various forms of program designs" (p. 166), and
for clarifying "the goals and objectives of federal programs" and for
incorporating "performance objectives and results as key elements
in budget and management reviews" (p. 161).

The Pentagon's chief response to the Gore Commission's invitation to reinvent itself has been to reaffirm its commitment to the
management initiatives of the Cheney era, especially the acquisition
reforms, the Business Operations Fund and unit costing, and the efforts designed to consolidate information, data processing, and telecommunications systems into a single system and standardize com-

puter procedures and software. To the previous administration's initiatives, Pentagon reinventors have added new commitments to
wholesale process reengineering, to franchising services, to competition, and to meeting customer needs.

It is our impression that there is lot more understanding of
the new public management and enthusiasm for it within the Department of Defense now than there ever was during the Cheney era.
Some of our sources within the Pentagon attribute this change to
the environment of benign neglect created by the Office of the Secretary of Defense under Secretary Aspin. Participation in the Gore
Commission effort forced large numbers of managers throughout
the Department of Defense to confront the missions performed by
their agencies and to think through their jobs. As a consequence,
many of them realized that reinventing government was precisely
what the Cheney-era reformers were trying to make them do. Many
also realized that, in the absence of a strong push from the top, they
would have to take ownership of the administrative reform process
if it was to go forward at all. Hence, the top-down initiatives of the
Cheney era have gained a substantial grassroots constituency—especially in the support agencies, but increasingly in the military
departments as well.

Whether this commitment will come to much of anything,
however, will largely depend on the willingness and ability of Secretary Aspin's successor William Perry to step forward at this time
and attend to top-management tasks—thinking through the Pentagon's structural relationships and clarifying its administrative
boundaries, functional roles, and mission responsibilities. This an
absolute prerequisite to developing a responsibility structure for the
Department of Defense that is aligned with American military strategy and to implementing a system of accounts that links each administrative unit and responsibility center to the overall defense
policies of the United States. Failure to sort out these relationships
will leave it an organization in which almost everything depends on
everything else, where nobody is responsible for optimizing much
of anything, and where decentralization remains counterproductive.

This problem is especially evident where the acquisition of
major weapons systems is concerned. As we show in subsequent

chapters, appropriate institutional arrangements and governance mechanisms have not been built into the acquisition structure of the Department of Defense. Nor have the military departments, the systems development commands, and program management personnel been provided with the means or the incentives to do the right things.

PART TWO

Strategies for a New Era

CHAPTER FOUR

Working with the Private Sector

Strengthening the Industrial Base

THE DEPARTMENT OF DEFENSE buys more merchandise than all the rest of the public sector of the United States put together. It bought $123 billion worth of goods and services in 1992. More than 30,000 firms provision the Pentagon; 15,000 are prime contractors. These firms employ hundreds of thousands of production workers, engineers, and scientists, as well as tens of thousands of accountants, lawyers, and lobbyists—altogether over three million employees (Field, 1990). The acquisition process also enlists the efforts of legions of Department of Defense personnel, both uniformed and civilian—over 580,000, according to the expansive Pentagon definition of acquisition, which comprehends research, development, procurement, logistics, distribution, and related maintenance activities (Cheney, 1989, p. 12).

Defined more narrowly, defense procurement generates about 250 million hours of paperwork a year, 90 percent of the federal government's total (Weidenbaum, 1992, p. 153). The Pentagon employs more than 100,000 men and women, uniformed and civilian, to produce this paper and pays them $5 billion each year. Nearly 50,000 of these employees (including 26,000 auditors) monitor and enforce compliance with procurement regulations and contractual terms.

101

Despite this huge commitment, the Pentagon has by no means extracted all the efficiencies that should be available from a defense industry as big as America's. Indeed, the *Economist* ("Slimming the General," 1993) claims that the whole process is in need of radical reform: "The Pentagon is the only western defence department with an entirely separate procurement machine for each of the country's service arms. Its methods make most other countries' defense establishments look like models of streamlined efficiency." Most acquisition experts would agree with this assertion. Most believe that the size and convolutions of the Pentagon's procurement machine are major obstacles to getting value for money. This view has been affirmed by a succession of blue ribbon commissions and endorsed by several serious students of the acquisition process who have published book-length studies of the difficulties (Fox, 1988; Gregory, 1989; McNaugher, 1989; Kelman, 1990).

These experts reject the notion that fraud and abuse significantly increase acquisition costs, *except insofar as efforts to stop these evils have seriously degraded the efficiency and effectiveness of the process.* They argue that fighting fraud and abuse has led to excessive reporting requirements, detailed contractual specifications, duplicative reviews, intrusive oversight—in short, excessive formalism and red tape—which has directly increased the size and complexity of the Pentagon's procurement machine. The result is delayed systems development and deployment and greatly increased weapons systems costs. As Steven Kelman (1990, p. 1)—the Clinton administration's chief procurement officer—eloquently explains,

> The government often fails to get the most it can from its vendors. In contrast to the conventional view, however, I believe that the system of competition as it is typically envisioned and the controls against favoritism and corruption as they typically occur are more often the source of the problem than the solution to it. The problem with the current system is that public officials cannot use common sense and good judgment in ways that would promote better vendor performance. I believe the system should be significantly deregulated to allow public officials greater discretion. I believe that the

ability to exercise discretion would allow government to gain greater value from procurement.

The experts are in general agreement about what hurts defense procurement, because they understand what it will take to improve it. There is only one way the United States can reduce significantly the costs of the weapons systems it buys: increase the *efficiency of the processes by which they are developed, manufactured, and purchased.* This means:

- Taking greater advantage of economies of scale and scope in systems development and production
- Enhancing manufacturing productivity by improving processes, reducing production cycle times and inventories, and increasing investment in new plant and equipment
- Reducing contractors' overheads and indirect costs
- Reducing the size of the acquisition establishment (while improving the quality and remuneration of its personnel)

In turn, these goals can be facilitated by:

- Redesigning the Pentagon's organizational structure to increase the personal authority and responsibility of acquisition personnel
- Simplifying and streamlining the processes through which contractors are selected and projects managed

Unfortunately, laws aimed at preventing fraud and abuse are among the principal stumbling blocks to these needed reforms. In some cases—for example, greater delegation of authority and organizational streamlining—they directly prohibit steps called for by the experts. In others, they serve as more oblique barriers to reform. For example, the individuals who represent the Department of Defense in the contracting process are often overmatched by their counterparts in defense firms, who are on average brighter, better paid, and more experienced (Kovacic, 1990b, pp. 112-113). Consequently, it is necessary to increase the skills and the experience of Pentagon's acquisition personnel. Of course, the best place to find the experienced acquisition personnel the Department of Defense needs is in private industry, but the revolving-door statutes have largely closed off the defense industry as a source of senior executives.

Weapons Industry

Before we can talk about improving the acquisition process, we must discuss the products themselves. In this chapter, we will describe the products the Pentagon buys, the industry it buys from, and the special problems that arise when it buys technologically advanced weapons. We also outline some positive steps that could be taken to improve the efficiency of the defense industry. In the next chapter, we explain how to streamline the procurement process and to redesign the Pentagon's management of it.

The Pentagon buys a bewildering array of things—everything from food to furniture to janitorial services. But more than half of its purchases are for weapons and weapons-related services. For the most part, the weapons it buys are of American design and manufacture, for two reasons. First, many of the weapons produced by America's arms makers are the best in the world in terms of quality or price—often both (Rich and Dews, 1986). Second, the Pentagon is predisposed by law, public policy, and the long-standing customs of the military departments to buy American-made goods and services even when they are inferior in quality or more costly (Thompson, 1985).

Product quality is the biggest competitive strength of the American arms industry. It is greatest where technologically sophisticated weapons—submarine finding gear, air-to-air missiles, stealthy aircraft, advanced rocket engines, communications paraphernalia, signals-intelligence equipment, and the like—are concerned. More than anything else, the excellence of these weapons reflects the level and quality of the Pentagon's investments in advanced research and development. In turn, the effectiveness of Pentagon research and development, especially in fields like military electronics, is a tribute to the scope and scale of America's research base, especially its numerous high-quality research universities. America's research base should remain a source of comparative advantage for the American arms industry well into the next century.

The size of the American military market is also a source of strength. Other things being equal, higher production volumes permit development costs and administrative overheads to be spread over a greater number of units. However, as domestic military demand falls and production volume drops, existing economies of scale will fade. Not only will reduced sales lead to increased production costs; by reducing resources available for research and development, they could also indirectly impair product quality. Furthermore, in many sectors of the industry, potential economies are further reduced by obsolete plant and high overheads, which can in part be attributed to the reporting requirements, detailed contractual specifications, duplicative reviews, and intrusive oversight that characterize federal acquisition regulation.

The proper response to these problems is a matter of considerable debate, even among the experts. So far the Pentagon has evidently been content to cut suppliers, shorten orders, cancel programs, and let the market pick up the pieces. This has been its policy since 1987 and has triggered a wave of horizontal and vertical integration in the defense industry, as firms have sought to cope with contraction by consolidating to maintain production economies and to amortize research costs and overheads as widely as possible and by acquiring suppliers to maintain profitability on reduced sales. Recently Loral, a leader in defense electronics, purchased LTV Missile; Martin-Marietta bought General Electric Aerospace; Lockheed acquired General Dynamics' military-aircraft division. One benefit to Martin-Marietta from its acquisition of General Electric Aerospace is that it now has its own electronics assembly plant and will no longer have to rely on potential competitors to assemble its gizmos and gadgets. Consolidation among subcontractors has been equally dramatic, and there is more to come ("Slimming the General," 1993, p. 63).

Rationalizing and Modernizing the American Arms Industry

One problem with the Pentagon's passivity is that it could easily degenerate into a program of across-the-board spending cuts, protectionism, restrictions on technology transfer, and thin research support. Furthermore, it does not address the problem of modernizing American defense production, which relies on some of the oldest manufacturing plant and equipment in the world, much of it dating to World War II. With plants designed for volume assembly of single designs over long periods, defense manufacturing in the United States is almost as inflexible today as it was then.

The U.S. Office of Technology Assessment (1984, pp. 60–62) defines flexible manufacturing as a system "capable of producing a range of discrete products with a minimum of manual intervention. It consists of production equipment workstations (machine tools or other equipment for fabrication, assembly or treatment) linked by a materials handling system to move parts from one work station to another, and it operates as an integrated system under full programmable control." Implementation of such a system can obviously yield a range of productive efficiencies, including increased machine utilization; reduced inventories, labor costs, and space-driven overheads; and higher product quality.

Most informed observers believe that, to remain competitive in world markets, producers must build flexible, state-of-the-art manufacturing plants in which economies of scope can be substituted for economies of scale and that use advanced technology—both product and process technology—to design and manufacture lower-cost products.

The Pentagon has encouraged investment in flexible manufacturing on the part of some of its suppliers, both because it is inherently more efficient and because, where the Department of Defense owns the design and manufacturing programs, it facilitates competition between producers—*second sourcing,* in Pentagon-speak (see Parker and Lettes, 1991; Haedicke and Feil, 1991). Unfortunately, America cannot afford to modernize everything. In recognition of this fact, Murray Weidenbaum (1992; see also Thompson, 1985) has argued that the way to overcome this constraint is to rationalize weapons making along transnational lines. This would permit production economies to be maximized and research costs and overheads spread as widely as possible. If America got rid of its export controls and domestic-content laws, it could also purge itself of some of the portions of its obsolete defense infrastructure that it cannot now afford to rebuild.

The logic of this suggestion is particularly apparent when

one looks carefully at America's domestic-content legislation. There one finds mention, not of America's highly competitive, technologically sophisticated weapons businesses, but its nearly moribund garment, watch, and metal-bashing industries (for example, the Preference for U.S. Food, Clothing & Fibers Act, the Required Source for Jeweled Bearing Act, the Preference for Steel Plate Act, the Required Source of Aluminum Ingot Act). Moreover, the firms that have received the greatest (or, at least, the most sustained) cosseting at the hands of the Pentagon are in the small-arms and ship-building industries, the duds of American arms making.

If product quality and price were the sole determinants of arms acquisition decisions, no nation's armed forces would purchase American small arms. They are generally inferior to those used by the rest of NATO and are clearly inferior to the best in the world. In belated recognition of this fact, the U.S. Army has recently adopted as standard issue light weapons developed in Italy and the United Kingdom and is seriously considering the adoption of infantry weapons developed in Germany and Sweden. Similar claims can be made with respect to most types of naval vessels, although the problem with American-made ships is price, not quality.

Hence, the logic of rationalizing weapons making along transnational lines goes beyond manufacturing weapons in the United States that were developed elsewhere, as the Army proposes to do. This logic calls for the Army to buy small arms in Europe and, presumably, to have the components of more complex systems made wherever their production would be most economical. Here, Japanese practice provides an eye-opening model. The Japanese Defense Agency uses the American-designed multiple-launch rocket system and Aegis destroyer, but it does not buy them from the United States. They are not built entirely in Japan, either. Rather, the Japanese Defense Agency buys the sophisticated electronics used by these systems from the United States and builds their engines and hulls in Japan ("Japan's Defence Industry: At War with the Budget," 1992). In one case, final assembly is in Japan, in the other, the United States. The result is that both the multiple-launch rocket system and Aegis are less expensive than if they had been built entirely in one country.

The gains from freer trade in this area are not limited to more

economical or better weapons, although this is an extremely important benefit. The end of the Cold War means that most nations are
reducing arms purchases. Thus, on top of decreased domestic demand, American weapons makers must also contend with declining
world demand—and with harsher world competition, in part owing
to the emergence of new arms producers and exporters (such as
Brazil, China, and Korea). It also means that their competitors
abroad face similar problems with production economies and
spreading research costs and overheads. Teaming up with foreign
partners is one way for firms to deal with these problems. Most
teams are currently based on existing weapons systems or components, because one of the goals of teaming is to convert existing
stocks of intellectual capital into cash flows.

If the barriers to free trade in weapons and their components
were lower, firms could also team up to reduce the cost of developing and manufacturing weapons systems—like Martin-Marietta and
General Electric Aerospace, but across borders, or, perhaps, more
like Ford and Mazda, since for the time being teaming must necessarily stop short of full vertical integration.

By focusing its defense policies and commitments along
these lines and by abjuring protectionism, America could help promote the efficient rationalization of its arms industry and those of
its allies as well. One can imagine an international arms-trading
regime in which the United States specialized in building radar and
sonar, air-to-air missiles and advanced aircraft, jet and rocket engines, communications equipment, and systems integration, Germany specialized in submarine hulls and diesel engines, the United
Kingdom in cannons, France and Sweden in airframes, and Taiwan
or Korea in tanks, combat vehicles, and the hulls of surface vessels.

Of course, it would penny-wise and pound-foolish to allow
freer trade to threaten industrial facilities that are vital to national
security. The weight of the evidence suggests that this need not be
the case, however (see Phelps, 1983). In the foreseeable future, wars
will almost certainly be fought using weapons from existing inventories or in production when hostilities commence, as was the case
with Desert Storm, Vietnam, the first six months of the Korean War,
and, so far as major weapons platforms are concerned, even the
naval war against Japan. In any case, it makes little sense to main-

tain obsolete industrial facilities that would have to be replaced anyway if it became necessary to fight a protracted war without allies.

Cost of Regulation

Rationalization will not ensure the continued competitive success of the American arms industry. Neither will modernization. Firms all over the world are using advanced technology to design and manufacture high-quality, lower-cost weapons. American manufacturers must modernize merely to keep up. Unfortunately, modernization appears to have the effect of accentuating the significance of overhead burdens, particularly those that are generated by the procurement process. This occurs because automation reduces variable costs but increases fixed costs. The effect of regulation tends to fall entirely on fixed costs. This means that, if changes are not made in the way the Pentagon buys weapons, the competitive position of the American arms industry could be seriously compromised, since it appears that procurement regulation is a greater burden in the United States than elsewhere.

One critical piece of evidence that procurement regulation is a greater burden in the United States than elsewhere was provided recently by a study described in the *Economist* ("Software Engineering: Made to Measure," 1993). This study was conducted by Software Productivity Research of Burlington, Massachusetts, and used a method called *function-point analysis* to estimate the productivity and cost-effectiveness of three kinds of software projects: small management information systems, large-scale systems, and military systems. Function-point analysis is widely used in the software business because it can be applied to any piece of software written in any computer language. Both Texas Instruments and Unysis sell computer-aided engineering programs that automatically compute five things in terms of a measure called *function points*: inputs, outputs, inquiries, files, and interfaces, weighted according to the complexity of the codes needed to provide them. Once a software project's function points have been measured, it is a simple matter to calculate its cost per function point, the standard measure of cost-effectiveness used in the industry, and the number of function points produced per systems engineer, a standard measure of productivity.

Applying function-point analysis to thousands of software projects selected from around the world, Software Productivity Research found that American military software productivity lags behind France, Israel, Korea, the United Kingdom, Germany, Sweden, and even Italy. The problem is not that American software engineers are inherently unproductive. On the contrary. The same study showed that the United States is in first place in the production of management information systems and runs a strong second to Japan in large-scale systems software projects.

Software Productivity Research also discovered that differences in cost per function point are due primarily to the amount of paperwork generated per point. Preparation of this paperwork takes a lot of engineering time but contributes no function points to the finished product. American military projects generate five times as much paper and cost twelve times as much per point as management information systems projects. They are six times as costly per function point as big systems software projects, which are arguably more comparable to military software projects.

This comparison is particularly telling for our purposes. Software production is more than 90 percent overhead, for product development, design, documentation, and administrative support; it involves no production labor, no capital, no materials. Once codes have been written and documentation prepared, software can be reproduced innumerable times at almost no cost. What this comparison suggests is that, where activities like software production are concerned, federal procurement procedures may account for as much as 80 percent of their cost.

There is a second reason for emphasizing this evidence. This is the only study we are aware of that directly estimates the cost burden imposed by federal acquisition procedures. There are other estimates, of course. William H. Gregory (1989, p. 3) estimates that they double the cost of the weapons the Pentagon buys. Weidenbaum (1992, p. 154) is more cautious; he estimates that they add about $50 billion to defense budget. These estimates are, to say the least, speculative. Weidenbaum bases his on the rule of thumb that says that monitoring and enforcing regulations impose private costs of about $10 for every dollar spent by the government (Weidenbaum and DeFina, 1978). Gregory provides no explanation for his estimate.

Aside from Software Productivity Research's, the only estimate of the cost of procurement regulation we have any real confidence in was provided by the Grace Commission (President's Private Sector Survey on Cost Control [Grace Commission], 1983, p. 146; see also MacManus, 1991; Lamm, 1988; Smith and others, 1988). The Grace Commission estimated that complying with procurement regulations accounted for at least 10 percent of the cost of the Pentagon's purchases, about $12 billion a year. The Grace Commission based its estimate on the observation that oil companies give substantial discounts to most bulk purchasers—up to 15 percent in some cases. However, because of the costs of complying with cumbersome procurement regulations, many suppliers refuse to offer similar discounts to the Department of Defense. Consequently, the Department of Defense pays market prices for about 80 percent of the gas and oil it buys.

Of course, petroleum products are at the other end of the spectrum from software engineering, since raw materials and processing costs account for nearly all oil company expenses. Perhaps when the Grace Commission and the Software Productivity Research estimates are taken together, they suggest that Weidenbaum's and Gregory's guesses are in the right ballpark after all. They also show why it is that good estimates of the cost of regulation are lacking: the accounting standards established by the federal government that tell defense contractors how to measure costs simply do not provide this information.

Accounting for Transaction Costs

Most overheads are transaction costs. They reflect the organization's policies, its operating and administrative procedures, and its customer relationships. They involve activities like purchasing, materials handling, marketing, accounting, and asset utilization. Nowadays these activities often have a greater effect on an organization's expenses than production volume. In the typical defense plant, direct manufacturing labor accounts for only 10 to 20 percent of costs; materials and purchased components typically account for 30 to 40 percent more. This leaves *at least* 40 percent for overheads. And that is the typical defense firm; as we noted earlier, direct labor costs are practically irrelevant in the increasing number of firms that rely on flexible computer-aided design and manufacturing— usually less than 5 percent of total costs.

Figuring out what drives overheads, identifying cost drivers that do not add value to end products, and changing them ought to be the purpose of cost analysis (Raffish, 1991). The software productivity study is useful precisely because it took this approach—paperwork was identified as a cost driver as well as a source of unproductive expense.

Unfortunately, this is not the Pentagon's approach to cost measurement. Its accounting standards require suppliers to focus on direct labor and materials costs and to treat most other costs as fixed. They call for overheads to be assigned to products on the basis of standard labor hours or machine time. This approach may have made sense twenty or thirty years ago, when efficient use of direct labor was the key to manufacturing productivity. But it is completely unrealistic today and it has probably always had the effect of diverting attention from costs that arise out of the procurement process. Until federal accounting standards are changed to focus on overhead and transaction costs, we will not know how much federal regulation of the procurement process really increases product costs.

For example, everyone knows that procurement regulation increases paperwork burdens—that is the gist of both the Software Productivity Research study and the Grace Commission's opportunity-cost analysis. But increased red tape is probably just the tip of the iceberg. Most of the cost of federal procurement regulation results from its effect on operating processes and the use of assets. This fact was forcefully brought home to us by our experience working with a small firm that makes trailers for the Army. Trailers are technologically unsophisticated and their manufacture appears to be a pretty straightforward exercise in metal bashing.

The company in question, which has asked to remain anonymous, operates two different production lines, one for its commercial business and one for the military. It established a second production line at a new location for its military business, because that was the easiest way to comply with federal cost-accounting standards and other Pentagon reporting requirements. Of course, duplication of facilities increases the average cost of the firm's trailers—an increase that should properly be attributed to the policies that caused it and not to the trailers themselves.

The firm tries to practice the principles of lean management and just-in-time inventory control. On its commercial side, it has succeeded fairly well. Its inventories have been cut to the bone, and manufacturing cycle time—the time from the start of production to shipment of the finished product—is usually less than thirty-six hours. Products are shipped to customers as soon as they are finished, which allows the firm to apply just-in-time inventory control to the production of finished goods as well as to raw materials, components purchased elsewhere, and work-in-progress inventories.

On its military side, total inventories were once twenty-five times higher. This doubled the company's working capital requirements and increased rents, insurance, utilities, and depreciation, since they also varied directly with inventory size. Inventory size was higher on the military production line because cycle time was higher; cycle time was higher because the Army required inspection at each stage of manufacture and because the Army preferred to take delivery in large batches. Increased cycle time also meant less intensive use of the firm's plant and equipment, which increased each trailer's capital cost. The same thing happened with management time. Consequently, although direct labor costs per trailer were not significantly higher, overhead costs per trailer were more than twice as high on the military line as on the commercial line.

This story actually has a happy ending. The Department of Defense exempts exemplary production facilities from direct oversight. With the help of the Army's contracting officer, the firm was designated an exemplary facility. Freed of intrusive oversight, it proceeded to apply to its military business many of the techniques that made its commercial activities so efficient.

Stories like this increase the appeal of claims like Weidenbaum's (1992, p. 148) that the best thing the government can do for the defense industry is "to administer a massive dose of deregulation to the entire military procurement process," or of his conclusion that many "defense contractors could adapt and survive if govern-

ment would simply get off their backs." Nevertheless, we do not
believe that it is quite that simple. To be sure, some deregulation
is called for, but what is needed is not so much deregulation as
rebuilding and restructuring. Positive steps must be taken to improve the efficiency of the defense industry. It is also necessary to
streamline the procurement process and to redesign the Pentagon's
management of it.

No Panaceas

Not everything the Pentagon buys is as easy to design or as simple
to make as a truck trailer. This means that it cannot simply buy the
high-tech weapons it needs off the shelf or from the lowest bidder,
but must instead often rely on incomplete, flexible-price contracts
with sole-source suppliers. It also means that the acquisition of
technologically advanced weapons systems is an inherently risky
business—characterized by technological unknowns, unanticipated
events, and an evolving product. These risks can be reduced by
sound project conceptualization and their consequences can be
minimized by skillful management, but they cannot be made to
vanish entirely, at least not at an economical cost. After all, information is costly. One can avoid surprises, but only at a cost. Efficiency is a matter of minimizing the sum of the costs associated with
surprise and the costs of avoiding surprise.

     Large-scale development projects seem inevitably to produce
surprises—and most are unpleasant. Few if any complex systems
initially work precisely the way they are supposed to; some never
do. Under the best of circumstances, unpredictable problems cause
some development projects to fall behind schedule or to exceed cost
targets.

Cost Overruns Happen

There is absolutely nothing new about this phenomenon, nor is it
a problem that is unique to the Pentagon. In 1794, Congress authorized construction of six frigates. To "spread the work among the
states as equitably as possible and with the greatest political advantage," six private yards were leased to carry out this task. Unfortu-

nately, the project soon fell behind schedule. The six keels were not laid until the end of 1795, seventeen months after construction had been authorized. Subsequently, mismanagement, delays, and cost overruns resulted in a cutback to three frigates (Smelser, 1959, p. 73). A few years later, Eli Whitney contracted with the war department to make 10,000 muskets using an untried new manufacturing system based on extensive division of labor, interchangeability of parts, and final manufacture by assembly rather than hand finishing. While the manufacturing system Whitney devised laid the foundations of American mass production, his contract called for completion of the full production run in two years. It took him nearly ten (Millis, 1956, p. 52).

In fact, the evidence suggests that nowadays the Pentagon's development projects experience on average fewer schedule delays and smaller cost overruns than similar large-scale, high-complexity projects carried out by either government or business. Moreover, the Pentagon has steadily improved its ability to avoid unpleasant surprises. Between 1960 and the mid 1980s, cost overruns, schedule slippages, and performance failures all decreased significantly (Rich and Dews, 1986). These improvements are due in part to its use of sophisticated should-cost and design-to-cost models to negotiate target prices and to enforce productivity standards during the execution of contracts.

The Monopsony Problem

The problems inherent in all large-scale development projects are further complicated by the role played by the Pentagon vis-à-vis its suppliers. Monopsony is the counterpart of monopoly on the demand side of the buyer-seller relationship. The Pentagon is the sole customer of its municipal suppliers—namely, a monopsonist. Monopsony often requires the development of idiosyncratic governance arrangements. Many of these are for the convenience of the monopsonist. Where the acquisition of technologically advanced weapons systems is concerned, replacing existing arrangements with standard commercial practices would probably be contrary to the government's interest and, in many cases, the broader national interest as well (see Gansler, 1980; Kettl, 1993).

For example, many students of the procurement process believe that the optimal strategy for the acquisition of technologically advanced weapons systems would feature a high degree of experimentation at the concept exploration and testing phase of the systems development process, carry at least two competitive systems to prototype development, and ruthlessly select systems for procurement from those available for production, producing a relatively small number of new systems at optimal production rates. This ideal is called the *acquisition funnel.* It is the method that the Packard Commission recommends and that was used successfully in the acquisition of the F-16 and later the F-22.

Why then does the Pentagon restrict competition at the wide end of this funnel by deciding which concepts to develop for testing and which to drop, by subsidizing prime contractors to perform them, and by setting limits on allowable costs for acquisition of concepts supplied by subcontractors? Why does the Pentagon not simply rely on small job shops to provide the bulk of this work? Indeed, since the production of these services does not require large fixed investments in highly specific assets and since the products themselves are fairly discrete and have many of the attributes of intermediate goods, why are their producers not allowed to market them freely to rival prime contractors? This is after all the standard arrangement in most industries.

The reason is obvious. The Pentagon does not rely on a freely competitive market for concept exploration and testing because it wants to deny substantial proprietary advantages to its suppliers. It makes perfect sense for the Pentagon to use its market power to capture for the government the economic surpluses accruing to the development of breakthrough concepts. Under more competitive arrangements, these would accrue to the developers (see Carlton and Perloff, 1990, pp. 548–551). Furthermore, Pentagon ownership of research produced under contract permits its widespread dissemination and avoids the barriers to free exchange of ideas produced by proprietary patents, trade secrets, and the like. More equal access to technology can also increase the benefits to the Pentagon from second sourcing.

The effectiveness of this approach ultimately depends on the soundness of the Pentagon's qualitative judgments about capabilities of rival design teams and the option values of alternative concepts. Hence, it makes no more sense for the Pentagon to award contracts for concept exploration and testing on the basis of the lowest bid from a "qualified" supplier than it would be for us to pick our spouses on that basis. Neither does it make sense for the Pentagon to hold weapons systems designers and developers at arm's length. That is no way to get to know someone's capabilities. Instead, what is called for is an ongoing working relationship—one that is close enough to keep up with material developments, but not too close to be suffocating. Where technologically advanced weapons systems are concerned, the Pentagon cannot simply get out of the way and let the market decide what is best.

Two Cheers for Cheaper, Simpler Weapons

If the acquisition of technologically advanced weapons systems necessitates special governance arrangements, one way to get rid of these difficult arrangements might be to stop buying technologically advanced weapons systems and to buy simpler, more specialized weapons instead. During the 1970s and early 1980s, one frequently heard that simpler weapons are easier to operate and maintain than complex, high-tech weapons, as well as cheaper to buy, and that America would be better off without its complex, high-tech weapons. This view was persuasively expressed by Pierre Sprey (see Merritt and Sprey, 1973) and Charles Spinney,[1] popularized in a brilliantly argued book by James Fallows (1981), and forcefully advocated in Congress by Senator Gary Hart and other members of the military reform caucus (see Smith, 1985).

While we believe that the existing procurement machine often encourages the acquisition of excessively complex weapons, we do not think that it would be wise for the Pentagon to eschew technologically advanced weapons systems. To see why, let us look more closely at the case for relying on simpler, cheaper weapons, which is essentially an argument against complex, technologically sophisticated, multipurpose weapons.

This case rested on three critical assertions. The first is that complex, technologically sophisticated, multipurpose weapons are inherently unreliable: even when they work the way they are supposed to, which is supposedly not often, they do not work because they are broken. Obviously, other things being equal, increasing a system's complexity tends to degrade its reliability. For example, consider the following calculation: there are 100 tanks, each tank has twenty components, and each component has a .01 probability of failure in 1,000 hours of operation. After 1,000 hours of operation about 82 of the tanks would be working. If, however, each of the tanks had 200 components, and each of the components had the same .01 probability of failure, after 1,000 hours, only thirteen would still be running. Assuming further that the military can afford only half as many of the more sophisticated tanks because they cost twice as much to buy, deploy, maintain, and support as the simpler ones, this calculation leaves only six tanks at the end of 1,000 hours. This calculation illustrates *Riccioni's law*, which states that "the number of weapons systems that can be employed in battle varies inversely as the *square* of the level of sophistication" (quoted in Fallows, 1981, p. 43; emphasis in the original).

It is also obvious that the technological sophistication and operational complexity of the weapons (and other) systems deployed by the Department of Defense have greatly increased in the last twenty years. The seventy-ton high-tech M-1A1 Abrams Main-Battle-Tank, with its target-stabilized turret, laser range finder, huge 120 mm smooth-bore gun, steel-ceramic composite armor, and turbine engine, is only one manifestation of a pervasive phenomenon. Recoilless rifles have been replaced by complicated rockets, towed artillery by self-propelled Multi-Rocket Launch Systems, radio direction finders by computerized signals-intelligence equipment, and human eyes by infrared imaging devices.

The second critical assertion is that the unreliability of America's high-tech weaponry imposes an intolerable logistical support burden on the armed forces—thereby fatally increasing the ratio of tail to tooth. This is a serious claim and it too deserves to be taken seriously. Logistics are the Achilles heel of every army. Rommel spent as much time in North Africa looking for fuel as he did attacking the British. Patton was stopped more frequently by logistical breakdowns than by the Germans. The multinational force in the Arabian Desert was successful only because its logistics were sorted out before the shooting started. Moreover, the reliability and maintainability of military hardware are directly relevant to the quantity of supplies needed to support operations and to the size, location, and composition of buffer stocks. It is common knowledge that the Russians replaced the T-64 tank with the retrograde T-72 primarily because the T-64 was too expensive to buy and too complicated to maintain in the field; it is not unlikely that their failure to deploy the T-80 in substantial numbers reflected similar considerations (Zaloga, 1990, p. 24).

Moreover, the complexity of modern weapons has clearly had a profound effect on the design of military organizations. Of the 1.85 million enlisted men and women in the American armed forces in 1988, 550,000 were repair technicians, an additional 166,000 were supply and other service personnel, and only 283,000 had combat jobs. One of the starker manifestations of technology's effect on combat strength was the experimental 9th High-Tech Division, a highly agile formation designed for ease in air transportability. Unfortunately, the High-Tech needed so many people to operate and maintain its equipment that it had almost none left over to put in foxholes—648, or 4.5 percent of its total personnel. In the mid-1980s, the High-Tech was reorganized as the 9th Mechanized Division, with a foxhole strength of about 5,000 (Dunnigan and Nofi, 1990, pp. 235, 267).

The third critical assertion is that training realism is directly related to technological complexity and the higher operating and maintenance costs that complexity induces. Other things being equal, complex weapons require greater skill to use effectively than simple weapons. Skill requires practice, but practicing with modern, high-tech weapons is prohibitively expensive. Consequently, the reformers concluded that, even if they were not broken, the armed forces would not know how to use their modern weapons. Furthermore, the performance of American forces relative to their NATO allies in various competitions during the 1970s—the Canadian Army Tank Gunnery Competition, the Boeslager Challenge Cup (an infantry competition), the World Helicopter Championships, the Tiger Meet (a tactical-fighter competition), the World Reconnaissance Air Meet—and in early Reformer exercises strongly suggested that they really were the "gang that couldn't shoot straight." In 1979, for example, the United States was an also-ran in the air force competitions; it was dead last in two of the ground forces competitions and could not even field a team for the third.

What Happened to Weapons Reform?

Serious as these concerns were, they have largely disappeared from recent discussions of the acquisition process. There are two reasons for this. First, the Pentagon adopted some of the weapons reforms. For example, the Air Force's F-16 broke the cycle of rising acquisition costs by stripping itself of many (but by no means all) of the nice-to-have gadgets. The F-16 is both relatively inexpensive to buy and reliable to operate, yet it is widely regarded as the best dogfighter in the world. The A-10 reflects a similar philosophy. Its designers set out to build a simple, sturdy, and cheap tank-buster. The fighting in the Gulf shows that they were successful. Second, the Pentagon took the symptoms identified by the weapons reformers very seriously, even when it rejected both their diagnosis and the proposed cure, and took drastic steps to improve the maintainability of the weapons it deploys and the training of the personnel using them.

Using Technology to Fix Technology

One of the solutions adopted by the Pentagon is to use technology to fix technology. Weapons from the first generation of high-tech systems were, in fact, excessively unreliable—a point Sprey, Spinney, and Fallows made with great vigor. (And also a certain amount of overstatement. It is revealing that many of the planes the weapons reformers described as hanger queens were double crewed during the Gulf War. Evidently they were able to put in far more hours of sustained operations than their more easily fatigued flight crews.)

To deal with the reliability problem, the military departments have made two adjustments to the high-tech systems they use. First, they now rely to a far greater degree on redundancy. If, for example, each of the components of the more complex tanks described in the previous illustrative calculation had a backup and if the probability of component failure were unchanged, the probability that both the original component and its backup would fail would drop to .0001. In that case, after 1,000 hours of operation, 98 percent would still be working. Second, the military departments now use solid-state circuits in their electronic components instead of wires, transistors, and tubes, which has greatly increased systems reliability.

The Pentagon has also put considerable effort into the design and development of systems that are easy to operate and maintain—using sophisticated technology to make it easier for combat troops to become skilled in the use of their weapons and to make it easier for maintenance and logistical personnel to become skilled at servicing them. For example, road wheel damage to an M-1 tank can be fixed in about three hours, using a simple procedure requiring no special tools; similar damage on other tanks requires highly specialized training and expensive equipment.

Arguably, in the case of the M-1, this virtue may have been practiced to a fault. Much of its sophistication was intended to make it easier to use. Not to put too fine a point on it, the Army designed the M-1 to be operated and maintained by dummies. It can be. The evidence shows that the M-1 outperforms the M-60 by a huge amount—when both are operated by personnel from AFT category III and lower (Scribner, 1986). Unfortunately for the cost-effectiveness of the M-1, Army enlisted personnel are much more capable than the Army expected them to be when it developed specifications for the M-1 and designed its maintenance/logistical organization (Horne, 1987; Gilroy, 1990). Given the AFT scores of the young enlistees in the armed services, it appears that, from a present-value, total-systems cost standpoint, it may not make sense to replace M-60s with M-1s before the end of the M-60s' service life, especially not when it is possible to up-gun M-60s and provide them with appliqué armor, laser range finders, and night-vision capability at a fairly low cost (Carter, 1988).

We should mention two key innovations here designed to increase reliability and make complex equipment easier to use and maintain. The first is widespread use of electronic diagnostic and test devices. These make it possible for moderately skilled technicians to identify the cause of most mechanical and electronic problems quickly and reliably. The second is modularization. This permits the entire complex of components containing the problem to be pulled and expeditiously replaced by a module off the shelf.

The M-1, for example, has roughly 200 of these modules. Even the M-1's $200,000, 1,500-horsepower gas turbine engine is designed to be rapidly replaced in the field.

Of course, there is no such thing as a free lunch. These innovations have created problems of their own. In the first place, the use of electronic diagnostics and modularization is expensive, both to acquire and to support. Their use has necessitated greater specialization of maintenance personnel and increased centralization of the maintenance function. According to Chris Demchak (1991), this has had the effect of greatly reducing the reliability and adaptability of the Army's maintenance/logistical organization and, therefore, of reducing its capability to carry out its assigned missions. Hence, she concludes, the Pentagon's technological fix has not eliminated operational unreliability, it has merely shifted its locus from its hardware to the organization.

Modularization has also increased the time it takes to fix some breakdowns. Much of this time is now spent getting replacements. Owing to the cost of replacements and their infrequent failure, modules are not held in inventory at the point of use, at least not in peacetime. Rather, the Department of Defense relies on its version of just-in-time inventory supply. It holds stocks of repair modules in central depots in the United States and air-ships them to users when ordered. The broken module is then exchanged for a spare and returned to the central depot for repair.

According to optimal inventory models, this makes a great deal of sense in peacetime when the units requiring replacement parts are dispersed all over the globe, breakdowns are relatively infrequent, and the opportunity costs of outages are low. In wartime, when forces are concentrated in a single theater of operations, breakdowns are more frequent (due to enemy action as well as higher levels of operational intensity), and the costs of outages are high, inventory models call for the location of large buffer stocks near the point of use. Consequently, the Gulf War saw the Department of Defense shift temporarily from a demand pull to a supply push system of parts replacement.

Finally, because component failures are rarer, information on mean time to failure is sometimes lacking. This means that surprises are fairly common, especially when systems are pushed to the limit in operations.

Despite these problems, however, contemporary weapons appear, on balance, to be far easier to maintain and use than their immediate predecessors. The M-1 tank illustrates the point about second-generation high-tech weapons systems. Despite its great complexity, it is highly reliable (Chalmers and Unterseher, 1988; McNaugher, 1989, pp. 73–74; Swales, 1989). According to official sources, its mean operating time to failure exceeds that of any of its predecessors (surprises are now relatively rare; after all, there are about 10,000 M-1s in use by the United States and its allies, and the Army has had over ten years operational experience in which to debug it). In peacetime operation, even high-intensity peacetime operations, the percentage of tanks that are fully ready for combat is higher in Army units equipped with M-1s than in Army and Marine units that still use the older M-60. In the Gulf War, M-1 operational rates exceeded 90 percent (Roos and Schemmer, 1991).

Competitive Strategies

The Pentagon has also tried to figure out how to use technology smarter—taking advantage of America's technological edge to defeat the Soviet Union's numerically stronger forces. The basic idea behind this effort was to identify critical weaknesses that American technology—combined with appropriate operational concepts, doctrine, and tactics—could exploit to disrupt Soviet combat operations and then to invest the Pentagon's scarce resources in those technologies. War gaming identified its highly centralized system of command and control as the critical weakness in the Soviet Union's war-fighting doctrine and demonstrated that it could be thrown into disarray by the clever use of systems then under development or, in some cases, already deployed. These include sophisticated intelligence gathering and distribution systems, stealth aircraft, large mobile conventional missiles (such as the MARS), scatterable mines (both smart and dumb), and smart munitions to ensure that once a target is located, it can be killed (Roos and Schemmer, 1988).

Most of these ideas were implemented in time to be used in the Gulf. Because the Iraqi military forces were organized along

Soviet lines, that experience generally confirmed the thinking behind the competitive strategies initiative. The combined application of stealth aircraft and highly accurate stand-off weapons, linked to modern intelligence and control systems, left Iraqi forces in shambles. Of course, to say that Iraq organized its forces along Soviet lines is not to say that they were nearly as good as the Soviets. Nevertheless, the lesson once more seems to be that quality, intelligently employed, will always defeat mere quantity.

Better Training

Even more important, the Pentagon has taken to heart the lesson that the principal determinant of combat success is not weapons, but the skill and determination of its personnel. It has made a profound commitment to high levels of realistic combat training. This includes authentic war play against tested adversaries, most notably at the Army's National Training Center at Fort Irwin, California. Mention should also be made of the Navy's Top Gun and the Air Force's Aggressor programs. In both, highly skilled opponents fly aircraft that perform similarly to those of the Soviet Union. Their function is to expose the pilots undergoing training to the closest possible imitation of actual warfare.

Here, too, the Pentagon has used technology to fix technology. Combat personnel now get reality in large doses from lifelike electronic combat simulators and training systems. Flight simulators to train pilots have been around for some time. Similar electronic scoring and recording devices are now also used to prepare tankers, artillery crews, and ground attack pilots for combat. By the late 1980s, these devices were organized into area networks such as SIGNET, permitting entire military units to get ready for the real thing by participating in realistic combat simulations (Ropelewski, 1988). Simulators are not cheap. The new F-15E fighter-bomber simulators cost the Air Force more than $45 million each, as much as an actual F-15. But they are a lot cheaper to use. Each F-15E simulator provides six or seven times as many training hours as an actual F-15, at an operating cost of $2,000 an hour—one-fifth of what it costs to fly an F-15 (Goodman, 1988).

As a consequence of all of these efforts, the combat skills of the armed forces have markedly improved. In recent years, American teams have been overwhelming in NATO maneuvers (Peters, 1988) and have completely dominated international competitions, most recently taking the top six places in the 1990 Tiger Meet—not to mention first place in the Gulf. During the Gulf War, we heard (on CNN) airmen and tankers, who had achieved remarkable feats of arms, say over and over again that "It was easy—it was just like in training."

Simpler Weapons Are Not Necessarily Better; They Might Not Even Be Cheaper

Eliot Cohen (1982, p. 124) has eloquently, perhaps even grandiloquently, explained the valid considerations that cause American defense planners to prefer flashy, multipurpose, and, therefore, more expensive weapons:

> It is the essence of America's geopolitical problem that her planners cannot know what kind of wars are ahead, or rather, that they must prepare for many different kinds of wars. . . . Because of the enormous diversity of possible enemies, climate, and terrain that its troops might have to cope with, the United States must strive to create an armed forces that can operate in all kinds of conditions. Small wonder that our military equipment is built to extraordinary and costly specifications, for who can tell whether a manpack radio set will be used in a steamy Asian rice paddy, in an Arabian sandstorm, or a Norwegian blizzard? Small wonder, too, that we build extremely capable but expensive weapons such as the F-15 fighter-bomber. The United States will probably have to fight the opening battles of a campaign at the end of a long logistical line: What weapons it can deploy had best be far more capable, pound for pound, than those of its enemies.

Cohen's point is amply demonstrated by the example of the F-16, one of the weapons reformers' favorite planes. Instead of the simple, austere, pure fighter it was originally planned to be, the Air Force made it into a dual-purpose aircraft, used to attack ground targets as well as being a dog-fighter. This increased its price 75 percent and increased its weight from ten tons to over twelve, with a proportional reduction in acceleration. It also increased the plane's complexity, owing to the installation of additional avionics, radar, and electronic countermeasures, with proportional reductions in reliability and maintainability. As result of these changes, Fallows (1981, p. 106) concluded that, while the F-16 remains a fine weapon, it is also "so much less than it might have been."

What Fallows's conclusion overlooks is that every dual-purpose F-16 can replace two single-purpose aircraft: a pure air superiority fighter *and* a dedicated ground-attack aircraft. This means that, even if the F-16 cost 75 percent more to acquire, operate, and maintain than the single-purpose alternative, a fixed budget could still be stretched 12.5 percent further in terms of mission capabilities by buying it instead. Since the true life cycle costs of the F-16 are only about 30 to 40 percent higher than those of dedicated ground-attack aircraft like the A-10 or the A-7, the actual payoff in terms of increased cost-effectiveness from the Air Force's decision to make a multipurpose aircraft out of the F-16 is probably at least 30 to 35 percent.

In the real world, utility depends on the jobs that actually have to be done. From this standpoint, the Air Force's decision to make a multipurpose aircraft out of the F-16 was clearly sound. F-16s assigned a ground-attack role performed yeoman service in the Gulf; those assigned a pure fighter role turned out to be superfluous. As it happened, the F-16's greatest successes in the Gulf were accomplished in tandem with one of the weapons reformers' least favorite aircraft, the Army's AH-64 Apache attack helicopter. The basic tactic was for the Apaches, with their terrain-following radars, infrared seeing devices, and laser rangers, to find the enemy and call in the F-16s. As the F-16s prepared to make their attack runs, the Apaches would pop up, illuminate targets, and disrupt the enemy's antiaircraft artillery with rocket and cannon fire. The F-16s would then zip in, deliver their payload of laser-guided bombs, and zip out again, their escape covered by fire from the Apaches (Roos and Schemmer, 1991).

If there were no trade-offs, the F-16 would be all things for all purposes, which, according to Bill Gunston and Mike Spick (1983, p. 193), means that:

1. It would be a good dogfighter, with a high combat cruising speed, good fuel economy at full military power, and excellent maneuverability. It would also have a good rate of climb and acceleration and a high ceiling (high maximum speed is not important). It would carry as many short-range dogfight missiles as possible, plus a gun or two with the highest possible rate of fire and the greatest possible muzzle velocity. It would have every possible device to warn the pilot of impending attack, including the elementary one of a good view from the cockpit. It would be as small as possible to avoid detection. (These were the attributes of the LWF, the direct antecedent of the F-16.)

2. It would also be a first-rate interceptor, which means that it would need clever electronics for long-distance detection and lots of long-range air-to-air missiles. Furthermore, it would be able to maintain high speed when giving chase and carry sufficient fuel to give it ample range. (These were the characteristics of the F-15 that caused it to account for nearly all of the allies' air-to-air kills in the Gulf War.)

3. It would be a superior attack craft. This means that it should be able to lift and carry a high bomb load to distant targets. To carry out the attack mission at night or in rough weather, it would be equipped with ground-following radars, infrared seeing devices, laser rangers, and marked-target seekers. To penetrate hostile airspace, it would have good electronic countermeasures, a secure communications system, and perhaps stealth technology. It should also be sturdy, with its vital components and the pilot well protected against ground fire.

4. It would still be cheap, both to fly and to buy, and highly reliable. It would be able to take off from and land on short airfields. These attributes give numerical strength and high sortie rates.

Unfortunately, these attributes are all in conflict with each other. Consequently, the Pentagon procures a variety of aircraft types, some that do each of these things superlatively and the majority, like the F-16, that do several well enough. The Pentagon's mistake lies not in preferring high-tech systems or in trying to use

one platform for multiple purposes, but in a propensity to carry
these preferences to extremes.

According to Thomas McNaugher (1989, pp. 128–129) this
often causes the Pentagon to "produce systems that are flashy but
not cost-effective and systems that perform so many functions they
perform none well." As an example of the former, he cites the F-
15's top speed of Mach 2.5. Its extra Mach probably increased total
life cycle cost 10 to 15 percent without significantly improving combat effectiveness. As an example of the latter, he cites the Bradley
fighting vehicle, which costs nearly twice as much as the armored
personnel carrier it replaced and is asked to do so many things that
it apparently does none very well.

In other words, even if defense firms were 100 percent more
efficient than they are and even if the Pentagon's contracting arrangements were all tip-top, the cost of technologically advanced
weapons systems would often still be too high, since many of the
determinants of program cost and performance have already been
decided when production contracts are negotiated. In the next chapter, we show how the architecture of the Pentagon's procurement
machine often causes the military to request extravagant weapons
and thereby causes technologically advanced weapons to be unjus-
tifiably expensive. We will also show how this propensity can be
reduced via the following administrative reforms:

- Reducing the size of the acquisition establishment and improving the quality of its personnel
- Redesigning the Pentagon's organizational structure to increase
  the personal authority and responsibility of acquisition personnel
- Simplifying and streamlining the processes through which contractors are selected and projects managed

CHAPTER FIVE

Streamlining Procurement

WHY DOES THE Pentagon so often try to build extravagant weapons that do, if not all things for all purposes, too many things at too high a price? Richard Stubbing (1986, p. 128) blames this propensity on the fixed force structure established by Secretary McNamara. He argues that, because quantity is fixed, the military departments try to get the best weapons they can, since they have nothing to lose thereby. Ex-Secretary of Defense Schlesinger evidently agrees. He is quoted as saying that "if you hand the military a force structure, you hand them a powerful incentive to build as much capability as possible into every weapon" (Alexander, 1985, p. 20).

While we hold McNamara responsible for a number of things, some good and some not so good, in this case the evidence shows that he is innocent. Based on an analysis of major weapons purchases between 1965 and 1987, we found that a 1 percent increase in the price of any given system reduced the total quantity acquired 0.64 percent and reduced annual unit acquisitions 1.5 to 2.5 percent. This means that cost growth reduces *both* the quantity of new weapons procured and the receiving unit's budget. What Stubbing and Schlesinger overlook is that only a small fraction of the weapons stock is replaced each year. Consequently, each new weapon must compete with other current weapons needs, the weapons already in the field, and even weapons still on the drawing board.

The main alternative to acquiring new weapons is upgrading existing systems. For example, the F-15 was initially deployed as a high-performance fighter weighing 28.9 tons and carrying 1.5 tons of weapons; the F-15E that served in the Gulf weighs forty tons and carries twelve tons of weapons. Upgrades should allow the F-15 to serve for another twenty-five years. Another example is the proposed upgrade of the thirty-year-old A-7, which would lengthen the fuselage by four feet, replace the single engine with two, and triple the electronics load. These changes would cost about $6.5 million each and keep the A-7 serviceable through 2010. In contrast, a brand-new F/A-18, with only a slightly longer expected service life and a far smaller payload, costs $24 million (Dunnigan and Nofi, 1990, pp. 157–158, 363). It would not take much of an increase in the price of F/A-18s to justify upgrading A-7s rather than buying new F/A-18s.

Another alternative to new weapons involves improving payloads rather than platforms. Given the existence of these real alternatives, it is hardly surprising that price matters to Congress, to the Office of the Secretary of Defense, or to the military departments. Even where the military is concerned, the existence of alternatives means that price is a proxy for opportunity cost.

Why then does the Pentagon have trouble making trade-offs? We think the basic answer boils down to organizational bloat. Some of the bloat is due to congressional micromanagement, but most is self-inflicted. McNaugher, for example, provides a finely nuanced discussion (1989, pp. 128–129; see also McNaugher, 1984) of how the Pentagon's oversized and overcomplicated acquisition organization induces "pressures for consensus [that] create a systematic tendency toward so-called gold plate." Of course, decision making by consensus is frequently inimical to performance. Consensus requires avoiding hard choices; getting things done requires clear choices and firm priorities.

The pressures inhibiting hard choices about trade-offs are hardest to control during the project definition phase of the acquisition process. This is when the need for a new system is demonstrated in terms of specific operational requirements, its cost-effectiveness is justified, and goals, timetables, and project milestones are established. In other words, it is when all the key elements of a development project are tied together into a single plan or budget that defines for both the Department of Defense and industry what is wanted, how it is to be designed and built, how it is to be used, what it will cost, and which procurement strategy will be used to manage the project.

No one suggests that there is anything inherently wrong-headed about putting together a project plan before initiating full-scale development. Quite the contrary, it would be rash of the Pentagon to do otherwise where large endeavors are concerned. However, each of the elements of such a plan is potentially controversial, *especially those having to do with the requirements of the system to be developed* (McNaugher, 1984; see also Holland, 1993).

The structure of the military departments' systems commands, the agencies with first-line responsibility for project definition and, subsequently, supervision of project acquisition, guarantees that the definition phase will generate conflict over operational requirements. This is because the departments' structures parallel the functional components of the systems they develop, which ensures that each command will house a substantial number of factions—each with its own doctrines, concerns, and interests. The size of the system commands helps to guarantee that these conflicts will be resolved by consensus and papered over. Unfortunately, conflict is all too easily avoided by accommodating every faction or interest, which leads to the elaboration of extravagant operational requirements.

The systems commands are huge. In 1984, the largest of them, the Air Force Systems Command, had a staff of 26,000, including 10,500 officers and 34 generals. Its central headquarters, at Andrews Air Force Base, was divided into sixty-eight directorates, which reported to the commander, a full general, the vice commander, a major general, and eleven deputy chiefs of staff, mostly brigadier generals. The actual work of the Systems Command was carried out by four operating divisions, each headed by a lieutenant general, space equipment in Los Angeles, electronics at Hanscomb AFB, aircraft at Wright-Patterson AFB, and armaments at Eglin AFB. Of course each of these divisions had its own headquarters. In addition, there were eight other lesser divisions and centers under the System Command, including the Contract Management Division at Kirtland AFB (Luttwak, 1984, pp. 166–174).

Moreover, their personnel are chronically underemployed. Between 1965 and 1984, the Aeronautical Division at Wright-Patterson, for example, developed only two bombers, three fighters, a transport, and a trainer. As Edward Luttwak (1984, 170) explains, "It is the . . . natural tendency of a chronically underemployed research and development bureaucracy to welcome exacting specifications that impose the need for a research-and-development program every time the Air Force needs some product or another. Finally it is also the natural tendency of an equally overstaffed supervising bureaucracy to impose all sorts of controls on manufacturers and to demand mountains of paper work."

Chronic underemployment also means that the myriad factions that comprise the systems commands can afford to participate at each of the multiple sites within the government where a project can be vetoed. These include not only those sites within the systems commands themselves, but also the offices of the military Department's Assistant Secretary for Research and Development and the Undersecretary of Defense for Research and Development, the Office of the Secretary of Defense's Department of Program Analysis and Evaluation, the Office of the Assistant Secretary–Comptroller, the Joint Chiefs of Staff, the Office of Management and Budget, and of course more than ninety committees and subcommittees of Congress.

Since disaffected interests within the systems commands cannot be excluded from these sites, and since their opposition could seriously damage a project's prospects, it is hardly surprising that project managers prefer to keep disagreements within the systems development community. The easiest way to get the potential participants on board is to give each of them a piece of the action by including their concerns in the operational requirements of the proposed system. Of course, the greater the number of participants, the greater the number of military requirements that must be accommodated.

The F-15 is a classic example of how this process works. According to McNaugher, the Air Force Systems Command was dominated by two competing parties, each with its own theory of air-to-air combat. Rather than deciding between these theories, producing a clear winner and a clear loser, the F-15's operational requirements reflected a consensus of both. As a consequence, the F-15 had all of the possible attributes of the ideal fighter-bomber, except that it was not small and it was not cheap and it was far less reliable than it could have been.

The problem of gold plating does not end with the completion of the definition phase of the systems development process. Turnover within the acquisition community means that development programs are constantly exposed to new managers who want to contribute to the program by changing and adding features or exploiting cost-reduction opportunities. Unfortunately, these well-intentioned efforts often disrupt design processes and exacerbate gold plating. Furthermore, as is true in the definition phase, the behavior of participants in subsequent phases of the systems development process often reflects the needs of their functional specialties rather than of the programs themselves. Each functional specialty tends to maximize the performance of its own subsystem according to the technical standards of the specialty. Thus, one specialty might spend a great deal of time trying to reduce power consumption in a circuit, while another is pushing the development of an electromechanical device whose power consumption will overwhelm anything the circuit could consume. George Stalk and Thomas Hout (1990, p. 131) might very easily have been describing the Pentagon when they described ineffective product innovators as "structured for functional control, cost efficiency, and risk avoidance, a structure that results in a slow and cumbersome development process. With the functional organization come multiple hand-offs that consume time, cause errors to occur and diminish overall accountability. Coordination and control can only be accomplished through elaborate review processes and documentation requirements. Quality seems to decline, not improve. . . . To help insure that budgets are met, performance targets are conservative. Senior management actively participates in program decisions, and . . . further slow the decision-making processes of the company." The consequences of conservatism and local optimization in every kind of development project are high costs due to gold plating, long development times, and reworking the individual components and subsystems designs, so that the performance of the system as a whole is closer to optimum.

In the private sector, the firms that do the best job of developing new products take an entirely different approach to the organization of the systems development process. They recognize that the development process is characterized by reciprocal rather than sequential interdependence and as a result they eschew the functional organizational structures preferred by the systems commands. Instead, they gather all the resources needed to develop a product in one group under a single head. Participants from a variety of functional areas work together on a full-time basis, scheduling is done locally, and all of the participants are usually located at the same site where the product is to be manufactured (Stalk and Hout, 1990, pp. 120–133). According to Hirotaka Takeuchi and Ikujiro Nonaka (1989, pp. 85–86), an

> emphasis on speed and flexibility calls for a different approach for managing new product development. Under the old approach, a product development process moved like a relay race, with one group of functional specialists passing the baton to the next group. The project went sequentially from phase to phase: concept development, feasibility testing, product design, process development, pilot production, and final production. . . .
>
> Under the [new] approach, the project development process emerges from the constant interaction of a hand-picked multidisciplinary team whose members work together from start to finish. Rather than moving in highly structured stages, the process is born out of the team members' interplay. . . . The shift from a linear to an integrated approach encourages trial and error and challenges the status quo. It stimulates new kinds of learning and thinking within the organization at different levels and functions.

The task-force approach has the further effect of focusing all of the participants' efforts on the team's goal rather on the narrower concerns of their individual functions.

Gold plating is also exacerbated by layers of oversight. The complexity of the program approval process and the turbulence caused by the proliferation of program hurdles reinforce the propensity to consensus building. If there were fewer bodies with the power to stop or hurt programs, program managers probably would not have to defer to so many special interests during program development. Moreover, at one time, when trade-offs had to be made during project execution, project managers were more or less free to make them. Nowadays, congressional and press scrutiny tends to deny project managers the discretion to make trade-offs between cost, schedule, and performance characteristics.

Nevertheless, the military departments themselves must take primary responsibility for the bloat that affects the acquisition process. Again, according to Luttwak (1984, p. 170), "Any Air Force Systems we might have, indeed any government buying outfit, would suffer from the same tendencies. But it is the great surplus of middle-ranking officers that has led to the luxuriant growth of the Systems Command bureaucracy we actually have, and then in turn to its grotesque overmanagement, which drives those natural tendencies to extremes." Like many of the excesses burdening the Pentagon, the officer surplus is a legacy of the postwar era. It is one that should not be permitted to survive the end of the Cold War.

Administrative Solutions?

According to the experts cited earlier, the systems acquisition process (although not its organization) should be a fun-house mirror image of the existing process—similar in form and content, but more streamlined and much, much slimmer. Most actually believe that the bones of the existing federal acquisitions regulations are fundamentally sound. The existing regulations prescribe the following actions prior to the award of a development contract:

1. Define the problem.
2. Clarify the user's basic need.
3. Establish operational requirements.
4. Based on user interaction, flesh out the specifications.
5. Perform should-cost analysis and determine availability of funds.

6.   Develop a procurement strategy (sole source or competitive, invitation to bid or request for proposals, flexible-price or fixed-price, step-by-step or total-package procurement) that reflects the attributes of the product sought and the capabilities of both potential suppliers and the skills of the acquisition team.
7.   Schedule the acquisition.
8.   Confirm with user the work schedule and the system's requirements.
9.   If the strategy calls for competition, develop evaluation criteria to be used in selecting one or more suppliers.
10. If the acquisition is not simply a low-bid auction, prepare, review, and release request for proposals; otherwise issue invitation to bid.
11. Establish evaluation team.
12. Conduct technical evaluation.
13. Determine competitive range and negotiate with contractors who are in the competitive range.
14. Review revised proposals including best and final offers.
15. Award contract(s) and debrief nonselected contractors (Crowley, 1984, p. III-1-20).

Each of these steps makes sense. Procedures should be in place to ensure that each is carried out properly.

The system fails not because these steps are overlooked or because acquisition officials are incompetent or corrupt, but because the individuals responsible for carrying them out are denied the discretion they need to do their job. Each of the required steps calls for the exercise of a high order of judgment, including making some choices that may be more or less arbitrary. As we will explain in the next chapter, the execution of contracts calls for highly skilled judgment. This is especially true of flexible-price contracts, but where a faulty decision has been made to rely on a fixed-price contract, it is true of fixed-price contracts as well.

A combination of three circumstances hampers the exercise of discretion on the part of the Department of Defense's acquisition officers. We have already mentioned the numbing effect induced by the overexpansion of the system commands and the numerous layers of review they impose between program managers and top Pentagon officials. In addition, program managers are forced to share their authority with contract officers and auditors, with a subsequent loss of needed control.

There is also the propensity of nearly everyone concerned with the acquisition process at each step in the contracting process to second guess the program manager's judgments. Every one of the program manager's judgments may have to be explained and defended at each of the many sites where the project could be vetoed. One result of the proliferation of review layers is that many program officers spend a lot more time explaining, justifying, and defending their programs than they do managing them. Furthermore, the acquisition officer's interlocutors frequently question the content of his judgments and not just the procedures followed in making them or their consequences, as would be proper.

Serious as these circumstances are, however, there is a third, which is even more fatal to the exercise of judgment: the statutes and internal Department of Defense policies that expressly limit the proper exercise of the acquisition officer's discretion. At several of the steps in the contracting process, Congress, the Office of Management and Budget, the Office of the Secretary of Defense, or the civilian secretariats of the military departments have prescribed the choices that they want the acquisition officer to make.

While the existing acquisition regulations grant the acquisition officer the nominal authority to overrule these choices, they impose on him the burden of showing the preferred alternative to be impractical or inappropriate. For example, in the selection of an acquisition strategy, existing regulations permit negotiations with a sole source, and also permit source selection to be based on factors other than price, but the acquisition officer must first prove, on the record, that his decision is justified. Not only is this requirement out of step with reality, it often forces the acquisition officer to tip his hand in negotiations carried out prior to and during the execution of a contract.

All the acquisition experts call for a substantial reduction in the size and scope of the systems commands, systems specifications, and evaluations teams, and in the number of criteria the evaluation teams consider in the source selection process. In addition to reducing gold plating, these changes would also elicit leaner responses to proposals from contractors, a step that would immediately reduce their paperwork burden. For example, the two competitors seeking the light helicopter–experimental (LHX) contract from the Army submitted proposals totaling 150,000 pages, 25,000 pages of answers to questions from the source selection evaluation board, and another 25,000 pages to substantiate their best and final offers—a grand total of six million pages for the thirty copies the Army required (Levens and Schemmer, 1991). In contrast, the Air Force limited responses to its RFP for the F-16 to sixty pages, fifty for technical considerations and ten to discuss the respondents' management plan (Kovacic, 1990a, p. 98)

Finally, the acquisition experts call for clear command channels, limited reporting requirements, and project teams with small, high-quality staffs.

Organizational Structure

According to Harvard Business School's J. Ronald Fox (1988, p. 306), the Pentagon's acquisition management structure should have the following elements:

- A single well-defined procurement chain of authority within the Department of Defense.
- Program managers with clear authority to override other interested parties within the Department of Defense (e.g., the user, functional specialists, advocates of competition, small business, and other socioeconomic programs).
- A single, well-defined monitoring and auditing authority.
- A single, well-defined channel for congressional inquiry and oversight.
- To address the problem of organizational proliferation and the diffusion of responsibility it engenders, the Department of Defense should identify each organizational unit influencing the acquisition process by name and define its role in unambiguous language.

Several of these organizational changes were adopted as part of Secretary Cheney's *Defense Management Report* initiatives. In addition, the Department of Defense has designated acquisition executives and established program executive officers with nominal authority over the various organizational layers that influence the acquisition process.

Despite these initiatives, flabby organization continues to be a major impediment to improving the effectiveness of the defense acquisition process. Clearly, the problems posed by the proliferation of interested parties have not been corrected by these initiatives. As one senior official in the Navy Department remarked, "Everybody is still falling all over everybody else; I just don't see any real changes." Moreover, the new acquisition executive officers still have limited authority regarding assignment and promotions of personnel, especially those not directly assigned to the program staff. In the meantime, the Department of Defense has broadened the definition of acquisition to cover almost any function that has to do with a weapons system or piece of equipment, not just their procurement, production, contracting, and research and development management.

Organizational Development and Staffing

Fox wants to give acquisition managers greater discretion and managerial authority. At the same time, he worries that they will not know how to use greater authority if they get it. Consequently, he stresses the importance of improving the quality and training of acquisition managers and of the processes by which they are selected and groomed to perform their roles. In addition, he argues that rigid pay scales and seniority-based promotion standards of civil service preclude the employment of the best people in the government acquisition system. He would substitute a personnel system that would provide far greater flexibility in status, pay, and qualifications, particularly at the senior level.

The model for the system Fox has in mind is the so-called China Lake project, in which employees—scientists and engineers, clerical personnel, and senior professional, administrative, and technical specialists—of the Naval Weapons Center at China Lake, California, and at the Naval Ocean Systems Center in San Diego received pay incentives and promotions based on performance under a radically decentralized personnel system (Fox, 1988, pp. 260–261, 314).

The China Lake demonstration project increased the authority of line managers to hire, promote, assign, and pay subordinates. This was done by grouping all the jobs at China Lake into five career paths and lumping the eighteen GS grades into a handful of broad pay bands. Managers were given the authority to meet market-determined pay levels to recruit and retain employees. They were also given the authority to increase the pay of outstanding individuals without having to justify promoting them to a higher grade or transferring them to a managerial position. Finally, they were given funds for incentive pay increases and performance bonuses. In its evaluation of this project, the federal Office of Personnel Management found that, in comparison with two similar Navy labs located on the East Coast, China Lake was better able to compete for talented engineers, had lower turnover rates, and did a better job of retaining high-performing individuals. Managers were unanimous in saying that the demonstration project helped them to maintain or improve the quality of their work force. The project also reduced personnel management costs and paperwork by 50 to 80 percent. As a result of its evaluation of the project, the Office of Personnel Management submitted legislation that would permit other agencies, including the Department of Defense, to adopt the China Lake plan (Wilson, 1989, pp. 146–48). So far, however, Congress has not acted.

Fox argues that, in addition to requiring both technical training and business skills, the Pentagon must provide a focused lifetime career path that progresses from technical work to assignments at laboratories, program offices, plant representative offices, to full management responsibility for small programs and, ultimately, large ones, if it is to develop fully qualified acquisition managers. "The challenge of managing the defense acquisition process effectively and efficiently requires a delicate balance between the adversarial role and the pure partnership role. . . . Achieving that balance requires years of training and experience to learn to cope with the complexities of the process, the day-to-day negotiations, and the marketing tactics within government, within industry, and between government and industry. What is needed is . . .

a business . . . partnership . . . characterized by rigorous bargaining, accompanied by tenacious regard for the best interests of one's own side" (Fox, 1988, p. 303)

With a lifetime of schooling and practice as his yardstick, Fox concludes that the Pentagon's current acquisition cadres are inadequately prepared to perform their proper duties. Moreover, he is skeptical that their scrimpy preparation can meaningfully be remedied by a twenty-week course at the Defense Systems Management College.

Using less exacting, but possibly more realistic standards, one would still have to conclude that many of the Department of Defense's program managers lack the technical proficiency and bargaining savvy they need to do their jobs. Over the last several years, we have talked with dozens of Department of Defense financial, program, and contract managers, as well as budget and cost analysts, both in uniform and out. While we have often been impressed by their dedication and commitment, and far more often than not by their intelligence, we have also frequently been amazed by the disparity between their actual theoretical and practical know-how and the expertise required of them by their assignments.

This is one area where the Pentagon has made a serious commitment to improvement. At the request of the Department of Defense, Congress passed the Defense Acquisition Workforce Improvement Act, which mandates increased training for acquisition personnel and established the Defense Acquisition University, a consortium of defense schools, including the Naval Postgraduate School and the Defense System Management College, to provide it. As for the military departments, the Air Force has gone farthest in its development of an acquisition career program, but the other services are not far behind. And all three services have evidently accepted the idea that developing adequate military program managers leaves candidates little time to become experts in a military operational specialty as well. Furthermore, the Pentagon is committed to providing the rank needed to secure and retain top-notch acquisition specialists.

However, a serious commitment is not the same as a sound program. The military departments still place far too much stress on ticket punching and not enough on job performance. For example, the Navy (Department of the Navy, 1989, pp. 6–7) plans to strengthen acquisition management by requiring "eight years of acquisition education and experience, a Masters' degree or its equivalent in a technical or management field, and graduation from the [Defense Acquisition University's] program management course prior to assignment to key positions." Moreover, the military departments often fail to understand the need for streamlining; they have a disturbing propensity to layer new acquisition programs atop existing organizations.

Would Streamlining Work?

Would the reforms proposed by the acquisition experts work to improve the efficiency and effectiveness of the acquisition process? Management theory says they would. Furthermore, clear command channels, limited reporting requirements, and small, high-quality project teams are characteristics of successful private sector project management efforts (Peters and Waterman, 1982). However, the best evidence for the efficacy of the proposed reforms is the success of acquisition programs such as the Polaris, the SR-71, and the F-16 that were shielded from bureaucratic oversight and the scrutiny of Congress (see Kitfield, 1989; Gregory, 1989, p. 167). These show what can be done when red tape is cut, authority and responsibility are coupled, and organization is decentralized to the working level. The successful and (for its time) highly sophisticated Polaris was completed as an operational weapon in about three and a half years, well ahead of schedule. Vice Admiral W. F. Raborn was given absolute discretion to manage this program and the full support of the Navy and the Department of Defense. The SR-71 "Blackbird," successor to the scandalous U-2 reconnaissance aircraft, was a secret project funded by the Air Force and the Central Intelligence Agency. With stable funding, full authority and responsibility, and a high degree of autonomy, Clarence L. "Kelly" Johnson of Lockheed's famed Skunk Works was twice able to produce world-beating planes—in the U-2 and the SR-71—under budget and ahead of schedule (Baldwin, 1965, p. 270). Gregory (1989, p. 67) quotes Ben Rich, Kelly Johnson's successor, as saying that the success of the Skunk Works was due entirely "to the fact that the Air Force's labyrinthian specifications, regulations and horde of blue light specialists and red light specialists could be bypassed in favor of a small group working informally."

The Polaris and the SR-71 were top-secret programs. The authority given their program managers, the streamlining of the acquisition process, and their small high-quality project teams were primarily by-products of the decision to restrict access to the project to those who had "a need to know." As a consequence of this restriction, program managers were just that. They ran projects, made decisions, sold them to a limited hierarchy, and rose or fell with the results. There was no second guessing the content of their judgments, no multiple layers of review. Project audits were few; audit teams had to be kept small and cost measurements simple. Their exploration of requirements had to be restricted to a small circle of users. Requirements were therefore kept to a minimum, as were the teams that evaluated them. Nonselected contractors could not complain to program managers' bosses or to Congress—at least not loudly—and program managers were entirely free from press scrutiny. For example, one of the CIA's surveillance satellite programs overran its cost target by $300 million, but that fact never made the newspapers. The managers of secret programs had to be guided by the armed services' procurement regulations, but the nominal discretion accorded program managers by those regulations was for them a reality.

Furthermore, research and development could easily be stopped if a program turned sour. It is often hard to kill public programs, in part because they are backed by hefty lobbies and in part because public debate distorts the acquiring agency's and the program manager's incentives away from managing programs to selling them. The legislative/bureaucratic process generates a great deal of misinformation, which makes it hard to distinguish good systems from bad ones. In contrast, when TRW's satellite program went bad, the Central Intelligence Agency simply replaced TRW— there were no public debates and no public appeals.

Most people we have talked with who have worked on both secret programs and those conducted in the open believe that the secret programs were once the better managed. Instead of being compelled to rely on the adversarial way of buying, with suppliers held at arm's length, frequent bidding contests, and orders shifted among suppliers chosen simply on price, managers of secret programs were free to follow businesslike practices and establish close working partnerships based on long-term mutual dependence, to nurture suppliers, and to fire them if they failed to produce.

In recent years, however, secret programs have been subjected to increased bureaucratic and congressional scrutiny. The General Accounting Office now audits secret programs, and those programs generally have to follow the same rules as those that are conducted in the open. According to Kitfield (1989, p. 27), the result of this added scrutiny has been that "added layers of oversight have slowed even the formerly streamlined Skunk Works process down. . . . The size of the government's program office at the Skunk Works has increased tenfold since 1965, and the subsequent number of military specifications and required reports have thus shown similar increases. Yet in 1987 the plant produced one-third the number of aircraft it did in 1965." Consequently, secret programs are probably managed now no better or worse than the Pentagon's other acquisitions (Morrison, 1986). Kitfield (1989, p. 25) quotes Jeffrey Phillips, a General Accounting Office analyst, as saying that "the kinds of problems we're now seeing in special-access programs are the same types of problems we've been seeing in similar, high-risk unclassified programs."

Lessons of the B-2

That programs such as the Polaris and the SR-71 were successful because of the way they were run, rather than because they were secret, is suggested by a comparison between the development of the B-2 bomber and the F-22 (Easterbrook, 1991). The B-2 program was secret from the very first. Nevertheless, it started with a set of detailed technical specifications, its prime contractor was selected through a paper competition, and its development was subject to high levels of bureaucratic and congressional scrutiny at every stage. Perhaps as a consequence, it took ten years to develop the B-2, the development was plagued by technical snafus, and it cost (counting to completion of the first four prototypes) $33 billion.

In contrast, the acquisition of the F-22 reflected the recommendations made by the Grace and Packard commissions, especially the latter. In addition to recommending that program managers be given increased personal authority and responsibility and that the processes through which contractors are selected and projects managed be simplified and streamlined, the Packard Commission emphasized the "funnel" approach to acquisition. The Packard Commission recommended that technological leaps not be funded until working prototypes demonstrated the practicality of the technology. The Packard Commission also criticized rigid specifications, recommending that contractors be told in general terms what was wanted and given wide latitude to devise solutions. The commission insisted that contract winners should be selected on the basis of head-to-head competition between working prototypes. Finally, the Packard Commission recommended that contractors be required to perform some research and development at their own expense.

That is precisely how the F-22 was developed. The contractors were freed from binding specifications: "The sole contractual requirement for the prototype was that it had to take off." And the program manager, General James Fain, Jr., dramatically reengineered the Air Force side of the effort. He set up product teams with responsibility for all aspects of particular components from blueprints to project completion, which had the effect of organizing jobs around an objective or outcome instead of single tasks. Under the old approach, development moved like a relay race, with one group of functional specialists passing the baton to the next group. Under the new approach, parallel activities were coordinated during their performance, thereby increasing speed, flexibility, and commitment to a common goal. Finally, he gave the people who did the work responsibility for making decisions. Team members voted on key decisions, "with more votes assigned to the working-level troops than the flag rank."

As a consequence, the F-22 was developed in only four years from inception of the program to first flight at a total cost (again counting to completion of the first four prototypes) of only $6 billion, $2 billion of which were provided by the contractors. The F-22 is a fine plane: stealthy, highly maneuverable, and capable of cruising at supersonic speed without running out of fuel. It has had few if any of the technical problems experienced by the B-2.

The Plural of Anecdote Is Not Data: The Case of the A-12

Regrettably, the empirical case for acquisition reform is based on experience with a very small number of programs, many of them secret. We do not have hard, quantitative evidence that acquisition programs are on average more efficient and effective when they are burdened with fewer bureaucratic gatekeepers and less micromanagement.

What we have to go on is hearsay. Indeed, most of what we think we know about acquisition is based on anecdotal evidence from case studies. Although volumes have been written that clearly demonstrate the dysfunctional aspects of the existing rule-bound procurement regime and some, such as Kelman's *Procurement and Public Management: The Fear of Discretion and the Quality of Government Performance* (1990), that provide a rich set of comparative cases, there is not nearly as much evidence about the effectiveness of alternative regimes as we would like. Furthermore, case studies are rarely conclusive—a point that is illustrated, although not proved, by the case of the A-12.

According to Chester Paul Beach (1990), author of the Department of the Navy's report on the A-12, this program had many of the characteristics advocated by the procurement gurus. The program's manager was an aviation engineering officer with three advanced degrees. His entire career had been in systems development and acquisition. He had been in charge of the A-12 program from its inception and was expected to remain with the project to its completion. He even picked his staff.

Moreover, the Navy gave the A-12 program its highest priority, and it enjoyed strong congressional support. The program was fully funded from its inception. It suffered few if any of the fluctuations in funding that destabilize many acquisition efforts or the logrolling that inflates systems specifications. Furthermore, Beach found no evidence of Office of the Secretary of Defense or congressional micromanagement that could have impeded the program manager's ability to manage the A-12 program or evidence that the program manager's Navy superiors interfered in any way with his decisions. Nevertheless Beach (1990, p. 34) sadly concluded that the A-12 proves those attributes do not guarantee program success: "The PM in this case is the archetype of the well-trained, highly motivated professional, fully empowered to fulfill his responsibility and be accountable for cost, schedule, and performance of his program, that we are trying to develop under the acquisition corps plans and matrix management approach reflected in the Defense Management Report. Nonetheless, it should be plain that neither he, nor the similarly well-qualified and dedicated officers in his chain of supervision, met the needs of senior civilian leaders within the DON and DOD for an accurate assessment of the program's status and risk."

According to Beach, the problem is that the program manager of the A-12 program, together with his uniformed superiors, were more concerned with selling the program than they were with managing it. They consistently cast the program in a positive, optimistic light. The data on program cost, schedule, and performance that the military managers communicated to their civilian superiors did not give them what they needed, but instead focused on securing continued support for the A-12 program.

Beach (1990, p. 34) believes that the solution is to create "appropriate incentives to enable senior leaders to rely upon responsible, accountable line managers for realistic perspectives on the cost, schedule and technical status of their programs. Only by doing so can we increase efficiency and accountability while reducing the burdens imposed by undue regulation and stifling supervision."

But was the Navy's approach to the A-12 development characterized by managerial failure? It is not clear to us that it was. When it became apparent that its development was over budget and behind schedule, the program was canceled. The program manager was punished for his failure to bring bad news promptly to the attention of his civilian superiors. He was fired from the project and a letter of censure placed in his personnel file. His superior, who actually suppressed the bad news about project cost and schedule overruns, was ordered to resign from the Navy. While it may be argued that these sanctions were inadequate, it cannot be concluded that they failed to provide responsible line managers with an incentive to furnish senior Pentagon officials with realistic information on the cost, schedule, and technical status of their program.

Frankly, we have a great deal of sympathy for the A-12's program manager and tend to believe that his lapse was both understandable and, to a degree, unavoidable. The A-12 was to be purchased using a fixed-price contract. Contrary to the assertion made in the Beach report, it is not the case that program managers are expected to monitor costs and schedules as closely under a fixed-price contract as under a cost-plus type contract. Fixed-price contracts are justified, at least in part, because they shift responsibility for managing costs from the government to the firm. The assumption is that a firm's managers are more competent to manage its operations than the government. Fixed-price contracts are designed in part to give them the discretion to do so. Moreover, a fixed-price contract puts the contractor's money at risk rather than the taxpayers'. This risk is supposed to provide the contractor with maximum incentive to do whatever is needed to stay under budget in terms of cost and schedule.

Up to a certain point, the General Dynamics/McDonnell-Douglas team was betting their own money on the success of the A-12. Perhaps they were hoping to get lucky and get back on schedule. Since the contractors had the primary responsibility for managing costs and schedule, was the A-12 program manager remiss in his duty when, in this case, he failed to second guess their judgment? The answer is not clear.

There is one area where the A-12's project manager was denied significant authority. Unlike his F-22 counterpart, he was not given discretion to choose an overall procurement strategy. Instead of the flexible-pricing approach recommended by the Office of the Secretary of Defense's acquisition specialists, the Navy's civilian secretariat mandated that the program be awarded on the basis of competitive bidding on a fixed-price contract. Moreover, like the B-2, the A-12 started with a set of detailed specifications and its development team was selected on the basis of a paper competition. Hence, this was a high-risk project.

Given the special risks associated with the development of the A-12 and the financial difficulties of McDonnell-Douglas, it is clear to us that once the wrong procurement strategy was adopted, the situation called for more careful monitoring and oversight of the project's budget than would be appropriate for most fixed-price contracts. Evidently this was not clear to the A-12 program manager.

We understand also why the A-12 program manager was

more concerned with getting the system developed and into the Navy's inventory than with meeting project cost or scheduled milestones. The A-12 was designed to meet very real military and institutional needs. Aircraft carriers are the Navy's centerpiece. A carrier's punch depends almost entirely on the potency of its attack planes. Many observers believe that, to ensure the continued viability of carrier forces, a new attack plane is needed to replace the long-in-the-tooth A-6s, many of which are now well over twenty years old (although some believe that the experience in the Gulf shows that the Navy would be wiser to invest its scarce resources in modernizing its payloads, rather than in new aircraft to deliver its inventory of obsolete iron bombs). In any case, the Navy has scheduled the A-6 to be retired in the not-too-distant future.

Certainly the Navy's top leaders believed that the future of the Navy depended on the success of the A-12 program. In the private sector, a project manager, especially the manager of a program crucial to the continued vitality of the firm, would be also be expected to play the role of program advocate. While private sector project managers are usually held accountable for the promises they make about the cost, schedule, and technical status of the programs they champion, ultimately so was the manager of the Navy's A-12 program.

Furthermore, as soon as it was apparent that General Dynamics/McDonnell-Douglas could not break even, let alone make money, on the A-12 development contract, the program manager blew the whistle. Based on the record, it is hard to see how he could have reached this conclusion much sooner. He reported his concerns to his superiors in April 1990. February would have been the earliest imaginable date for him to have surmised that the development team would be unable to meet its obligations. Even then, a reasonable doubt would have remained.

A key failure occurred at the next level, however, when his uniformed superior suppressed the A-12 program manager's April report.

Incompetence Is More Common Than Conspiracy

It is possible, as suggested in the Beach report, that in the A-12 case the contractor intentionally sought payment for work that it had not done and that it intentionally misinformed the Navy about its plans in an attempt to maximize cash flow (in the form of progress payments). It is also possible that the contractors knew that they could not meet the terms of the contract, that they expected the contract to be canceled, that top executives from both General Dynamics and McDonnell-Douglas lied when they said they were committed to the program, and that they were merely stringing the Navy along to keep the money flowing as long as possible. These possibilities require us to believe, however, that the executives of both General Dynamics and McDonnell-Douglas consciously considered the risks they were facing by pursuing such a dangerous strategy: that they discounted the Navy's efforts to obtain reimbursement for overpayment, plus any applicable penalties, the likelihood of suit under RICO, and the possibility of prosecution for both statutory and common-law fraud. Perhaps. But, given the risk of penalties to the firms involved and to their managers, we are inclined to believe it more likely that their sin was wishful thinking than fraud.

It is somewhat more likely that General Dynamics and McDonnell-Douglas believed that the Navy had so much invested in the A-12 that it would quietly renegotiate the A-12 contract, perhaps on a cost-plus basis, despite their troubles with schedule and costs. This possibility requires us to accept that the contractors believed the Navy would have willingly repeated the whole sordid history of the C-5A to get its hands on the A-12. Such a belief might have represented poor judgment on the part of the management of both General Dynamics and McDonnell-Douglas, but bad judgment is also far more common than conspiracy.

One real problem that is addressed by neither the Beach report nor most of the literature on acquisition reform is suggested by the possibility that the Naval Air Commander fully understood the gravity of withholding information from his civilian superiors. It is likely that he willingly risked his career for the good of naval air (assuming he would have had a career if the A-12 went down). It is hard for us to see how, given the importance of the A-12 to naval air and the military's tradition of self-sacrifice for the good of the service, incentives could have been put in place that would have motivated him to provide realistic information to his civilian supervisors.

We believe that part of the solution to this dilemma must go to broader questions of organizational structure such as the matrix-management concept outlined in the Packard Commission report, not just to incentives to tell the truth.

Experimentation

It would, of course, be better if the conclusions outlined in this chapter were based on the results of a careful program of experimentation to determine how weapons costs actually vary with acquisitions policies. According to research carried out at the Naval Postgraduate School by Mark Robert Radice (1992), just such a program of experimentation, the Defense Enterprise Program, was launched during the last decade, although it never really got far off the ground. This program was designed to say whether regulatory relief and streamlined management—short lines of communication, clear responsibility, accelerated schedules, and a modicum of congressional neglect—would, in fact, produce better, cheaper weapons. Authority to experiment with simplified acquisition strategies and structures was granted the Pentagon by the Defense Authorization Act of 1986, under the terms of which Congress waived its supervision of selected acquisition programs. The military departments selected ten major programs for participation, including the SSN-21 Seawolf submarine.

By 1990, the Defense Enterprise Program was for all practical purposes dead. Acquisition personnel in the Pentagon blame the House and Senate Appropriations Committees for this fatality. They claim that the key to the success of the program was milestone-to-milestone funding, which guaranteed program participants freedom from direct congressional supervision and oversight. They argue that the refusal of the House and Senate Appropriations Committees to fund on a milestone-to-milestone basis or to suspend congressional oversight of the Defense Enterprise Program, as the law required, rendered the whole experiment moot and that the Pentagon was forced to withdraw its support from the Defense Enterprise Program in protest.

Later, Deputy Secretary Donald Atwood made an attempt to revive this initiative. He envisioned a set of procurement experiments designed to test the utility of short lines of communication, clear programmatic responsibility, and relief from congressional micromanagement. But he was persuaded to abandon this attempt by Donald J. Yockey, the Under Secretary of Defense for Acquisition—in part because Yockey's office already had a full plate and was reeling from the implementation of the *Defense Management Report* initiatives.

Instead, Yockey's office threw its weight behind the implementation of advanced cost systems. These efforts culminated in a July 1990 meeting with representatives of the defense industry to talk about the implementation of activity-based costing in a Federal Acquisition Regulations–governed environment. While the participants agreed to work toward modernizing the Pentagon's approach to cost measurement, this meeting failed to produce any substantive changes in federal cost-accounting standards. Regrettably, the Pentagon has apparently decided not to pursue this initiative.

Yockey's office also promoted the establishment of a Defense Acquisition archive—a central repository of all acquisition-related studies, reports, records, and memoranda open to the public, with a restricted-access companion archive for classified material. This more modest effort has continued and may ultimately bear fruit.

The Accountability Problem

Since the Pentagon is formally committed to streamlining and restructuring its acquisition process, many observers now believe that the main bulwark against reform of the procurement process is Congress (see Jones and Doyle, 1992; Jones and Bixler, 1992). It would be hard to deny the congressional predisposition to overcontrol (in this vein, one of the very best analyses remains Ackerman and Hassler, 1980). Indeed, the belief that the best way to attack an abuse or to do good is to make a rule prohibiting or requiring some behavior seems to be especially robust on Capitol Hill, perhaps because so many of its denizens are lawyers, who are accustomed by training and professional experience to dealing in mandates.

Nevertheless, while we do not deny that Congress too often fails to consider alternative governance designs or that its concern with the details of administration often leads it to overcontrol, we would also stress that Congress is not alone in this. These are recurring problems in most organizations. Superiors are nearly every-where more confident of their own competence than they are of their subordinates'. Most are also far more cognizant of their own decision-making abilities, responsibilities, and prerogatives than they are of their ignorance of the nitty-gritty ramifications of their choices or of the massive paperwork burden that management by fiat imposes on an organization. One of the major aims of manage-rial training is overcoming this bias

There is, however, a darker alternative: political authorities, especially legislators, know exactly what they are doing. They favor administrative controls that are ineffective by design. This view implies that no amount of evidence would be sufficient to persuade Congress to back away from direct supervision of the systems acqui-sition process—the procurement process is staggeringly Byzantine not by accident but by design and procurement reforms are inevi-tably destined to fail, because they leave in place the political in-stitutions and bureaucratic incentives that created the problems in the first place (Moe, 1989, 1990).

Obviously, we do not agree with this assessment. Indeed, it reminds us of the pessimistic assessments of the political feasibility of transportation deregulation that were made by many of our aca-demic colleagues during the struggles of the late 1970s. At that time, there was much talk among academics about iron triangles, about the demand for and the supply of regulation, and about how, de-spite the strength of the theoretical case for deregulation, regulatory reform was not feasible. In fact, those assessments were never more widely accepted or endorsed than at the moment Congress acted (Robyn, 1987; Jones and Thompson, 1984).

We will deal further with the question of the political feas-ibility of implementing the new public management in the Depart-ment of Defense in Chapter Eight. Nevertheless, we would note here that the congressional response to the Pentagon's internal regula-tory relief effort, which was carried out between 1990 and 1992 un-der the direct supervision of Deputy Secretary Donald Atwood, strongly suggests that Congress might be receptive to evidence that restructuring and redesign would work. As part of the Department of Defense's internal regulatory relief effort, the Pentagon's basic acquisition guide was revised, canceling fifty directives, fifteen policy memoranda, and all Service Supplementing Guidance. As a result of this effort, the defense acquisition regulations now explicitly permit program managers to pay attention to past supplier performance in making source selection decisions and to reward good performance. Congress was fully informed of these changes and enthusiastically approved them. Furthermore, Congress has singled out the sections of the *Gore Report* dealing with procurement reform for its special approval.

Nevertheless, the refusal of the House and Senate Appropriations Committees to fund the Defense Enterprise Program on a milestone-to milestone basis or to suspend oversight of them serves to remind us that congressional concerns must be allayed if the new public management is to be successfully implemented. In the case of the Defense Enterprise Program, several of the members of the appropriations committees expressed approval of its goals, but they indicated that their job did not end with enactment of the budget—that they were also responsible for ensuring that the budget is executed as enacted—otherwise Congress would lose control of the uses to which taxpayers' dollars are put (Radice, 1992). The implication here is that that congressional preoccupation with the details of administration is somehow ordained by the division of powers found in the Constitution, and that congressional micromanagement of the budget is a direct consequence of the exercise of Congress's substantive powers.

Of course, this view would be correct if the system of line-item encumbrances and reports that legislative bodies have used since the seventeenth century to exercise control over the executive were the only mechanism of administrative governance available to Congress. As we show in the next chapter, however, that is most assuredly not the case.

CHAPTER SIX

Redesigning
Control Systems

THE PROPENSITY TO devise inflexible and comprehensive rules is, perhaps, nowhere more irresistible than where military procurement is concerned. As an example, consider the MIL-F-1499 (Fruitcake), 250 tons of which were recently purchased by the Army. To preclude abuses on the part of unscrupulous bakers, to make sure there really are some candied fruits and nuts in the fruitcake, to guarantee adequate shelf-life and resistance to handling, and to ensure palatability in all the far-flung places of the world where the American Army celebrates Christmas, the specifications for the MIL-F-1499 (Fruitcake) were eighteen pages long. Plastic whistles take sixteen pages of specifications, olives seventeen, hot chocolate twenty, chewing gum fifteen, condoms thirteen, and so on (Adelman and Augustine, 1990, pp. 126–127).

Not so long ago, the late Frederick C. Mosher (1980, pp. 545–547) observed that government has experienced a sea change in its responsibilities and tactics and concluded that these massive changes have rendered obsolete the traditional administrative controls that we inherited from our forebears. In a similar vein, Allen Schick (1978, p. 518) has noted with concern that changes in the reach and scale of government have been accompanied by massive growth in the scope and content of rule-bound governance mechanisms: reporting

155

requirements have multiplied, auditors scrutinize more closely the accounts of federal agencies and contractors, and direct controls in the form of rules and regulations have proliferated.

Schick concluded that we cannot afford to go on imposing direct controls over an ever-widening sphere of activities—that new solutions to the problem of administrative governance must be sought. He finished with a reminder that in many cases individuals can be more effectively influenced to serve the public interest "by inducements which allow them to pursue their own interests than by constraints which try to bar them from behaving as they want."

Remarkably, many of the participants in contemporary debates over defense management and operations are unfamiliar with the alternatives to rule-bound governance mechanisms. In this chapter, we describe the basic management control systems designs[1] that are available for influencing people to advance the policies and purposes of the institutions they serve. We then show how these mechanisms can be executed to enforce efficiency in the delivery of services and outline the circumstances under which each has a comparative advantage over the others. We also show what happens when these designs are misused—and overused.

Control Systems in General

The design and implementation of control systems is a ubiquitous problem. It is encountered by engineers, planners, and regulators as well as management controllers. The purposes of various kinds of control systems differ, as do the details of their execution, but all control systems designers face the same key choices: what, where, when, and, in the case of human systems, whom to control. The choice of what and where to control is reasonably self-evident. Management control should be primarily addressed to the behavior of service suppliers (that is, the military departments and defense agencies, other departments of government such as the General Services Administration, and contractors), the efficiency with which they produce goods and services, and ultimately the efficiency with which they use the assets at their disposal.

The choice of whom to subject to controls and when to execute those controls is far less self-evident. In the abstract, a control systems designer has four sets of options, comprised of two choices of subject and two of timing: (1) the subject may be either an organization or an individual, and (2) controls may be executed either before or after the subject acts.

Before-the-fact controls are intended to prevent subjects from doing undesirable things or to compel them to do desirable things. These controls necessarily take the form of authoritative mandates, rules, or regulations that specify what the subject must do, may do, or must not do. The subjects of before-the-fact controls are held responsible for complying with these commands and the controller attempts to monitor and enforce compliance with them.

After-the-fact controls are executed after the subject, either an organization or an individual, decides on and carries out a course of action and, therefore, after some of the consequences of the subject's decisions are known. Because bad decisions cannot be undone after they are carried out, after-the-fact controls are intended to motivate subjects to make good decisions. Hence subjects are made responsible for the consequences of their decisions, and the controller attempts to monitor those consequences and to see that subjects are rewarded or sanctioned accordingly.

Combining the choice of subject with that of timing, we find that the control systems designer must choose among four distinct institutional alternatives: individual responsibility, before-the-fact or after-the-fact, and organizational responsibility, before-the-fact or after-the-fact. In this chapter, we will try to explain the significance of this choice, its relevance to management control, and the economic logic that should guide it.

Privatization

The significance of these alternative designs is partially reflected in the debate over the merits of privatizing the delivery of public services. Proponents of privatization imply that we have a choice between rule-governed, often overregulated, monopolistic public bureaucracies and freely competing private firms. They conclude that the latter will usually be more efficient than the former. If that were our choice, it is difficult to see how privatization could be wrong, since it resolves to a simple question of monopoly or competition.

Other things being equal, provision by competing private firms will usually be more efficient than provision by a public monopoly.

But other things are not equal. Consequently, the distinction often drawn by proponents of privatization between public and private production is inordinately simplistic. It is simplistic because many of the advocates of privatization implicitly assume that governments are flawed and markets are perfect: that participants are perfectly informed, that transactions are costless, and that they involve the exchange of a discrete product for cash. However, when the choice of governance arrangements is at hand, that is precisely what we must not do. In the real world, where the production of a good or service may be characterized by increasing returns to scale or scope, a high degree of lumpiness in production (or consumption),[2] asset specificities, or the absence of close substitutes, the purchaser must expend resources shopping and bargaining over prices and terms. If the item or service is to be made available at a later date, the purchaser must expend resources to ensure that the supplier adheres to the terms of the bargain or contract. That is, to avoid costly mistakes, the purchaser must incur search, bargaining, monitoring, and enforcement costs.

These control or transaction costs are part of the cost of acquiring an item. It does not matter whether they occur inside of government or out; ultimately the government as purchaser pays. Consequently, the distinction between provision by a public agency and provision by a private entity fails to capture the full range of choices available to the management controller. It also fails to reflect all of the factors that are relevant to his or her choice.

First, although it is true that most goods and services purchased with public money are produced by organizations and not individuals, effective control ultimately presumes individual accountability. The distinction drawn by the proponents of privatization between public and private provision ignores the management controllers' capacity to hold managers of public organizations under their jurisdiction personally responsible for their behavior and, thereby, the controllers' capacity to influence directly the rewards and sanctions that accrue to those individuals, such as salary and opportunities for advancement.

Controllers cannot possibly hold managers personally responsible where their relationship to the supplying organization is at arm's length and the structure of individual responsibility is veiled by the organizational form. The only way an organization can be rewarded (or punished) is by increasing (or reducing) its revenues. An organization's revenues can affect an individual manager's welfare, but only indirectly.

The difference between holding individuals and organizations accountable or between direct, personal influence and indirect influence is straightforward. Take the following example: if the quality of services supplied by an agency, the Defense Logistics Agency for example, is grossly unsatisfactory, the controller can recommend the dismissal of the agency director. Where the Department of Defense has an arm's-length relationship with a service supplier, McDonnell-Douglas for example, and the relationship is unsatisfactory, all that the controller can do is recommend termination of the relationship. The controller can punish the supplying organization but cannot punish the manager responsible for the failure—although his or her actions might well lead the organization's board of directors to do so. Unfortunately, punishing a monopoly (that is, any sole-source supplier) is like cutting off your nose to spite your face; rewarding one is like eating an eclair to celebrate staying on a diet. Consequently, where the supplying organization is a monopoly, the capacity to influence managers directly will have considerable utility, particularly where the controller can stimulate and exploit competition between alternative management teams.

This claim can be verified by reference to the private sector. In the private sector, most real natural monopolies make intermediate products—that is, goods that are used to produce consumer goods or services. Natural monopoly (decreasing costs as output increases) can usually be attributed to spreading large, lumpy investments in specialized resources—technological know-how, product-specific research and development, equipment—over additional output. Investment in specialized resources often inspires a process called *vertical integration* ("backward" if initiated by the consumer goods producer, "forward" if initiated by the intermediate goods producer) (Joskow, 1988). The new economics of organization tells us that vertical integration occurs because it permits transaction or control costs to be minimized, in part through the substitution of direct supervision for indirect influence (see Williamson, 1985; to understand better the relevance of transaction cost economics to public administration, see Maser, 1986, Vining and Weimer, 1990, and Ferris and Graddy, 1991; see also Friedman, 1981, and Borcherding, 1988).

We use the terms *transaction cost* and *control cost* interchangeably. For the purposes of this volume, we prefer the latter term. Controls have costs even where transactions fail to occur. The rules governing the disposition of federal lands to private commercial interests discussed in the next chapter provide an example. These rules were intended to protect the public patrimony by making it impossible for corrupt or fraudulent real estate speculators to profit at the public's expense. In this, they have succeeded and have done so without imposing substantial direct costs on either the Department of Defense or business. This is the case because they are so sweeping that they have prevented almost all transfers of public property to private owners. Consequently, the Department of Defense has not expended resources negotiating property transfers or monitoring and enforcing compliance with the rules governing these transactions. Neither has business expended resources to comply with these rules. But insofar as these resources have alternative uses, there is still a cost. Nevertheless, the branch of economics that is concerned with these issues is not called *control-cost economics*, it is called *transaction-cost economics*.

In the language of transaction-cost economics, investment in specialized resources is called *asset specificity*. An asset is said to be specific if it makes a necessary contribution to the provision of a good or service and has a much lower value in alternative uses. The corollary of asset specificity is bilateral monopoly, a circumstance that provides an ideal environment for opportunistic behavior on the part of both the intermediate product supplier and his customer.

For example, once an intermediate product producer has acquired a specialized asset, his customer may be able to threaten to switch suppliers to extract discounts from him. In that case, the supplier may find it necessary to write off a large part of his specialized investment. Or, if demand for the final good increases greatly, the intermediate product supplier may be able to use his monopoly power to extort exorbitant prices from his customer. Hence, where the relationship between the intermediate product supplier and his customer is at arm's length, the threat of opportunistic behavior may be sufficient to eliminate the incentive to make what would otherwise be cost-effective investments. Vertical integration can eliminate this threat. Indeed, where the intermediate product producer provides homogeneous goods or services (that is, outputs that are easily monitored), total production volume is specified, and technologies are mature, vertical integration permits a bilateral monopoly to be governed satisfactorily by unbalanced or two-part transfer prices.

Vertical integration is, of course, only one way to deal with asset specificity. Some firms invest in specialized resources and own design-specific assets, which they provide to their suppliers. This is called *quasi-vertical integration*. It is common in both the automobile and the aerospace industries, and, of course, it is standard procedure for the Department of Defense to provide and own the equipment, dies, and designs that defense firms use to supply it with weapons systems and the like (see Monteverde and Teece, 1982). Other organizations that rely on a small number of suppliers or a small number of distributors write contracts that constrain the opportunistic behavior of those with whom they deal. A well-executed contract can approximate the outcome from vertical integration (although such contracts are often hard to write and, where one of the parties is inclined to exploit the other, prohibitively costly to enforce) without incurring the very real costs of vertical integration.

In other cases, desired outcomes can be realized through alliances based on the exchange of hostages (for example, surety bonds, exchange of debt or equity positions) or just plain old-fashioned trust based on long-term mutual dependence. In Japan, for example, buyer-seller relationships tend to be based on mutual confidence. Toyota relies on a few suppliers that it nurtures and supports. It maintains tight working links between its manufacturing and engineering departments and its suppliers and explicitly eschews opportunistic behavior in the interest of maintaining long-term relationships ("A Guide to Better Buying," 1986).

Nevertheless, in one study of vertical integration in the U.S. aerospace industry, Scott Masten (1984) unambiguously demonstrated that asset specificity and, therefore, decreasing cost is basic to the make-or-buy decision. Where intermediate products were both complex and highly specialized (used only by the buyer), there was a 92 percent probability that they would be produced internally; even 31 percent of all simple, specialized components were produced internally. The probability dropped to less than 2 percent if the component was not specialized, regardless of its complexity.

Furthermore, the proponents of privatization err in their implicit claim that responsibility can be vested in organizations if and only if the organization is private, and in individuals if and only if the organization is part of the public sector. The absurdity of this claim becomes clear as soon as it is explicitly stated; it is consistent with neither theory nor practice. For example, many state legislatures base their relationships with public entities such as universities or hospitals on arm's-length relationships that are guaranteed by self-denying ordinances, which exempt the managers of these public entities from detailed oversight and direct control. Indeed, the Department of Defense's decisions about base closure and realignment are exempted from direct congressional control by just such a self-denying ordinance (see Chapter Seven). Similarly, the recurring procurement fraud cases show that the managers of private entities that supply services to the Department of Defense can be held directly and personally responsible for their behavior when it violates federal law.

Finally, most of the proponents of privatization implicitly presume that the services provided to or for government are homogeneous or fungible, which implies that the problem of identifying the most efficient supplying organization or management team resolves to a simple question of price search, an elementary control mechanism that reveals information about the "customer's" demand for the service. In fact, many of the organizations supplying goods or services to or for government supply bundles of more or less heterogeneous products—many of these products are hard to measure and costly to evaluate, some prohibitively so.

Choosing Between Alternative Institutional Designs

The proponents of privatization do, however, make one significant, unexceptionable claim: that the choice of institutional designs should depend on the cost and production behavior of the good or service in question. However, they frequently fail to carry this claim to its logical conclusion. At least two factors are relevant to this choice: the ease with which the consequences of operating decisions can be monitored and the desirability of interorganizational competition.

Most management control theorists believe that where consequences (that is, an organization or responsibility center's outputs) are easily monitored, control should focus on the consequences of the subject's decisions; where they are not, control should focus on their content (inputs). Because consequences are easily monitored where entities produce homogeneous outputs or where a responsibility center within an entity performs fungible activities, it follows that controllers should rely on after-the-fact controls where homogeneous outputs are supplied. In contrast, it follows that they should rely on before-the-fact controls where each item supplied is, from the "customer's" perspective, intrinsically unique. Furthermore, this view has been reinforced by recent findings in transaction-cost economics and agency theory.

At the same time, industrial organization theory tells us that interorganizational competition is desirable only where costs are constant or increasing as quantity of output (rate or volume) increases. Where economies of scale or scope cause costs to decrease when output is increased, monopoly supply is usually appropriate (Barzelay [1992] refers to entities that have this characteristic as *utilities*; see also Kettl, 1993). Because responsibility can be effectively vested in organizations only where customers or their agents are ultimately indifferent to the survival of one or more of the supplying organizations, the implication of this line of reasoning is that controllers should vest responsibility in organizations only where interorganizational rivalry is practical and likely to be effective— and in individuals, where it is not.

These normative prescriptions are summarized in Figure 6.1.

Execution of Alternative Control Systems Designs

These four basic sets of controls are all employed by the Department of Defense. But is each appropriately employed? Before we can

Figure 6.1. The Microeconomics of Control Systems Design.

COST

	Decreasing	Increasing
Unique	Individual Responsibility/ Before-the-Fact Controls	Organizational Responsibility/ Before-the-Fact Controls
OUTPUTS Homogeneous	Individual Responsibility/ After-the-Fact Controls	Organizational Responsibility/ After-the-Fact Controls

answer this question, we must first show how these designs are used and explain the practical logic of their implementation. Our discussion will concentrate on the use of before-the-fact controls. This does not mean that we particularly like them. On the contrary, we believe that controllers should resort to before-the-fact control designs only where the cost and production behavior of the good or service in question makes their use the least objectionable alternative.

We concentrate on the use of before-the-fact controls because it seems to us that their implementation is not well understood, especially by those who most rely on them. Many participants in the policy process believe that before-the-fact controls not only safeguard against abuse, but also, by reducing costs, improve mission performance. If failure occurs nevertheless, they tend to believe the solution lies in still more or better rules.

One possible explanation for the persistent faith in the efficacy of before-the-fact controls is that its devotees just do not understand how hard it is to execute them efficiently. For example, they appear to believe that the subjects of before-the-fact controls will comply with them simply because they are morally obligated to do so. Obviously, however, not everyone is inclined to respect moral authority, to respect the law, or to obey rules. It is necessary to monitor and enforce compliance with rules and to ferret out and punish noncompliance. It is also necessary to specify the content of before-the-fact controls—to tell subjects what to do and what not to do in such a way as to find and enforce efficiency, which is no easy matter.

Moreover, many of those who believe in the potency of before-the-fact controls fail to understand that moral authority is all too easily eroded by an oversupply of rules. Moral authority, respect for the law, and the inclination to obey rules are of critical importance to the stability and the efficacy of social arrangements. We believe that they are far too important to be frittered away where other mechanisms of social control will suffice. Rather they ought to be carefully husbanded so that they will be available when and where they are really needed (see Tyler, 1990).

Before-the-fact controls are like after-the-fact controls in that they ultimately rely on incentives and sanctions for their effectiveness. The difference is that after-the-fact management controls are incentive- or demand-revealing mechanisms, while before-the-fact management controls are incentive- or demand-concealing mechanisms. As we will explain, this means that opacity is an essential characteristic of before-the-fact controls. The incentive aspects of before-the-fact controls are thus less clear than the incentive aspects of after-the-fact controls. This means that their effectiveness is hostage to the skill with which they are executed. It also means that the incentive aspects of before-the-fact controls are easily overlooked, which might explain why they are not better understood. In order to show how demand-concealing mechanisms work, we will first try to show how demand-revealing mechanisms work or, at least, what they are.

After-the-Fact Control Systems Designs

By demand-revealing mechanisms, we mean those in which customers (or their agents) declare their willingness to pay for various quantities of goods, services, or activities. Customers transparently reveal a demand schedule that fully expresses their wants and preferences to their suppliers. Then they let suppliers figure out how best to satisfy those wants and preferences. The classic demand-revealing mechanism is the competitive spot market, where customers buy from any number of anonymous firms. When many suppliers are disposed to satisfy customer wants, customers simply choose the best price and quantity combination offered—the one that moves them farthest down their demand schedule. In so doing, the customers reward the organizations that are willing to do the most to satisfy their preferences and implicitly punish the rest. For example, they might order wheat from a broker, at the market price payable on delivery. In that case, there would be no formal contract. The customers would put no restrictions on the producer. In fact, the customers will probably not even know who grew the wheat. But the wheat farmer is nevertheless rewarded. The Department of Defense relies on spot markets when, for example, it purchases electrical components off the shelf.

After-the-Fact Controls Transparently
Reward Measured Performance or Results

The spot market is by no means the only demand-revealing mechanism that is used to govern relationships between buyers and sellers. There are many variations on the basic theme of reliance on transparent rewards. But all of these variations have one common attribute: rewards are provided after operating decisions have been made by the producer, after his or her asset acquisition and use decisions have been carried out and outputs have been monitored. Because they are executed after asset acquisition and use decisions have been carried out, we refer to them as *after-the-fact* controls.

A close analogue to a spot market is seen where government uses prospective price mechanisms to reimburse freestanding service providers. The system used by the Health Care Financing Administration to pay hospitals for treating patients is an example. The enrollment-driven funding formulas used by some states to compensate postsecondary institutions for teaching students is another (Jones, Thompson, and Zumeta, 1986). In both of these instances, the subject is a freestanding organization, and the structure of authority and responsibility within the supplying organization is assumed to be a purely internal matter. The government or its agent, say a controller, announces a price schedule and specifies minimum service quality standards (or a process whereby these standards are to be determined) and the time period in which the price schedule will be in effect.

Under prospective pricing, all qualified organizations will be paid a stipulated per-unit price each time they perform a specified service, such as enrolling a full-time equivalent student or treating a heart attack. This means, among other things, that the government's financial liability is somewhat open ended. It depends on the quantity of service actually provided, although not directly on the costs incurred by the organizations supplying the service.

Another close relative of the spot market is the fixed-price contract. Under a fixed-price contract, the price to the customer should not be affected by the supplier's actual costs of providing a service. (In contrast, under a flexible-price contract, those costs are shared with the customer. The limit is reached in the case of a cost-plus fixed-fee contract, where the customer assumes full responsibility for all legitimate, measured costs.)

Under a fixed-price contract, the government buys from numerous suppliers held at arm's length. Frequent bidding contests are held and orders are shifted among suppliers chosen simply on price.

In practice, these price schedules entail all sorts of complex arrangements, including rate, volume, and mix adjustments as well as inflation adjustments and sometimes default penalties. Moreover, under a fixed-price contract, government may grant a selected organization a franchise to provide a specified service, perhaps at a specified location, for a fixed period of time—garbage collection at a military base, for example. But when the contract is completed, the Department of Defense again puts the franchise out to bid to all comers.

Under all of these demand-revealing mechanisms, the government relies on interorganizational competition, combined in most instances with the profit motive, to motivate service suppliers to produce efficiently and therefore to make wise asset acquisition and use decisions. If interorganizational competition is effective, organizations that do not make wise asset acquisition and use decisions will fall by the wayside.

Demand-Revealing Mechanisms
in Vertically Integrated Organizations

In some cases, even where the cost behavior of the service in question renders vertical integration and therefore monopoly supply appropriate, demand-revealing mechanisms or after-the-fact controls can still be effectively employed. Where the supplier is part of the same organization as the customer, the organization rewards managers who do the best jobs of satisfying their customers' preferences and explicitly punishes the rest. This is done in businesses and businesslike public sector organizations by holding a manager responsible for optimizing a single criterion value, subject to a set of specified constraints.

This control mechanism is known as *responsibility budgeting* (Anthony and Young, 1988, pp. 365–386; Thompson, 1991). In the public sector, responsibility budgeting is more often called *output budgeting*. We prefer the former term, because it is more widely used in the American management-control literature and also to distinguish it from output-oriented approaches to budget formulation (as opposed to budget execution, which is the focus of administrative control), such as performance budgeting, PPBS, and zero-base budgeting.

Examples of governments that have experimented with responsibility budgeting as the term is used here include New Zealand and Australia (Schick, 1990; Goldman and Brashares, 1991) and the City of Fairfield, California (Osborne and Gaebler, 1992, pp. 138–165). (Indeed, the public sectors of New Zealand and Australia have both embarked on a comprehensive redesign of their governance arrangements based on the new institutional economics outlined in this chapter [Scott, Bushnell, and Sallee, 1990]. As a result, their public bureaucracies have been rapidly downsized to more efficient types of organizations and their reliance on monopolistic agencies replaced by policies favoring competition and contracting out on the assumption that competition, both of advice and delivery systems, is essential to efficient service provision.)

Under responsibility budgeting, the manager of a cost center, for example, is given the authority to make spending decisions—to acquire and use assets, subject to exogenously determined constraints on the quality and quantity of output—and is held responsible for minimizing costs. Note that, in contrast to other demand-revealing mechanisms, under responsibility budgeting an organization's financial liability will depend on the costs actually incurred providing the service to the customer and not merely on its quantity or quality.

Under this control systems design, the structure of authority and responsibility within the organization is of crucial interest to the management controller. The effectiveness of responsibility budgets depends on the elaboration of well-defined objectives, accurate and timely reporting of performance in terms of those objectives, and careful matching of spending authority and responsibility. Their effectiveness also depends on the clarity and transparency with which individual reward schedules are communicated to responsibility center managers and the degree of competition between alternative management teams.

Before-the-Fact Control Systems Designs

Before-the-fact management controls are demand-concealing mechanisms. Their distinguishing attribute is that they are executed before public money is spent. That is, they govern a service supplier's acquisition and use of both short-term and long-term assets, which means that the controller retains the authority to preview these decisions. Examples of before-the-fact management control include object-of-expenditure appropriations and encumbrance accounts. These govern the kind of assets that can be acquired by governmental departments and agencies; apportionments, position controls, and the fund and account controls that regulate the rate, timing, and purpose of public spending (Pitsvada, 1983; Schick, 1964, 1978); and the similar rules and regulations that govern the behavior of private contractors (Goldberg, 1976; Kovacic, 1990b).

Readers will recognize the combination of before-the-fact controls and individual responsibility in traditional defense budgets. Most will also recognize the combination of before-the-fact controls and organizational responsibility in the so-called cost-plus contract—the most notorious member of the administered or flexible-price contract family. We generally prefer the term *flexible-price contract* to *cost-plus contract,* because we are concerned primarily with distinguishing these contracts from fixed-price contracts. Flexible-price contracts comprehend a variety of incentive and cost-sharing contract designs other than the classic cost-plus contract. In turn, flexible-price contracts are included in the much broader category of administered contracts (see Goldberg, 1976).

Traditional governmental budgets are basically spending plans. To distinguish them from responsibility budgets, we will use the term *outlay budgets*. Under outlay budgets, supplying organizations are guaranteed an allotment of funds in return for providing a service for a stipulated period. They usually receive the allotment regardless of the actual quantity or quality of services provided.

Flexible-price contracts are basically production plans. They fully specify product or service characteristics and a usually a delivery schedule. Under flexible-price contracts, supplying organizations are guaranteed reimbursement (complete or partial) for any legitimate expense incurred providing the service. Hence, the prices they are paid for providing services are determined retrospectively according to settled cost-accounting standards and the specifics of their contracts.

To say that controllers focus their attention primarily on a supplier's asset acquisition decisions does not mean that they ignore performance in executing outlay budgets or price in executing flexible contracts. Controllers usually take account of information about the future consequences of a supplier's decisions as well as information on its current and past behavior. Their attention to performance may be tacit, as in the execution of traditional line-item budgets, rather than express, as in the execution of performance, program, or zero-base budgets. But the consequences of asset acquisition decisions usually matter a great deal to controllers. What is crucial is that, under these control systems designs, attention to the performance consequences of spending decisions is necessarily prospective in nature. Controllers will not reveal a demand schedule that fully expresses customer wants and preferences to suppliers or leave it to suppliers to figure out how best to satisfy those wants and preferences.

Even under these control systems designs, the service provider, whether a department or an outside contractor, must assume some responsibility for managing output levels and delivery schedules, service quality, or price. Nevertheless, as we will demonstrate, the logic of demand-concealing oversight requires supplier discretion to be carefully restricted. This means that suppliers must be subjected to fairly extensive, fairly detailed before-the-fact controls. An agency's outlay budget, for example, should clearly identify all the asset acquisitions that it is to execute during the fiscal year, specify their magnitudes, and make it clear who is responsible for implementing each acquisition.

Of course, constraining managerial discretion is not the only function that before-the-fact controls perform. If it were, it would be hard to claim that they ever represented a least-objectionable alternative, let alone explain their widespread use. Rather, as we will explain, constraining managerial discretion is chiefly a means to an end, not an end in itself. To show how subjects can be told what to do in such a way as to enforce efficiency, we will outline in detail the logic of employing the two basic before-the-fact control systems designs: flexible-price contracts and outlay budgets.

Flexible-Price Contracts

There is a difference in the role that competition plays under fixed-price and flexible-price contracts. The difference is not that it takes place before the production of the service in question. (Economists refer to such a competitive regime as competition *for* the market, to distinguish it from competition *in* the market.) The recipients of fixed-price contracts often receive exclusive franchises prior to the delivery of services.

The difference between the role played by competition under fixed-price and flexible-price contracts is that, under flexible-price contracts, competition cannot be relied on to keep prices low, let alone to enforce efficiency. Once a flexible-price contract has been signed, the supplier is free to dip his hand into the customer's pocket. Because the supplier is spending somebody else's money, the normal incentives to cost effectiveness largely disappear. Decisions that affect cost, service quality, or price (that is, asset acquisition and use decisions) must be made during performance of the contract, but once the contract is signed, the supplier can no longer be fully trusted to make them. This conclusion holds especially where the customer ignores information regarding the performance of incumbent suppliers on earlier contracts or cannot (will not) promise to award future contracts based on good performance. Even where fixed-price contracts are concerned, the refusal to take past performance into account discourages supplier loyalty and eliminates any incentive to improve the quality of the product delivered (see Kelman, 1990).

Why, then, would a customer ever sign a flexible-price contract? Why not simply write fixed-price contracts? The answer is that a fixed-price contract is the mechanism of choice where controllers know precisely what their principals want and there are several potential service suppliers who know how to meet those preferences. Under those circumstances, service quality attributes offered, promised delivery schedules, and bid price allow us to evaluate proposals satisfactorily. Regrettably, these conditions are likely to obtain only where the service supplied is fairly simple and relatively standard—garbage collection, for example.

Technological Uncertainty and Financial Risk

In other cases, neither the controller nor the service supplier will have enough knowledge of the value of product attributes or production processes prior to performance of the contract to employ a fixed-price contract. It is a simple fact of life that considerable experience is usually required to manage to a narrow range of outcomes; where specialized or unique services are involved, no organization is likely to have the required experience. Consequently, any organization that agreed to produce a unique service, according to a specified schedule, at a fixed price would incur a large financial risk. This risk can be shifted, but it cannot be eliminated.

The Department of Defense can often bear financial risks better than supplying organizations. This is the usual case because of the size of the assets the federal government commands and its ability to pool risk. Consequently, the cost to the Department of Defense will often be lower if it assumes a portion of the risk associated with acquisition of the service. Flexible or retrospective pricing is one way for the Department of Defense to assume this risk. Moreover, the preferences of the Department of Defense may change during performance of a contract. Under a fixed-price contract, it might not be possible to secure desired changes in service attributes if they involve increased costs for the vendor.

Of course, the indifference of the Department of Defense to financial risk is easily exaggerated. Government is not immune to financial risk; otherwise it would never make economic sense for it to rely on outlay budgets (Carlton and Perloff, 1990, p. 503). Moreover, while it may be true that doing business with the Department of Defense is risky, the risk is mostly unsystematic, and may, therefore, be diversified away. This especially the case with respect to major defense contractors, whose financial statistics typically exhibit two distinctive characteristics: low price-earnings ratios and even lower levels of undiversifiable risk. According to the capital-asset pricing model, such firms should be far less averse to financial uncertainty than average.

Nevertheless, our point remains: customers should prefer flexible-price contracts to fixed-price contracts where it is cheaper for the customer to deal with uncertainty than it is for the contractor to do so or where the customer is more concerned with the ability of the contractor to provide a product that works than with price. The question is, Can before-the-fact controls be used to ensure that the seller retains an interest in cost-effectiveness?

Using Before-the-Fact Controls to Enforce
Efficiency Under Flexible-Price Contracts

Execution of a flexible-price contract must begin with a fully specified project spending plan detailing work to be performed, personnel, material, and equipment to be used, input quality standards, and scheduled milestones. This plan provides a basis for the enforcement of efficiency through bargaining and negotiations carried on during the performance of the contract.

This process can be compared to a repeated prisoner's dilemma game, in which both parties have a common interest in reaching agreement but also have antagonistic interests with respect to the content of agreements. In this game, customers try to get as much of what they want as they can at a given price, and suppliers try to get the highest possible price for providing the service (Hofstede, 1967). Bargaining power in a prisoner's dilemma game depends on the information available to each party. In particular, the customer's power is greatest where the customer (or the customer's agent) knows the supplier's true cost schedule but can withhold full information as to preferences or demand schedule (Morgan, 1949).

This is simply a more formal way of saying that strategic advantage accrues to the party that can best look ahead and reason back. To do so, one must be able to put oneself squarely in the other party's shoes (that is, one must know the other party's costs under a variety of contingencies). This is one purpose of "should-cost" models. It is also one of the purposes behind selecting agents who have walked in the other party's shoes (promoting trust is another)—purchasing agents in manufacturing plants, for example, are usually recruited from the ranks of industrial salespeople and process engineers and vice versa. (The federal government's revolving-door laws enjoin this kind of personnel exchange, however. These laws probably increase the government's power to set an agenda but undoubtedly reduce its ability to understand or use the information that power confers.)

In a repeated game, the information available to the customer (or agent) will depend on the customer's ability to control the sequence of moves and countermoves that comprise the game. Public choice theorists refer to this condition as *agenda control* (Hammond, 1986). Given comprehensive before-the-fact controls, under which changes can be made only with the prior approval of the other party or agent, the party suggesting or initiating a change must necessarily reveal valuable information to the other. This can work to the advantage of the customer or the supplier, or both. For example, consider the following situation: "Contracts and specifications are drawn for . . . a ship and agreed to. . . . The contractor discovers he can do the welding of some plates less expensively by another means. About that time the client decides that some room on the ship should be larger. . . . The contractor can plead that he cannot easily change the room size: however, if the client will permit the altered welding maybe a deal can be struck" (Stark and Varley, 1983, p. 132). But when flexible-price contracts are appropriately employed, there is every reason to believe that most change proposals will be initiated by the service supplier. Competition for the market provides an incentive to potential service suppliers to promise more than they can deliver, since contracts are usually awarded to the service suppliers who promise the most. Consequently, few contract winners can make good on all their promises, especially where their managerial discretion is severely restricted by a full set of before-the-fact controls. This fact will usually become evident to the service supplier during performance of the contract. The service supplier will also learn of the trade-offs between cost, service quality, and delivery schedule available to it and will eventually want to (or in some cases have to) change its promises or its plans.

Under a full set of before-the-fact controls, such changes are contingent on prior approval. To secure that approval, the service supplier must reveal information about its capabilities and trade-off possibilities. As a result, power to enforce the preferences of the Department of Defense will over time pass to the purchasing officer—but only if she knows what she is doing and how to make it happen. A practical example of this process can be seen in the development and production of the Army's multiple-launch rocket system, where the relative expertise of the program manager permitted not only a confident source-selection decision but also highly effective contract management (John F. Kennedy School of Government, 1987).

Outlay Budgets

A similar logic (Wildavsky and Hammond, 1965) applies where outlay budgets have a comparative advantage—under decreasing costs to scale over an array of specialized or unique services. Outlay budgets can help to keep prices low and to encourage efficiency where large, lumpy investments in specialized resources are needed in order to provide services, where each problem, client, or task performed is in some sense unique, and where the most serious problems are supposed to be dealt with first. Many organizational units in the Department of Defense have these attributes. They supply outputs that are heterogeneous, hard to define, and nearly impossible to measure. As a consequence, "Such bureaus seem always to be near the beginning or end of a comprehensive dismantling and restructuring since there is usually a sense that performance is not all that it might be. The performance of such bureaus can only be improved by budget augmentation. And, of course there are no guarantees in budget augmentation alone" (Thompson and Zumeta, 1981, p. 43).

Under outlay budgets, the purchasing officer retains the authority to review all significant asset acquisition and use decisions. Presumably, therefore, this individual would like to know as much as possible about alternative choices and their consequences before the manager of an administrative unit decides or acts. That is, the controller would like the service supplier to reveal a comprehensive menu of all possible actions and a price list identifying the minimum cost of performing each action under every possible contingency. But there is no way to compel the manager of an administrative unit within an organization to reveal her unit's true production function—even if she knows what it is (and in most cases, she will not).

Consequently, the controller must usually settle for a practical approximation of this ideal. Here too, the controller's authority provides a basis for the enforcement of efficiency through bargaining carried on during the execution of the budget. If controllers are skillful, if they play their cards right, their principals' preferences may be approximated, if not fully satisfied. That is, over time, they may be able to compel supplying organizations to address the "most important" problems and to address these problems at a reasonable cost.

The more pressured the unit, the faster its movement. But here, too, as with flexible contracts, the impetus for change must come from the operating manager. That is, responsibility center managers must have an interest in increasing their budgets. Otherwise they will be indifferent to circumstances in which low-priority problems drain resources from problems that are of greater importance to their superiors or legislative sponsors. And here, too, a full set of before-the-fact controls must be in place. At a minimum, this means that controllers must specify when, how, and where assets are to be employed and how much the subordinate can pay for them. In addition, money saved during the budget period from substituting less costly or more productive assets for more costly or less productive assets must revert to the treasury. Money lost in failed attempts to improve operations must be found elsewhere, and new initiatives requiring the acquisition of additional assets or reallocation of existing assets must be justified accordingly.

These constraints are necessary because they prevent the operating manager from overstating asset requirements in high-priority areas to get resources for use elsewhere, thereby creating a precedent for higher levels of support in the lower priority area. They are also necessary to force the operating manager to seek authorization to make changes in spending plans and, therefore, to reveal hidden preferences, capabilities, and trade-off possibilities.

Where these conditions obtain, where a budget maximizer is subject to tight before-the-fact controls, the controller can enforce efficiency during the budget period by requiring affirmative answers to the following questions: Will a proposed change permit the same activity to be carried out at lower cost? Will higher priority activities be carried out at the same cost? Will the proposed asset acquisitions or reallocations of savings support activities that have lower priority than those presently carried out? When operating managers know and understand these criteria, the controllers will approve most changes in spending plans that the managers propose—because managers will propose only mutually advantageous changes.

Paradoxically, to say that before-the-fact controls are needed to reinforce the controller's bargaining power where outlay budgets are called for does not mean that the controller must administer before-the-fact controls directly. Under certain necessary and sufficient conditions, authority to spend money, transfer funds, and fill positions can be safely delegated to operating managers. The threat that direct controls might be reimposed can be sufficient to ensure that the operating managers ask the right questions of themselves and get the right answers to those questions before they take action—which should go a long way toward ensuring that managerial behavior corresponds to the customer preferences. This is obviously also the case where flexible-price contracts are appropriate. For example, as we have noted, the Department of Defense has a program that designates exemplary production facilities and exempts them from direct oversight.

The necessary conditions are: reimposition of controls must

be a credible threat; the gain to the operating manager from delegation must more than offset the associated sacrifice in bargaining
power (the manager of an aging agency in the stable backwaters of
public policy, for example, may have nothing to gain from relief
from before-the-fact controls, if the price of such relief is a change
in business as usual); and the controllers must be confident that
their monitoring procedures, including postaudit, will identify vi-
olations of trust.

As A. Breton and R. Wintrobe (1982; see also Gormley, 1989)
explain, the sufficient condition is that the controller and the operating manager trust each other. Trust requires mutual respect and
understanding and a common sense of commitment to a joint enterprise. In this context, its corollary is a willingness on the part of
both the controller and the operating manager to eschew opportunistic behavior that would be costly to the long-term well-being of
either the operating unit or the organization as a whole, including
a willingness to forgo opportunities to exploit events for personal
advantage. Trust in a bargaining relationship can be poisoned by
a single lapse of honesty or fair dealing, by contempt on the part
of one of the parties for the abilities, judgment, or ethical standards
of the other, by an excess of zeal or an overtly adversarial or con-
frontational approach, or by a simple lack of communication. In
other words, the kind of trust that is needed to realize the best
possible outcomes under a spending budget, or under a flexible-
price contract for that matter, can be threatened by the very same
conditions that threaten a business partnership—or, more famil-
iarly, a marriage.

Of course, these conditions also apply where contractual relationships are concerned. According to the original manager of
Lockheed's Skunk Works, Kelly Johnson, there are fourteen rules
for running a successful systems development project, including
complete control of the program, small military project offices,
specifications agreed to in advance, timely funding, and minimal
inspections and reports, but the most important is: "mutual trust
between the military project officer and the contractor" (Kitfield,
1989, p. 28).

All long-term buyer-seller relationships ultimately rely on
incentives, even those governed by outlay budgets and flexible-price

contracts. As we have seen, the difference is that when these control systems designs are employed, the incentives are deeply embedded in the process of budget or contract execution. Consequently, they are often overlooked. External observers fail to understand how they work; they also fail to understand how hard it is to make them work well. Effective execution of demand-concealing control systems designs—flexible-price contracts as well as outlay budgets—requires a great deal of skill and savvy on the part of the controller. The skills required to execute demand-concealing control systems designs properly are certainly far rarer and more remarkable than are those needed to design and execute after-the-fact controls, for which a modicum of technical expertise will suffice. It usually takes years of training and practical experience, combined with a lot of common sense, to manage the complexities of bargaining in this context.

Costs of Overcontrol

All long-term buyer-seller relationships rely to a degree on standards and rules. Even where the Department of Defense uses prospective price mechanisms to reimburse freestanding service providers, quality standards must often be specified and enforced. But demand-concealing control systems designs require considerably higher levels of reliance on before-the-fact controls and also on monitoring and enforcing compliance with them than do demand-revealing designs. At the very least, adoption of one of these control systems designs means that controllers must take steps to ensure that suppliers fairly and accurately recognize, record, and report their expenses. This, in turn, requires careful definition of costs and specification of appropriate account structures, bookkeeping practices and internal controls, direct costing procedures, and the criteria to be used in handling overheads.

But accurate accounts will not guarantee efficiency. Even if—as is unlikely to be the case—the service supplier's financial and operational accounts completely and accurately present every relevant fact about the operating decisions made by its managers, they will not provide a basis for evaluating the soundness of those decisions. This is because cost accounts can show only what happened, not what might have happened. They cannot show the range of asset acquisition choices and trade-offs the supplier considered, let alone those that should have been considered but were not. As we have noted, under outlay budgets and flexible-price contracts, asset acquisition decisions must be made, but the supplier cannot be trusted to make them efficiently. Consequently, suppliers must be denied some discretion to make managerial decisions.

Hence, the federal acquisition regulations state: "Although the government does not expect to participate in every management decision, it may reserve the right to review the contractor's management efforts." In fact, where government decides which costs are allowable under the terms of a contract and which are not, it has the power to determine which activities and what items of expenditure the source will undertake. Furthermore, defense contracts typically assign to government the right to review make-or-buy decisions, to approve subcontractors and suppliers, to specify internal financial reporting, operational, cost accounting, and planning systems, wage rates, and so on.

A fundamental question is how far should this participation go; that is, to what extent should the Department of Defense replace or duplicate the supplier's managerial efforts? It is necessary to pose this question because before-the-fact controls are costly—both in terms of out-of-pocket monitoring and reporting costs and in terms of opportunity costs—benefits lost owing to the customer's inability to exploit fully the supplier's managerial expertise. The Department of Defense or its agents will very seldom be more competent to make asset acquisition decisions than suppliers. The answer to this fundamental question is obvious: the minimum necessary, given the motivations of service suppliers and the incentives confronting them. Sometimes, "the minimum necessary" is a great deal indeed. How much depends on circumstance and the controller's skill in exploiting the opportunities created by the supplier's response to institutional constraints.

The problem of figuring out how much constraint is necessary is perhaps best expressed in terms of minimizing the sum of the costs that arise out of opportunistic behavior on the part of suppliers (that is, to use the language of public discourse, waste, fraud, and abuse) and the costs of control, both direct and indirect. Economic theory tells us that this optimum is to be found where the marginal costs of controls equal their marginal benefits, as shown in Figure 6.2 (from Breton and Wintrobe, 1975; see also Williamson, 1985; Masten, Meehan, and Snyder, 1991).

The benefits produced by administrative controls are characterized by diminishing marginal returns. This is simply an abstract way of saying that controls that produce the greatest payoffs in terms of waste, fraud, and abuse avoided should be executed first. In contrast, the costs of control (the sum of direct and indirect cost of their execution) are characterized by increasing marginal costs. This assertion is, of course, debatable. To the extent that we are talking about the direct cost of controls—the out-of-pocket search, bargaining, monitoring, and enforcement costs that they impose on buyer and seller alike—it might be more reasonable to presume constant marginal costs. However, it seems to us that the indirect costs of control, at least those that take the form of stifled initiative, dulled incentives, and duplicative effort (Marcus, 1988), do increase at an increasing rate as the quantity of controls is increased. Hence,

Figure 6.2. Costs and Benefits of Administrative Controls.

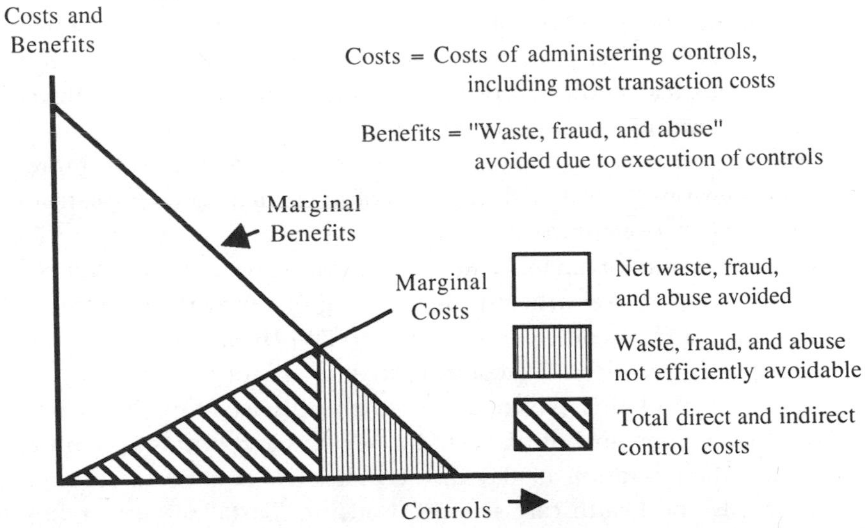

the total cost of controls is depicted by the triangle marked with diagonal lines in Figure 6.2. The lightly shaded triangle represents the total benefits from controls. These consist primarily of avoided waste but also of circumvented fraud and abuse. The darker triangle shows the quantity of waste remaining.

The figure indicates that it almost never makes sense to try to eliminate abuse altogether. If the sum of the costs of opportunistic behavior on the part of suppliers plus the direct and indirect costs of controlling their behavior is minimized, some abuse must remain simply because it would be dreadfully uneconomical to eliminate it. Controls contribute *nothing* of positive value; their singular purpose lies in helping us to avoid waste. To the extent that they do what they are supposed to do, they can generate substantial savings. But it must be recognized that controls are themselves very costly.

What Difference Does It Make?

How much more efficient would the Department of Defense be if control systems designs were carefully tailored to circumstances? Unfortunately, we do not have an unambiguous answer for this question. The theory outlined here states that both the ease with which the consequences of operating decisions can be monitored and the desirability of interorganizational competition matter. But most empirical studies overlook the distinction between the subject and the timing of controls. Hence, they do not relate the cost of supplying services to the choice of governance mechanism. Moreover, we would distinguish the costs of mismatching controls from the costs of overcontrol or micromanagement. The nasty consequences of micromanagement are far more frequently denounced than measured. Nevertheless, our reading of the evidence suggests that mismatched controls may add 5 to 20 percent to the real cost of supplying services; overcontrol can add far more.

Some of this evidence goes to the efficiency of privatizing various services, including custodial services and building maintenance, the operation of day-care centers, fire protection services, hospitals and health care services, housing, postal services, refuse collection, security services, ship and aircraft maintenance, wastewater treatment, water supply, and weather forecasting. Because these are common, homogeneous services that do not require large, lumpy investments in extraordinary assets—indeed, most have direct commercial counterparts—the logic outlined here indicates that they are appropriate candidates for a combination of organizational responsibility and after-the-fact control.

Not surprisingly, the evidence shows that shifting from individual responsibility and before-the-fact controls to organizational responsibility and after-the-fact controls does reduce the cost of delivering *these* services. In his evaluation of the Navy's commercial activities program, Paul Carrick (1988) of the Naval Postgraduate School found that the introduction of competition reduced service cost in 80 percent of the cases studied, with average savings of nearly 40 percent—the greater the number of competitors, the greater the average savings. Carrick also found that Navy teams won over one-third of the competitions carried out under OMB Circular A-76, achieving productivity improvements of 13 percent on average. In these latter instances, the only significant change in governance relations was the shift from a demand-concealing to a demand-revealing control systems design, since the winning in-house teams were usually the incumbent suppliers.

In a second relevant study, which was carried out under the auspices of the Defense Enterprise Program, Scott Masten, James Meehan, and Edward Snyder (1991) carefully analyzed the determinants of control costs, holding production costs constant, in the construction of the SSN-21 Seawolf. Looking at seventy-four components—forty-three "make" items and thirty-one "buy" items, classified using benchmarks similar to those outlined here—they determined that control costs represented about 14 percent of total costs: about 13 percent for make components and 17 percent for buy components. They also determined that the proper choice of governance mechanism permitted control costs to be substantially reduced. Making the right decisions resulted in control costs that were a third less than if all components had been made internally and half what they would have been if all components had been contracted out.

Several analysts have found that, where appropriate, the substitution of after-the-fact for before-the-fact controls produces similar productivity gains. David J. Harr, for example, reports that replacing standard outlay budgets with responsibility budgets in Defense Logistics Agency depots was associated with efficiency increases of 10 to 25 percent (Harr, 1990, p. 36; Harr and Godfrey, 1991a, pp. 68–69). Other analysts who have looked at the issue outside the defense arena make even stronger claims about the significance of the nature and timing of controls. For instance, Chase's law asserts that "wherever the product of a public organization has not been monitored in a way that ties performance to reward, the introduction of an effective monitoring system will yield a fifty percent improvement in the product in the short run" (Allison, 1983, p. 16). Productivity increases of this size are not, in fact, unheard of.

One frequently cited example of such an increase is the central repair garage of the New York Sanitation Department, which replaced its standard municipal outlay budget with a well-designed responsibility budget. Robert Anthony and David Young (1988, pp. 356–357) claim that this reform increased productivity by nearly 70 percent—from a high of 143 percent in the machine repair center to a low of 19 percent in the motor room.

William Turcotte's classic matched comparison of two state liquor agencies reports even larger productivity differences caused by the substitution of after-the-fact for before-the-fact controls (Turcotte, 1974). The organizations studied by Turcotte ran sizable statewide programs featuring large numbers of local retail sales outlets. Furthermore, both defined their missions in identical terms—maximization of profits from the sale of alcoholic beverages to the public. According to the theory outlined here, this situation called for the use of a rather simple, straightforward responsibility budget to govern local retail sales outlets. One of the states (Turcotte refers to it as *state B*) did in fact adopt this approach to governance—treating each outlet as a profit center, holding the outlet's manager responsible for meeting a profit target, and granting her the operational discretion needed to meet it. The other state (Turcotte refers to it as *state A*) relied on standard outlay budgets and a comprehensive set of before-the-fact controls. Turcotte reports that one consequence of the difference in the control strategies used by the two states is that direct control costs were twenty times higher in state A than in state

B. The indirect costs of control were somewhat less disproportionate, but absolutely far greater in state A than in state B. Furthermore, individual stores in state B were twice as productive as stores in state A. Operating expenses for each dollar of sales in state A were 150 percent higher than in state B, administrative expenses were 300 percent higher, and inventory costs 400 percent higher.

However, Turcotte, like Anthony and Young, appears to conflate the choice of governance designs with their intensity. New York's garages and state A's liquor stores were subject not only to the wrong kinds of controls but probably also to an excess of controls. One of the more melancholy properties of before-the-fact controls is their propensity to proliferate—excess controls cause failures, which leads to more controls, and then more failure. We would not be surprised if two-thirds of the productivity differences reported here were due to overcontrol.

Unworthy Candidates for After-the-Fact Controls

The evidence also shows that some goods are unworthy candidates for after-the-fact controls. The case that has been given the greatest amount of attention by industrial-organization economists is where customers artificially maintain rival suppliers where a single supplier could more efficiently supply the entire market (Anton and Yao, 1990). There is, however, a more interesting case. Consider what can happen when rivals are invited to bid on a fixed-price contract to supply an advanced and, therefore, highly risky or uncertain technology. They will likely respond to such an invitation in one of two ways.

First, if they bid at all, they will bid high to protect themselves against the risk of failure; this means that the price of the service to the customer will be excessively high. Alternatively, and even worse, one or more of the bidders will underestimate the difficulty of the contract (or overestimate his capacity to meet its terms). He will often be the low bidder, of course, and win the contract. If he is not very lucky, he will then be cursed by his victory. When he fails to deliver, as he mostly will, or threatens to slide into bankruptcy, his customer may have to step in to rescue the project and, in some cases, the contractor as well.

Alas, open-bidding contests tend to select suppliers for their optimism (or their desperation), since the bidder with the most optimistic view of a project's feasibility will usually win the contract. Unfortunately, the most optimistic (or most desperate) bidder is unlikely to have the best understanding of the contract's technical feasibility. Indeed, he may overestimate its feasibility precisely because of his incompetence to carry it out. This likelihood probably does not matter much where all of the bidders have the experience needed to manage to a narrow range of outcomes. In that case, either comparative advantage will trump optimism or, if not, the advantage will usually be borderline. But this likelihood is crucial where bidders lack the experience needed to manage to a narrow range of outcomes—as will usually be the case where advanced and, therefore, highly risky technologies are concerned.

Indeed, where a product or service is highly specialized, a single organization is often uniquely qualified to produce it. Identifying the right supplier is, therefore, frequently the key to getting the best product on time and at a reasonable price. In the private sector, this process is often fairly informal. Firms tend to rely on experience and reputation to pick suppliers. A decision to invite a proposal is usually tantamount to a promise to do business. And proposals are more often than not jointly developed.

In the public sector, the process tends to be more formal. Potential suppliers must appear on a list of qualified vendors. Customers must usually request proposals from more than one organization. Requests for proposals (RFPs) are supposed to provide detailed explanations of what proposals should include and how they will be evaluated. Evaluations tend to be highly ritualized, with each section of a proposal assigned an explicit numerical score and its overall evaluation based on the weighted sum of these scores. Only after evaluators have identified the best proposal will the Department of Defense's representatives engage in ex parte conversations with the vendor to work out contractual details and nail down a best and final offer.

Nevertheless, these processes have similar aims and, we believe, more often than not produce similar outcomes. Where the program manager is authorized to issue an RFP rather than an invitation to bid, the formality described here is probably more apparent than real. Indeed, where a single supplier has an acknowledged technological lead, the law permits the request of a single proposal and a sole-source contract. Even where that is not the case, the purchasing officer probably has a pretty good idea of the identity of the most qualified supplier. The RFPs cannot but reflect the purchasing officer's subjective judgments about the importance of various product attributes and the competence of alternative vendors to deliver on their promises. The formality with which proposals are evaluated also serves to insulate purchasing officers from the consequences of choice and, therefore, to protect them from the complaints of rebuffed vendors. This is especially important when, as happens in the best of circumstance, things go wrong.

We sympathize with procedures that work to minimize criticism and keep hard-working contracting officers out of trouble. Unfortunately, there is a tendency for RFPs to swell out of control, particularly where major projects are concerned. These RFPs tend to be very detailed; in response, proposals expand to carload size, and armies of evaluators are needed to score them. This is clearly wasteful, although probably less wasteful than when the contract is awarded solely on the basis of price and the winning contractor turns out to be incompetent.

Unfortunately, this happens sometimes. For example, Gansler (1989, p. 141) observes that in 1989, under pressure from the Competition in Contracting Act, "The Navy made awards for professional engineering services at $7.29 an hour. Many wondered whether these same procurement officers would have acquired a heart surgeon for their family on the basis of the lowest bid price."

It is generally acknowledged that the worst defense procurement fiasco in recent memory, Lockheed's default on the C-5A program and the subsequent Department of Defense bailout, occurred because Lockheed misread the difficulty of designing and building the C-5A. Consequently, Lockheed submitted a bid on a fixed-price, total-package procurement contract to design and deliver 150 C-5s that was 50 percent less than Boeing's, the next highest bid. Evidently, even if Lockheed had known what it was doing, which as it turned out it did not, its bid would have been half-again too low. By the time the Department of Defense and Lockheed discovered the magnitude of their error, they were in too deep to get out (Gregory, 1989, pp. 107–117).

Something similar happened with the Navy's A-12 program. Fortunately, when the A-12 development team got into trouble, the Department of Defense decided the A-12 was expendable and canceled the contract, thereby avoiding the worst aspects of the C-5A case. Nevertheless, this was evidently a near-run thing. In the mid 1980s, Boeing took a bath on a series of fixed-price development contracts that it sought and won despite lack of expertise. Again, fortunately for Boeing and ultimately for the taxpayer, Boeing's civilian profits were sufficient to make good its military losses.

The lesson suggested by the example of the C5-A is that the total costs arising from mismatched controls are asymmetrical in their composition: if other things were equal, it would probably be far more prohibitive to rely on after-the-fact controls where before-the-fact controls are called for than vice versa. This lesson is reinforced by Masten, Meehan, and Snyder's (1991) finding that, although making "buy" components would have caused control costs to be about 70 percent higher than they actually were, contracting out "make" items would have caused control costs to increase even more—nearly 200 percent, from 13 percent of the total value of the items to over 30 percent. But other things are not all equal. Not only are after-the-fact controls easier to use, they are also self-limiting. Where the purchaser relies on demand-revealing controls, overcontrol produces negative feedback in the form of higher prices or reduced output that causes controls to be cut back. Before-the-fact controls often produce positive feedback that leads to their multiplication. Hence, their costs are subject to no natural limits.

Carrying Legitimate and Necessary Controls to Self-Defeating Extremes

Organizational theorists have long understood that failure induces certain predictable responses—and that these responses, in turn, produce certain equally predictable consequences. Pradip N. Khandwalla (1978), for example, observes that threatening situations always generate pressures for direct controls: standardization of procedures, institution of rules and regulations, and centralization of authority. Michael Crozier (1964) argues that failures to meet expectations almost inevitably produce a cycle of rule making, more failure, and then more rules. Anthony and Young (1988, p. 562) claim that detailed rules result from encrustation—an abuse occurs, someone decides that "there ought to be a law," and a rule is promulgated to avoid the abuse in the future—but such rules often continue after the need for them has passed. No one who has the power to rescind the rule may ever consider "whether the likelihood and seriousness of error is great enough to warrant continuation of the rule."

Jack H. Knott and Gary J. Miller (1987, pp. 108, 257, 262–265) observe that stricter rules and tighter oversight often produce positive short-term results, but that they also exacerbate the factors that cause organizational failure. Furthermore, extra supervisors giving more orders and monitoring efforts more closely may make subordinates "even more resentful of their status than before, which may make subordinates even more unwilling to trust or cooperate with management. Which leads to more stringent rules, greater reliance on hierarchy, and more hostility on the part of subordinates and on and on." Robert Merton (1957; see also Marcus, 1988) concludes that reliance on rules and regulations reflects a concern with error prevention and that an emphasis on error prevention, rather than measured performance, tends to result in organizational rigidity and ultimately total ineffectiveness.

In other words, the inclination to respond to abuses with calls for more and better rules is normal, as is responding to repeated failure with calls for ever more inflexible and comprehensive rules, greater oversight, and closer supervision. William Kovacic (1990b, p. 112) provides an example here of the cyclical process by which before-the-fact controls induce failure and thereby additional controls: "Because DOD's contracting personnel are overmatched by their industry counterparts, Congress and DOD have sought to rebalance the playing field by mandating layers of procedural safeguards and intricate review processes. By having large numbers of less talented eyes look long enough at a given problem, it is assumed that DOD can prevent Contractors from picking its pocket." In other words, asymmetries in human capital between the Pentagon and its suppliers help to explain the size and content of the existing regulatory regime.

Kovacic (1990b, pp. 112-113) further observes that "this strategy has enormous costs. Programs proceed at a glacial pace as contractors and Department of Defense purchasing personnel carry out required review and auditing procedures. Authority is dispersed so widely among a large collection of program managers, contract officers, senior Pentagon executives, auditors, and inspectors that accountability vanishes. Department of Defense payrolls expand, and contractors hire legions of contract administrators to respond to the requirements of large multitiered DOD procurement organizations."

To say that controls have enormous costs does not necessarily mean that they cost too much. Evidence of overcontrol requires information on the benefits as well as the costs of control. For example, at the beginning of this chapter, we used fruitcakes to illustrate the ludicrous extent of procurement regulation. But we have to acknowledge that the Department of Defense pays only $1.50 a pound for its fruitcake—about half the price in civilian markets (Dunnigan and Nofi, 1990, p. 360). Are the benefits of control generally proportionate to their costs?

One agency, as an example—the Defense Contract Audit Agency—proudly claims that it saved the American taxpayer about $7 billion in 1988 and cost only $1 billion. Its criminal investigations generated an additional $300 million in fines and penalties and cost only $84 million (Dunnigan and Nofi, 1990, p. 368). This sounds like a pretty good deal, even if one allows for the source of the claims. However, the rule of thumb is that monitoring and enforcing regulations impose private costs of about $10 for every dollar spent by the government (Weidenbaum and DeFina, 1978). Since these costs are ultimately borne primarily by the regulated firm's customers and since in this case the customer is the Department of Defense, this multiplier implies that Defense Contract Audit Agency regulation imposed costs of $10 billion to save $7 billion in the first instance and $1 billion to save $300 million in the second—in other words, it cost an average of over $1 to save $1, which is consistent with marginal costs of $2 and $4. Evidence that marginal costs are greater than marginal benefits, let alone four times greater, is prima facie evidence of overcontrol.

Looking beyond the Department of Defense, it is not hard to find evidence that the marginal benefits produced by some before-the-fact controls are actually negative. Alfred A. Marcus (1988), for example, shows that increasing the number of safety rules governing the operation of nuclear power plants, together with greater oversight and closer supervision, actually had the effect of degrading reactor safety. Anecdotal evidence suggests that this is often the case where defense procurement is concerned, especially where demand-concealing governance mechanisms are called for but where a plethora of rules deny the program managers the authority to trade off costs, schedules, and performance (Weidenbaum, 1992).

Finally, excessive reliance on rules often produces organizations that are simultaneously overcontrolled and out of control. Again looking outside the Department of Defense, Turcotte (1974, p. 69), for instance, found that the managers of retail stores in state A were subject to many more rules and far stricter executive and legislative oversight than their counterparts in state B, but, even so, were far less responsive to the wishes of their political masters. Evidently the managers of retail stores in state A were subject to so many rules that none of them mattered much. Consequently, over-control led straightaway to loss of control.

How Well Are Control Strategies Matched to Circumstances?

We do not observe a perfect match between the control strategies used by the Department of Defense and the cost behavior of the goods and services it produces and acquires. Yet the mismatches are perhaps not as pervasive as one might fear. Among the services that the Department of Defense now contracts out, there are very few it should perform for itself. And while there are many minor services that the Department of Defense performs for itself that should probably be let to contract, there are very few critical ones.

At the same time, we would stress that there are clear opportunities for subjecting many of the common, everyday services used by the military to competition. Many of these services do not require large, lumpy investments in extraordinary assets and already have direct commercial counterparts. At this time, however, only 58,000

Department of Defense employees are subject to A-76 competitions under the Pentagon's commercial activities program, about one-tenth of the 540,000 currently performing activities with private sector counterparts (Carrick, 1988, p. 521). Congress has formally exempted 250,000 Department of Defense employees from the commercial activities program. But most of the rest of the Department of Defense's employees are effectively exempted from competitive challenge by the absence of good cost information. In far too many cases, the Department of Defense simply does not have the unit-cost information it needs to implement the A-76 program.

Flexible-Price Contracts

Department of Defense policy currently restricts the use of flexible-price contracts to situations characterized by considerable procurement risk. In other contracts, the degree of incentive is supposed to be calibrated to the project's riskiness. The first ship in a multiship construction program, for example, is supposed to be constructed under a cost-plus contract, while later editions are required to be built under under incentive and eventually fixed-price contracts, on the assumption that experience permits the service supplier to manage to a narrower range of cost outcomes and, therefore, to assume a greater share of the risk burden. Where production volume is sufficient, Department of Defense policy calls for the maintenance of long-term contractual relations with two or more producers, since second sourcing permits renewed competition at each renegotiation of production contracts. On the face of it, these look like sound policies. Moreover, we believe that the Department of Defense generally makes the proper transition from cost-plus to award-fee contracts as it moves from design to prototype development.

During the mid to late 1980s, however, the Department of Defense was under excessive pressure to sign fixed-price contracts awarded by competitive bidding on major systems development projects—the big-ticket projects that account for 80 percent of procurement spending. Some of this pressure was internal to the Pentagon, but much of it was a consequence of the Competition in Contracting Act. The intensity of this pressure is reflected in the decline in flexible-price contracts from 60 percent of the Department of Defense's major purchases in 1978 to 20 percent in 1988 (Pilling, 1989, pp. 3–7).

We think this is excessive. Although some of the adverse effects of favoring fixed-price contracts and competitive bidding, regardless of circumstances, have been mitigated by Department of Defense–sponsored changes in production technology and by its imaginative use of quasi-vertical integration, they have not been eliminated altogether (Pilling, 1989). Besides, multiple sources are required to exploit competition, and that runs counter to the need for a drastic culling of defense firms.

Responsibility Budgeting

One of the biggest needs of the Department of Defense is a modern activity-based costing system. Obviously, better cost information is necessary to carry out make-or-buy decisions under the A-76 program, but that is not the most important use for such a system. Rather, adequate cost accounts are needed to implement a sound responsibility budgeting system, and the lack of a sound responsibility budgeting system is by far the greatest mismatch between control systems design and circumstances that we have observed in the Department of Defense. We also think it likely that such a system would show that many of the activities performed by the Department of Defense, especially overhead and supply activities, are essentially unproductive and could be eliminated.

In any case, it is inarguable that the Department of Defense overuses before-the-fact controls—rules and regulations—when other governance mechanisms would be more appropriate. Why and what to do about it are the subjects of the remainder of this book.

CHAPTER SEVEN

Cutting Overheads

The Politics of Downsizing

THE AMERICAN military base structure comprises 5,600 bases and installations around the world. They occupy twenty-four million acres in the United States alone. This is an area larger in size than Maryland, Massachusetts, Connecticut, New Jersey, and Rhode Island combined. Of the more than 4,000 domestic bases and installations, the Pentagon acknowledges that only 300 or so are "essential for national defense" (Murphy, 1986, p. 63). Like the defense-industrial base, this structure was established during World War II, and, like the industrial base, its retention was justified after the war by the possibility of a similar conflict. Today, again like the industrial base, it is both too large and inappropriate to military realities. Nevertheless, despite the improbability of another world war fought by conventional forces, the training camps, technical centers, headquarters facilities, and supply depots established during the war remain largely intact (Luttwak, 1984, chap. 2).

    The current military base structure imposes two kinds of costs on the American public: opportunity costs—that is, the sacrifice of any better or higher uses to which these millions of acres of real estate could be put—and excess operating costs. Because federal lands are inventoried at historical cost, which does not reflect the present market values of these assets, we have no accurate, agreed-on data on the opportunity cost of these lands, but it is unquestionably large. Based on the work of M. J. Boskin (1986), it may be inferred that military land is worth at least $50 billion and, if one accounts for the urban/rural composition of military land, perhaps as much as $100 billion. Even the latter figure may be too low. Boskin implicitly assumes that all urban land is equally valuable. In fact, much of the urban real estate occupied by the military is concentrated in the rapidly growing, high-value areas of the Sunbelt. Hence, it is possible that the correct figure is as high as $150 billion.

Based on an analysis of a random sample of the assets inventoried in *Detailed History of Real Property Owned by the United States and Used by the Department of Defense for Military Purposes Throughout the World as of September 30, 1982* (General Accounting Office, 1983), we determined that the most valuable 10 percent of the real property held by the Department of Defense represents 90 percent of its total market value—$45 billion to $135 billion. Allocating the two million of these acres with the highest market values to their best alternative economic uses would, therefore, reduce the opportunity cost of maintaining the existing base structure by at least $35 billion and perhaps by as much as $90 billion.

Excess bases must also be operated and cared for. The Grace Commission concluded in 1983 that a 10 percent reduction in the existing military base structure would reduce outlays for operations by at least $2 billion per year without harm to national defense (President's Private Sector Survey on Cost Control [Grace Commission], 1983, p. 13)—which implies a discounted present value of approximately $20 billion. This conclusion has been confirmed by the General Accounting Office (General Accounting Office–Congressional Budget Office, 1984) and endorsed by knowledgeable officials in the Department of Defense.

Conventional Wisdom

The federal government's inability to close unnecessary military bases is often attributed to self-interest on the part of Congress or the bureaucracy. This explanation is particularly popular with cynics and conservative ideologues, but it is widely accepted. It is also wrong, or at least not entirely correct, and it is definitely not a useful guide to reform.

Clearly, the persistence of an inappropriate military base structure serves the selfish interests of many, both in government and outside (see Twight, 1990, 1989). It would be surprising to discover otherwise. As students of public choice point out, "rent seeking" is a fact of political life. Public choice is the branch of the new institutional economics that deals with the intersection between economics and political science. It involves the application of economic logic—methodological individualism and rational, self-interested choice—to problems that are normally dealt with by political scientists and students of public administration. A fundamental premise of economics in general and public choice in particular is that "bad outcomes" (that is, inefficiencies) are not the result of bad acts by bad men—or even foolish or incompetent men—but are the result of the cost-reward structures facing the participants in the decision-making process. This means that if different outcomes are desired, the solution lies in altering the costs and rewards faced by the participants in the process.

The question of responsibility is relevant to public-choice theorists, not because they are concerned about blame, but because it is the first step in the redesign of incentives to produce the desired outcomes. Of course, inefficiency often results from ineptitude as well as evil—otherwise, incentives would never have to be reevaluated or reformed.

This chapter questions the relative importance, not the fact, of individual and organizational self-interest for an understanding of military land-use policy. It argues that the federal government's inability to close unnecessary military bases results *less from selfish motives than from good intentions gone awry*. Besides, self-interest is a given. It should be understood, anticipated, and exploited for the public good. In this case, good intentions have gone awry partly because decision makers have failed to understand how the institutions they created have shaped individual and organizational self-interest.

Furthermore, it is generally agreed that congressional resistance to the closure and realignment of military bases constitutes the best evidence of congressional pork-seeking behavior in the field of defense policy.[1] If it can be shown that, even with respect to this issue, motives cannot be easily reduced to parochial self-interest, perhaps readers will be more inclined to credit the argument made in the conclusion of this volume. We argue that congressional involvement in the details of administration, particularly detailed line-item budgets, generally results from the best of intentions, which, like the best-laid plans of mice and men, do often go awry.

The cynic's allegation that our "bloated military base structure" is somehow due to self-aggrandizement on the part of the military departments is clearly flawed, but it rests on a valid premise: the military departments have no reason to use land efficiently or to transfer it to higher-valued nonmilitary uses (see Niskanen, 1967). It costs them nothing to hold land—once they have acquired real property, it ceases to be reflected in their operating accounts, except insofar as its use induces outlays for operations and maintenance. Moreover, in the past, the military departments gained nothing from the sale of land; receipts from land sales went not to the military branch holding the asset but to the Land and Water Conservation Fund of the Treasury.

The military departments do not merely hold land, however; they also use it. Land may be free; using it is not. Its use induces outlays for logistical support and base operations and maintenance. These costs are evident to the military departments and, while organizational self-interest might lead them to substitute land for labor or capital, to do so beyond the point of negative returns would actually be inimical to their own interests. Yet the hundreds of millions of dollars in operations outlays that could be saved by closing unneeded military bases is prima facie evidence that the returns *to the military* from use of this resource are negative.

Moreover, prior to 1981, the military departments lacked the opportunity to influence land-use policy. Base closure decisions were made by the Office of the Secretary of Defense, not by the uniformed services. Throughout the postwar era, the Office of the Secretary of Defense has supported an aggressive policy of base closures and realignments. It is true that Secretary of Defense Caspar Weinberger assigned this responsibility to the military departments. It is also true that the response of the military departments to Weinberger's 1981 request for closure nominations—to which two responded that no further reductions were advisable and the third responded with less than 40 percent of its quota—was less than enthusiastic. However, the services' lack of enthusiasm for Weinberger's base closure program might be attributed to an understandable willingness on their part to cater to congressional preferences.

Congress and Military Bases

Cynical claims about Congress's responsibility for the failure to reduce the military base structure are much harder to dismiss—that is, claims that "to politicians . . . military bases are considered first and foremost local jobs programs, and no congressman worth his pork will let one close without a battle" (Murphy, 1986, p. 62). Indeed, the best scholarship on the base closure issue tends to confirm the cynics with respect to the responsibility of Congress and the hoggish motives of its members. According to Douglas Arnold (1979, p. 146), legislators must "protect the military installations in their districts, because local beneficiaries see such installations as semi-permanent benefits. . . . Adverse decisions may suggest incompetence or lack of interest in their constituents."

Arnold's conclusions are highly qualified. For example, he acknowledges that during the period he studied, congressional influence was largely restricted to the members of the Armed Forces and military appropriations subcommittees and that it was not necessarily decisive—hundreds of bases and installations of various sizes were closed during this period by Secretaries McNamara and Laird, who perfected the tactic of acting first and answering to Congress later. Nevertheless, he observed that decisions to close military bases "are not in congressmen's interests. . . . Congressmen have fought them for years. Congressmen have never been sympathetic to imposing substantial local costs on their districts in return for modest economies. Even the most fiscally conservative legislator can instantly make an impassioned speech on 'false economy' when his district's interests are at stake" (p. 146). Consequently, he predicted that "if Congress were to make the closing decisions, the most likely consequence would be that the economy would take the back seat—most bases would remain open. It is far easier for affected rank-and-file congressmen to defend their local turfs when Congress makes the decisions than it is when they must somehow coalesce to reverse bureaucrats' decisions'' (p. 154).

Arnold's prediction was evidently confirmed after 1977 when Congress enacted legislation (10 U.S.C. §2687) empowering the Armed Services Committees to review all decisions to close or realign military installations, thereby giving Congress the final authority to make these decisions. And, as Arnold predicted, all major closures and realignments stopped.

It would be naive to deny this evidence. Clearly some legislators are preoccupied with providing private, divisible benefits to their constituents—with where federal dollars are spent and who gets them rather than with what those dollars buy. And clearly these parochial, location-specific concerns have helped to turn the military authorization and appropriations process into something resembling a giant pork barrel. It is even possible that the cynics and the conservative ideologues are correct when they claim that the provision of collective goods is merely a by-product of constituent demands for collectively financed private benefits—that we have national defense because Congress buys aircraft carriers, bombers, and military bases and that we have weapons and bases because congressional decision makers respond to constituent demands for government contracts and jobs (as argued in Aronson and Ordeshook, 1978). Nevertheless, it seems to us that this is not the whole story and is perhaps not even the most interesting one.

Triumph of Parochial, Special Interests?

That parochial interests are not the only impediment to reducing the military base structure is suggested by the consequences of Congress's 1985 decision to make base closure proposals part of the budget process, ensuring that every proposal from the Department of Defense would be voted on within a year. Congress also exempted the nearly 4,000 bases in the United States with fewer than 300 civilian employees from most of the requirements of its 1977 legislation. While the Department of Defense still had to give Congress sixty days' notice of its intention to close one of these bases, "the only way Congress [could] stop the closure is to pass specific legislation forbidding it" (Murphy, 1986, p. 65; see 10 U.S.C. §2687, as revised November 8, 1985). In other words, the 1985 act gave Secretary Weinberger the authority to close over 90 percent of all domestic installations, but he never used it. Clearly, not all the blame for foot-dragging belonged to Congress.

An even more telling flaw in the cynics' argument is that it is based on a credulous and unsophisticated analysis of the interests of the members of Congress and their constituents. The cynics' story stresses constituent demands for jobs and contracts, but surely concern for the plight of civilian workers discharged as the result of the closure or realignment of an active military installation is merely a disguise for broader, more influential interests. One of the basic lessons of public choice is that the benefits of federal boondoggles— pork-barrel spending, tariffs, agricultural marketing orders and production quotas, and the like—accrue not only, or even primarily, to their nominal recipients (Buchanan, Tollison, and Tullock, 1980). Most of the quasi-monopoly rents created by government action are capitalized and/or competed away. Instead, federal boondoggles increase local cash flows and thereby asset values, particularly real property values, throughout congressional districts, benefiting large numbers of influential constituents—land owners, renters, and developers.

Military bases, for example, do not appear to provide substantial benefits to their local civilian employees, most of whom could obtain comparable employment elsewhere, or to the few nearby businesses that cater to service personnel and their families, since their owners by and large do not earn extraordinary returns on their investment. But the existence of a military installation may quicken local economic activity and thereby substantially increase location-specific wealth.

This view of the interests of members of Congress and their constituents is manifestly inconsistent with the notion that they would oppose the transfer of military land holdings to higher economic uses, however, since such transfers increase local wealth. For example, there is a small Veterans Administration medical facility located on Wilshire Boulevard in Los Angeles, adjacent to the UCLA campus. This facility occupies about 120 acres of real estate acquired during the Philippine Insurrection, when there was nothing nearby but sand dunes, lizards, and scrub. Today, according to a real estate market analysis reported by the office of the UCLA Vice Chancellor, this property would be worth $200 million if it were sold as a block and without substantial use restrictions—that is, nearly $10 million an acre (memorandum from Tallman T. Trask III, Associate Vice Chancellor, UCLA, April 1986). Nearly everyone would benefit if the activities carried out at this facility were transferred elsewhere and the 120 acres were allocated to uses compatible with those of nearby properties—high-rise hotels and commercial buildings, fancy shops and restaurants, and ultra-low-density housing. This is precisely the kind of location-specific benefit that members of Congress are supposed to pursue with unrestrained vigor. Why don't they?

The fact is that we know of no evidence that they do not— although we have evidence that they do. Charlotte Twight (1990, p. 52) provides examples of local representatives who have tried to get military facilities closed so the property could be transferred to a better or higher-valued use—unsuccessfully. In fact, there is no evidence of effective congressional opposition to the closure of any base that would be put to higher-valued uses.

What the evidence clearly shows is that Congress often opposes closing military bases that have little or no value in alternative, nonmilitary uses and sometimes opposes closing bases where impenetrable roadblocks prevent transfer of the facilities to private uses. Loring Air Force Base in Maine is a good example of the kinds of bases that Congress has tried to protect. Indeed, it was the Air Force's attempt to close Loring that inspired the 1977 legislation that transferred effective authority to close bases from the Secretary of Defense to Congress—10 U.S.C. §2687 (Mayer, 1982, p. 463). While this site may be appropriate to a variety of alternative military uses, it is no longer needed as a bomber base, and the Air Force slated it for closure in 1976.

Loring had little or no value in any alternative use; it had no conceivable nonmilitary use and its closure would have devastated the local economy (Hellman and Wassall, 1982). Recognition that congressional opposition has been concentrated on attempts to close bases like Loring throws a new light on its behavior. Since the principal cost of maintaining the existing military base structure is the opportunity cost of not putting valuable, scarce resources to

their best and highest uses, congressional opposition to base closures may have actually prevented a serious misallocation of resources. A correct interpretation of the evidence makes it seem
unlikely that Congress would object if the military tried to close the
bases that ought to be closed and could guarantee that sites would
be speedily transferred to higher and better uses.

Of course, closing a military base may cause visible and dramatic losses for civilian employees and local service suppliers. Some
economists view these kinds of losses with equanimity—observing
that when the economy is adapting to economic change, jobs are
not really lost to workers, who, given a car and a full gas tank, can
move to other jobs in expanding organizations, industries, or sectors, and that the new jobs will be more productive and perhaps
even better paid. The simple fact is that existing jobs are eliminated
and movement is often painful. One of the lessons learned closing
military bases is that it is necessary to mitigate the adverse consequences for those who are least capable of bearing them—primarily
civilian workers—or these consequences will give rise to political
pressures that are hard to resist.

Fortunately, the Department of Defense has designed highly
effective programs that mitigate the more dramatic adverse consequences of base closures. The Pentagon's Office of Economic Adjustment has an outstanding record of providing retraining and
relocation assistance for workers who have to adjust and of making
other visible losers whole (see Behar, 1985, p. 82).

Why Does the Military Try to Close Bases Like Loring?

In the case of Loring AFB, congressional pursuit of self-interest
evidently promoted efficiency. The same cannot be said of the military's behavior. Organizational self-interest leads the military departments to be far more concerned with closing bases than in
transferring them to higher uses. Consequently, they suboptimize
when they select potential candidates for closure—identifying candidates by criteria that are dominated by a desire to minimize outlays for construction, operations, and maintenance and not to
maximize the value of the assets at their disposal. Since only by
chance is a good candidate for transfer to an alternative use also a

good candidate for closure, the base closing efforts under McNamara and Laird probably exhausted the set of potential candidates that are both operationally inefficient and highly valued in available alternative uses. Consequently, it is not surprising that the military departments want to close bases that ought to remain open and are not interested in closing bases that ought to be closed. It is also likely that this situation will persist as long as the military is not charged for holding real property and cannot benefit from transferring it to higher uses.

The military departments suboptimize, however, not only because of self-interest—because land is free and because they wish to hold stocks of it as a buffer against uncertainty—but also because suboptimization is mandated by the federal regulations governing the disposition of public lands. These not only complicate the disposition of military bases, they also require a lexicographical approach to the selection of candidates for disposal, whereby the agency holding the asset is required to consider its own operating needs and costs first and *private uses last*.

The regulations governing the disposal of military property were established by the Federal Property and Administrative Services Act of 1949 (10 U.S.C. §2667; 40 U.S.C. chs. 3, 4, 6, 10, 11, 12, 14, 15, 16 [1970]; 43 U.S.C. §1701; 41 C.F.R. subtitle C [1976]). This act declares that "public lands [should] be retained in public ownership, unless . . . it is determined that disposal of a particular parcel will serve the national interest" (43 U.S.C. §1701 [a][1]). It establishes administrative procedures for identifying the "national interest," including specific provisions for a planning body to develop "long range goals" and to coordinate federal and state land-use planning agencies. It also limits disposal of lands to the following situations (43 U.S.C. §1713 [a]):

1. Because of its location or other characteristics, the site is uneconomic to use and is unsuitable for management by the military or another federal department or agency;
2. The parcel was acquired for a specific purpose and is no longer needed for that or any other federal purpose; and
3. Disposal will serve important public objectives, including economic development, which cannot be realized "prudently or

feasibly on land other than public lands" and "which outweigh
other public objectives including . . . recreation and scenic
values, which would be served by maintaining such tract in
Federal ownership."

Finally, the statute requires congressional approval of sales of 2,500
acres or more and, to ensure compliance with congressional intent,
provides for judicial review of all administrative actions (3 U.S.C.
§1701 [a][6] and §1713 [c]).

    The process of disposal begins when the military department
using a property certifies that it is excess. This means that the user
plans to curtail the activities carried out on the parcel or that the
plant and equipment on the site are obsolete and would be more
costly to repair than to replace elsewhere. Then the other military
departments must be screened, as must all other nonmilitary departments and agencies. If no new requirements arise, the land may be
disposed of under the supervision of the General Services Administration, the Public Land Law Review Commission, the Federal
Property Review Board, and in some cases the Office of Management and Budget. The General Services Administration's screening
process consists of the following steps:

1. It notifies all other federal agencies, including the Postal Ser-
    vice, of the availability of the property.
2. It conducts an on-site appraisal of the property.
3. It screens the requests of all interested federal agencies.
4. Based on its determination of the use that "will best serve the
    interests of the government," the General Services Administra-
    tion transfers the property to a requesting agency or, if no
    agency has requested the property, declares the property
    surplus.

The Office of Management and Budget must also approve the
transfer if the appraised value of the property exceeds $1 million
(Federal Property Reserve Services, General Services Administration, 1980; see also 587 F.2d 428 and 486 F. Supp. 18).

    Moreover, the using department and the General Services
Administration must comply with the requirements of the Toxic

Substances Control Act and the National Environmental Policy Act, which requires the preparation of an Environmental Impact Statement to assess the environmental consequences of potential reuses of the land (42 U.S.C. §4331 *et seq.*). Environmental Impact Statements are reviewed by the Council on Environmental Quality, and their adequacy is subject to judicial review. The Environmental Impact Statement does not have to consider all possible uses, but no use, public or private, that has not been evaluated in the Environmental Impact Statement is permissible (707 F.2d 626).

Once declared surplus, the property is available for transfer to state and local governments or to private persons. Generally speaking, the more valuable the property is in a private use, the more onerous the regulations governing its disposal and the more ponderous the procedures to be followed. The General Services Administration is authorized to delegate the administration of public benefit conveyances of the land to the military department in possession of it (41 C.F.R. §101-47.303-2 and §101-47.30-7[m] 1983; 40 U.S.C. §484[k][2][C][i] and §484[b] 1987). But even this can be a highly protracted process. For example, in 1959 the General Services Administration gave the Navy permission to convey certain lands to Kern County in California for the purpose of providing local recreational facilities. Despite the enthusiastic support of California's congressional delegation, it took nearly *fifteen years* to consummate this transfer (Minasian, 1967, p. 243). Transfers of public land to private individuals are even harder; they must be for cash, following a public invitation to submit sealed bids or sold at a public auction (41 C.F.R. §101-47.308-7[m] [1976]).

Of course, Congress is responsible for these impediments to a rational program of base closure and disposal. It is appropriate to inquire into the motives behind the elaborate web of rules and regulations that governs the disposition of federal property. Here, what one finds is not parochial, selfish interests, however, but a record of well-intentioned, albeit possibly misguided, actions.

Protecting the Public Patrimony

The basic aim of these actions has been to protect the public patrimony by eliminating opportunities for corruption on the part of public officials, who might otherwise exploit their official discretion for private profit. Of course, the obvious way—not the best way—to eliminate temptation is to eliminate discretion. Hence Congress has elaborated an extensive array of rules telling officials what they must do, may do, and must not do, and to enforce the rules, has set watchdogs "to watching watchdogs who watch watchdogs" (Kaufman, 1972, p. 54). The Treasury, the Office of Management and Budget, and the General Accounting Office have been authorized to monitor all pecuniary transactions involving the U.S. government, the General Services Administration to stand guard over federal property, and the Property Review Board to maintain surveillance over the General Services Administration. Herbert Kaufman, in his important book *Red Tape: Its Origins, Uses, and Abuses* (1972, p. 52), reminds us that historically the sale or gift of government land and the disposition of government resources were "riddled with corruption . . . as government agents were bribed to overlook wholesale perversions of the law." For example, George Bernard Shaw tells the story of a quartermaster who sold a gunboat to a speculator just before the Civil War battle of Fort Donelson. Three days later, during the height of combat, the Union Army commander was forced to buy the gunboat back for an enormous sum. The figures given by Shaw make it clear that the speculator came out considerably ahead of the Army in terms of dollars and does not seem to have been at any appreciable moral disadvantage, since the affair was a put-up job (Shaw, 1965, p. 103).

Shaw proposed to eliminate corruption by eliminating the opportunity for private gain at public expense—by eliminating private property. Kaufman does not go that far, but he also argues that it is not enough to outlaw giving or taking bribes: "Criminal penalties deter only if there is a good chance that the forbidden acts will be detected. Corrupt bargains, however, are difficult to detect. We have therefore gone beyond deterrence; we have tried to elaborate procedural safeguards, to make the commission of these acts almost impossible" (p. 52).

Fraud, Waste, and Abuse Revisited

A story from a later time, but one when the military departments were still responsible for disposing of properties in their possession, is more relevant to the issue at hand—the story of the Teapot Dome Scandal (Noggle, 1962; Mowery, 1958, pp. 60–63, 72–73). This story is frequently cited as evidence that public officials cannot be trusted to dispose of government property without careful supervision. According to the conventional telling of this story, Albert Fall, Secretary of the Interior, Edward Doheny of the Pan American Petroleum Company, and Harry F. Sinclair, representing the Continental Trading Company—with the acquiescence of the unsuspecting and pitifully incompetent Secretary of the Navy, Edwin Denby, and President Warren Harding—plundered the oil reserves held in trust to meet the future needs of the Navy at Elk Hills in California and the Teapot Dome in Wyoming. Given the conventional way of telling this story, there is little room for doubt that Congress was justified in transferring responsibility for the disposal of government property to the General Services Administration and in increasing the procedural safeguards governing its disposal.

There is, however, another way of telling this story, one that makes Congress's decision less clear. It is true that Doheny paid Fall a bribe of $300,000—$100,000 in cash and $200,000 in Liberty Bonds—and that Sinclair presented Fall with some stock and, after he left office, with a gift of $85,000. It is also true that Fall persuaded Denby to transfer administration of the oil reserves to the Department of the Interior and, after receiving this authority, that Fall promptly leased the Elk Hills reserve to Doheny and the Teapot Dome reserve to Sinclair.

What is usually omitted from this story is that the Navy received a substantial quid pro quo for making the transfer. In return for giving up its reserves in Wyoming and California, the Navy received from Doheny and Sinclair a "tank farm" on Oahu. As Eliot Cohen and John Gooch (1990, p. 48) point out, the Japanese could have changed the outcome of the Pacific war by attacking not the battleships at Pearl Harbor but the Pacific Fleet's oil supplies. They quote Admiral Chester Nimitz as saying, "All of the oil for the fleet was in surface tanks at the time of Pearl Harbor. We had about four and a half million barrels out there and all of it was vulnerable to .50 caliber bullets. Had the Japanese destroyed the oil it would have prolonged the war another two years." Given the strategic value of Doheny and Sinclair's tank farm, it seems that the Navy at least made a good trade.

This conclusion seems even more firm when it is realized that the Wyoming and California oil reserves were being drained by private wells on adjacent properties. When Elk Hills and the Teapot Dome were finally leased to Arco during the oil shocks of the 1970s, secondary and tertiary recovery methods were needed to extract the remaining oil. These methods were not available until long after World War II.

Furthermore, Fall was convicted of taking a bribe, fined $100,000, and sent to jail for a year. Doheny and Sinclair had their leases canceled and were required to make a complete restitution for their illegal use of government property (the Navy got to keep its oil and oil storage facility). Perhaps additional procedural safeguards were not really necessary.

Furthermore, it is possible that the Teapot Dome Scandal was ultimately caused by too much red tape, not too little. Corruption is often a price signal about where resources should go. Perhaps existing procedural safeguards meant that the Navy could substitute a more productive asset for a less productive asset only by a highly roundabout method. If so, given the transaction costs associated with roundabout methods, it is hardly surprising that it took some grease—"collusion and conspiracy" in the Teapot Dome case and "fraud and conspiracy" in the Elk Hills case—to bring it off. Clearly, the Elk Hills and Teapot Dome reserves were not originally allocated to their best and highest uses. Perhaps it took a slippery operator like Harry Sinclair to find a way to make the proper transfer. And perhaps it was the rules being broken that needed a closer look, not those breaking them.

A second story from the same period is also relevant here. It is well know that Senator George Norris of Nebraska prevented Secretary of War John Weeks from handing over the nitrogen extraction plants built during World War I to manufacture explosives at Muscle Shoals, Tennessee, along with the nearby Wilson Dam, built to power their operation, to private exploitation. Norris's key objection to this deal was that the best bid offered for these resources was a small fraction of what the government had expended for their construction. However, the price offered the Department of War for its assets at Muscle Shoals was a direct consequence of restrictions governing the transfer of these assets to private use—they could only be leased, not sold outright; the lease could be unilaterally canceled during a national emergency; failure to utilize the facility could result in loss of the lease; and the lease could not be transferred to another holder without the approval of federal authorities. Furthermore, the Department of War persisted in bundling the nitrogen extraction plants with the power source, despite the fact that the Wilson Dam was far from completion and that, given the private cost of capital, completing it would be a money-losing proposition. Rather than writing off the wartime acquisition of the assets at Muscle Shoals as a sunk cost, Norris kept them idle for nearly twenty years. In this case, good intentions clearly resulted in pure waste, but Norris probably could not have blocked the transfer of these assets to private use if the Department of War had not already been constrained in what it could transfer and how (Mowery, 1958, p. 73).

Public Values and Public Property

The real question is why these facts are not usually mentioned in the retelling of these stories. According to Kaufman (1972), the answer is simple: government waste, especially when it results from an act of omission rather than of commission, is less important than the moral integrity of public officials. Kaufman alleges that public discretion and public property have a special moral status, that "abusing them eats away at the foundations of representative government," and that we ought to be "willing to put up with a lot to safeguard their integrity" (p. 52). He claims that the comments of the economist Arthur Okun typify American attitudes toward the protection of the public patrimony. Okun categorically stated that the guardians of public resources *"should* spend $20 to prevent the theft of $1 of public funds" (Kaufman, 1972, p. 52).

In the case of public lands, Americans may be fortunate that the Office of Management and Budget, together with other watchdogs, can avoid spending funds to thwart corruption merely by preventing transactions that might permit private profit—a variant of the Shaw solution. Unfortunately, as we have seen, that is not elsewhere the case. Unfortunately too, the military properties that have the highest-valued alternative uses and that are, therefore, the most suitable for disposal are also those that have the greatest potential for private profit.

The point of this discussion is that America's oversized military base structure is less the result of demands for collectively financed private benefits than it is the result of an aversion to fraudulent gain at public expense. If this claim is true of military bases, can it be doubted that the aversion to public rip-offs also plays a leading part in explaining the overregulation of defense procurement or congressional micromanagement of the defense budget and its execution?

Anyone who is inclined to doubt that this aversion is nearly universal need only recall that Harding and Denby continue to be regarded as dupes (or worse) or that Shaw could select out from all the terrible waste and carnage of the Civil War the illicit sale of a gunboat as deserving special attention (or that his account of the transaction could be read without our questioning his sense of proportion). And even the most conservative public-choice economist—hard-headed, tough-minded, and well schooled in the Coase theorem—would probably hesitate to acknowledge, let alone to proclaim, that Doheny and Sinclair were public benefactors.

Nevertheless, while it might under certain circumstances make sense to spend $20 to prevent the theft of $1—and frankly, we do not really see how—we know that it would *not* make sense to spend $200 billion to prevent the theft of $10 billion. The United States does not, of course, spend $200 billion, or more than two-thirds of the defense budget, to prevent defense fraud and abuse. But it has clearly gone too far in that direction.

Recent Developments in Base Closure

The analysis presented in this chapter suggests that Congress would, in fact, support the closure of military bases—if it were persuaded that the Pentagon had selected the right bases for closure, that it had adopted procedures that would permit properties with high alternative uses to be identified and promptly allocated to those uses, and that it could ensure the propriety of such transfers.

The events of the 1988–1993 period go a long way toward confirming this analysis.[2]

In 1988, the Pentagon cut a deal with Congress, whereby a bipartisan commission (the Defense Secretary's Commission on Base Realignment and Closure) would produce a list of proposed base closures and realignments. The commission was charged with specifying a set of criteria and procedures for evaluating candidates for base closure and with applying the criteria and procedures to the array of candidates to select a final list for closure and realignment. Once the list was approved by the Secretary of Defense, who could reject it and send it back to the commission but could not alter it, Congress was obliged to reject it in its entirety within forty-five days or it would automatically go into effect (the Base Closure and Realignment Act, Title II, P.L. 100-526, 10 U.S.C. §2623).

In January 1989, the Secretary of Defense accepted the commission's recommendations and forwarded to Congress the list of bases to be closed. Howls of anguish were heard following release of the commission's hit list, especially in the Senate and House Armed Services Committees, which were responsible for initiating the joint resolution of disapproval needed to call off the process. Opposition centered on the validity of the commission's selection criteria and the methodology and information it employed in reaching its conclusions. Opponents also argued that commission members were biased and that the procedure for making appointments to the commission was flawed. Much of this opposition came from representatives of the districts affected by the commission's list and was intended to show constituents that they were making a brave effort on their behalf. However, this effort failed to generate sufficient votes to disapprove the list inside the forty-five-day period within which Congress was required to act.

The commission slated eighty-six facilities for closure, of which sixteen were considered major bases. An additional fifty-four were to be realigned and five others partially closed. Realignments and closures were to commence on January 1, 1990, and be completed by September 30, 1995, producing estimated annual savings of about $700 million.

In early 1990, Secretary Cheney submitted a second list of bases to be closed directly to Congress. Congress turned his proposal down cold, partly because it thought that the Pentagon was playing politics by targeting facilities in congressional districts whose representatives had a record of voting against defense budgets. Congress also wanted more say in the composition of the commission, which it got in November 1990, when it established a second Base Realignment and Closure Commission to recommend additional facilities to be closed. This commission was reduced in size but was given its own staff. Congress also included the General Accounting Office in the base closure process, calling for it to preaudit the commission's selection procedures. This legislation also directed the convening of two additional commissions to consider further closures in 1993 and 1995 (Title XXIX Part A, P.L. 101-510, 10 U.S.C. §2687; "Military Bases: Not on My Toe," 1991).

Secretary Cheney announced a third list of bases to be closed in April 1991. The new Base Realignment and Closure Commission then held public hearings, in which it was greeted by community leaders objecting to the Pentagon's proposals wherever it traveled. It also requested additional data from the military departments (for example, from the Navy on the Philadelphia Naval Shipyard). Nevertheless, the commission essentially approved the Secretary's proposals and sent its recommendations to the president in June 1991. The president endorsed the list on July 10 and sent it to Congress. Congress then had forty-five days to vote a joint resolution to reject the list. Again, despite significant lobbying, Congress failed to do so. The Department of Defense began the third round of realignments and closures in 1993.

The second commission's list recommended closing thirty-one major bases and a dozen minor ones and cutting twenty-eight others. According to the Pentagon (Office of the Assistant Secretary of Defense [Public Affairs], 1991a), carrying out this recommendation will cost $5.7 billion during fiscal years 1992–1997. It will reduce operating costs $6.5 billion during the same period, for a net savings of about $850 million. The Pentagon further estimates revenues from land sales of $1.9 billion and reductions in future annual operating costs of $1.7 billion in 1998 and beyond (which implies a net benefit in present-value terms of about $30 billion).

Base cleanup, including hazardous and toxic waste mitigation and regulatory compliance, is projected to grow from about $3 billion in 1991 to $12 billion by 1995. The cost of environmental cleanup remains a point of contention between the Pentagon and Congress. The Pentagon maintains that in order to clean its facilities for closure it needs additional funding. Congress agrees with the need for cleanup but has not appropriated funds to perform this work. Instead, it has insisted that the cleanup process be supported through transfers from other Pentagon accounts, a practice that the Pentagon has continued to resist.

The principle that base closure costs money up front in order to achieve longer-term savings is only grudgingly accepted by Congress. Three sources could provide support for base closures: funds specifically appropriated for that purpose, reprogramming from funds appropriated for other purposes, and Base Closure Account receipts. So far, the Department of Defense has had to rely on the second and third sources, since Congress has been unwilling to appropriate funds for the specific purpose of closing bases.

Base Closure Account receipts have also been minimal. They are earned from the sale "of excess and surplus real property and facilities located at a military installation closed or realigned" under the authority of the Base Closure and Realignment Act. In other words, the base closure act allows the Department of Defense to realize a direct benefit from the transfer of property to private uses. These receipts can be used for purposes of military construction, to facilitate realignment, to comply with federal, state, or local environmental standards, to ease economic adjustment for affected communities, community planning, and employment assistance for civilian personnel displaced by base closures, and to cover the costs of selling property.

Receipts from the sale of closed bases have been minimal, in part because many of the cumbersome procedural requirements that govern the disposal of federal property still remain in effect, although the Department of Defense has been given responsibility for the functions usually performed by the General Services Administration (Twight, 1990, p. 269). Twight notes that the original Armey-Roth Bill, the precursor of the base closure act passed by Congress, explicitly waived these requirements, but this provision was not enacted.

Compliance with environmental standards is another impediment to the sale of closed bases. The Pentagon is authorized to shut bases down without first preparing and filing a full-fledged Environmental Impact Statement. But it must still satisfy all federal, state, and local environmental standards, including those prescribed under the National Environmental Protection Act, before a facility can be sold or otherwise converted to nonmilitary uses. However, some representatives from districts suffering closures are touting legislation that would permit the Pentagon to sell off the parts of bases that meet existing standards, even where the entire facility has not been cleaned up. The objective of this proposal is to speed up the sale of shutdown bases and, therefore, their allocation to alternative uses.

Even if these impediments did not exist, base closure receipts would still be much less than they should be. This is a result of military departments' continued reliance on lexicographical selection of candidates for closure. They first look at the military value of facilities and, only after all militarily valuable facilities have been excluded from consideration, at the extent and timing of potential costs and savings from closing, cutting, or changing the facilities that remain. Moreover, in estimating returns on investment from shutdowns, the military departments still pay far more attention to reducing operating costs than they do to potential receipts. This fact is also reflected in the Pentagon's low estimates of revenue to be earned from sale of property.

Finally, many of America's bases are in the wrong places. Some of these are overseas, in places where forward deployment is no longer required by American defense policy. Others are hemmed in by urban encroachment. Hence, a sound base closure program calls for extensive realignment and perhaps in a few cases the acquisition of new sites.

Realignment abroad is on track. There is little (perhaps too little) congressional opposition to closing overseas bases, since the interests of foreigners generally lack standing in American political forums. Through mid 1993, the Department of Defense had announced decisions to end or reduce operations at over 300 foreign facilities. Reductions in America's base structure abroad mean that reductions at home may not be directly proportional to the reduction in force structure. Nevertheless, as the United States scales back its forces over the coming decade, more domestic bases will have to go. Despite anguished cries from Capitol Hill, most observers believe that they will.

Final Comments

This chapter has attempted to explain why our military base structure is larger than needed and how it can be and is being reduced. Given this objective, our findings are encouraging: it is possible to design procedures that permit military bases to be closed. It may also be feasible to change the incentives facing the military departments to give them a greater interest in economizing on their use of real property by permitting them to benefit from transferring unneeded land to higher-valued nonmilitary uses.[3]

Our findings are encouraging in a second way. In this instance, Congress has enacted self-denying ordnances that have curbed its ability to interfere with base closings. Congress would never have passed this legislation if its members were exclusively concerned with the generation and distribution of pork. It seems more accurate to characterize this legislation as simply good public policy. We do not believe that this is an isolated example.

One final factor deserves emphasis: the propensity of nearly everyone concerned with the disposition of federal property—members of Congress, bureaucrats, and cynics—to take the path of least resistance, to see only those issues bringing themselves forcibly to their attention and corresponding to their particular understanding of right and wrong. That the conduct of the public's business is or should be invested with special moral values is obvious. The cost of these special moral values is often not. Laws and regulations that interfere with the possibility of economic choice necessarily result in inefficiency. Rules intended to thwart corruption ought, therefore, to be a red flag alerting decision makers and budget and policy analysts to the possibility of substantial waste. In this respect, the regulations governing the disposition of public lands are unfortunately not unique.

CHAPTER EIGHT

Reinventing the
Department of Defense

FROM THIS VANTAGE POINT, one fact stands out: the combatant commands are the principal instruments of U.S. defense policy. Flexible response requires organizational responsibilities to be divided along geographic lines. This fact is the key to closing the gap between defense organization and strategic purpose that appeared in the wake of the Eisenhower/McNamara reforms. In recognition of this fact, William A. Niskanen, now chair of the Cato Institute, suggested that a major reorganization of the Department of Defense may be in order—one in which far greater emphasis is given to the combatant commands. According to Niskanen (1988, pp. 18–19), the Department of Defense "is now the third-largest command economy in the world. No command economy works very well, and Americans are not especially efficient at managing a command economy. One approach that should be considered is to improve the buyer-seller system within DOD. Most of the defense budget could be allocated directly to the unified and specified commands, which would maintain their own organizations for testing and evaluation. The four services would then compete to provide forces, weapons, and supplies to the commands." He further recommended ending the Key West Agreement to permit the services to compete more effectively with each other and changing the system of personnel evaluation to reward superior performance in joint command.

In a similar vein, Jacques Gansler (1989, pp. 135, 325–330) proposed that multiyear spending authority be allocated to the combatant commands rather than to the military departments, as is now the case. Gansler calls this *mission budgeting*. One of the coauthors of this volume has published a book explaining how budgeting by mission would work and how it would make things better (Jones and Bixler, 1992; see also Jones and Doyle, 1992). Moreover, the *Gore Report* has recently endorsed the idea of mission-driven, results-oriented budgets, decentralizing decision-making power, and using market mechanisms to solve problems.

How Should the Department of Defense Be Organized?

Many of these concepts were adumbrated nearly fifty years ago by Abba P. Lerner. Lerner was both a socialist and a great economist. As a socialist, he believed that government should set goals and objectives for the economy as a whole. But as an economist, he recognized the dysfunctions produced by comprehensive state allocation of productive assets. He was especially critical of the system of detailed centralized planning and before-the-fact control used by Gosplan, the central planning agency in the Soviet Union, to implement its long-term policies. Consequently, he devoted himself to designing an institutional arrangement that would reconcile unity of command with the market and, thereby, provide a socialist alternative to state allocation of productive assets. In 1944 he published his classic work, *The Economics of Control*, which outlined a fully decentralized approach to socialism.

While he was inventing market socialism, Lerner observed that Gosplan's approach to economic planning and control was merely an adaptation of the *Kriegwirtschaftsplan*, the planning and control system used by the General Staff under Ludendorff to mobilize Germany's resources during World War I. Not surprisingly, Lerner concluded that if his proposal would work better than state central planning and allocation of productive assets for the economy as a whole, it should also work better than the system of state allocation of productive assets in the conduct of war. (Unfortunately, Lerner's 1942 essay, "Design for a Streamlined War Economy," has never been published, but it is discussed at length in

Hitch and McKean, 1960, pp. 220–224; see also Spulber and Horowitz, 1976, pp. 338, 352–358.)

Lerner believed that the bulk of defense spending authority should be allocated directly to the combatant commanders, who would use the funds to purchase personnel and equipment from the military training and support commands and to lease logistical and support facilities and weapons systems from the private sector. According to his scheme, purchasing and leasing would be carried out by means of arm's-length transactions, and the whole military establishment of the United States would be organized as a network of markets that would operate like the private American economy does. Combatant commanders would bid for supplies of materiel and skilled personnel. Military suppliers would sell their services to the highest bidder. And prices would be used to bring demand into line with supply.

Lerner made only one concession to centralized planning and control. He proposed to assign what we would now call the Joint Chiefs of Staff responsibility for allocating the military budget to the combatant commands. Based on their net assessment of the strategic situation, which would take account of the capabilities of potential enemies, the contribution of allied forces, the significance of the missions assigned to the combatant commands, and the relative effectiveness of their commanders, the Joint Chiefs of Staff would identify the force thresholds needed to hold risks to acceptable levels. The Joint Chiefs of Staff would then ration spending authority between missions so as to equate costs and risks at the margin (that is, equate the marginal utility of the contribution made by each of the combatant commands to the overall defense strategy of the United States).

Lerner claimed several apparently plausible advantages for his proposals. Combatant commanders would be able to make full use of their specialized knowledge of enemy, terrain, and weather conditions to tailor their force structure and logistical support facilities to the contingencies they faced. The network of markets and arm's-length transactions through which resources were allocated would supply the information needed by procurement and training units and private suppliers regarding the relative utility of various kinds of military units, capabilities, equipment, and skills. Finally, the budgeting and pricing procedures would maximize the Department of Defense's capability to carry out its assigned missions and responsibilities. That is, marginal rates of substitution or trade-offs between different military resources would tend toward equality in all missions and functions—the necessary condition for efficient allocation of resources.

The Lerner Scheme and Transaction-Cost Economics

Despite Lerner's claims, we believe that the implementation of military strategy must be carried out within the bounds of a single organization. We have given a great deal of space to Lerner's ideas because they go to fundamental principles of military organization and institutional design and because in many ways they point in the right direction. What Lerner proposed for the U.S. military establishment is decentralization—total, complete, and without qualification. We believe that decentralizing the Pentagon makes good sense. Its size and complexity argue against centralized direction and, in any case, we believe that organizations should be as decentralized as possible. But our starting point is the Pentagon's existing, extremely centralized regime. It is probably not possible to take decentralization of the military as far as Lerner would have. Nor would it be desirable to do so.

The defense establishment is not—and probably cannot be made to mimic perfectly—a market economy, with many freely competing buyers and sellers. This is the case not only because of the need for a single set of foreign policy objectives to define the Department of Defense's purposes and strategies, but also because of the special interdependencies that are created in the implementation of those policies.

It is clearly unrealistic to imagine that Lerner's scheme could work in time of war. The notion that spot-market prices involving arm's-length transactions between independent entities would satisfactorily allocate resources in wartime is clearly contradicted by the extreme interdependence that characterizes combat operations, its short time horizon, the strategic uncertainty that arises from enemy efforts to anticipate and frustrate operations, and the spillovers produced by success or failure in one theater of operations on the conduct of operations in other theaters. At best, implementation of the Lerner proposal in wartime would increase transaction costs without any commensurate increase in military effectiveness, as happened in times past when something very much like it was used (see Corvisier, 1979; Frey and Buhofer, 1988).

But even in peacetime, Lerner's approach would be defeated by the functional interdependencies—reciprocal and sequential, as well as pooled—that pervade defense strategy. Combatant commanders, for example, have their major responsibility in the present or near future; according to Hitch and McKean, they can therefore be expected to heavily discount the new and untried and to avoid investments with distant payoffs, regardless of their size. They are perhaps even more likely to eschew shared forces, multipurpose weapons, and standardized military formations and equipment, despite the lower acquisition, supply, maintenance, and repair costs that a degree of standardization confers on the military establishment as a whole (Hitch and McKean, 1960, p. 224).

The problem is that, like the advocates of privatization discussed in Chapter Six, Lerner implicitly assumed perfect markets. Because he did not imagine the possibility of market failure or recognize its implications for the efficiency of arm's-length transactions, he could not comprehend that organization was the solution to those problems. Yet there are three basic market failures that arise from the integration of activities and assets with military missions: the supplier-switching problem, the monopoly/monopsony problem, and the asset accounting problem. Based on the insights of several of the leading contributors to the new institutional economics—especially Oliver Williamson (see also Vining and Weimer, 1990; Friedman, 1981)—in each case, the solution is organization.

Lerner simply ignored questions of product or service quality, availability, reliability, and supplier loyalty. But these are potentially serious issues where the supply of combat forces is concerned. Combatant commanders cannot afford to risk disruption of supply when their need is greatest. Yet that is precisely the risk they would run if service suppliers were free to enter or exit the market at will, selling their services to the highest bidder. We will not carry this point to absurdity, arguing that suppliers would go out of business to avoid damage to their persons, their employees, or their assets, let alone offer their services to the enemy—like Lieutenant Milo Minderbinder in *Catch 22*. The behavior of the merchant marine in wartime shows that these concerns are groundless. Nevertheless, one should be mindful of the fact that private contract forces are likely to be less reliable than government forces; that, at least, seems to be history's lesson. For example, during the Thirty Years War contract armies often sold out to the highest bidder, changing sides for higher pay and bonuses. Even when they remained loyal to their employers, they avoided fighting whenever they could and battles were routinely decided by counting lances rather than by combat (Corvisier, 1979, p. 45).

On the other hand, if combatant commanders were free to shift suppliers whenever they wanted, suppliers of combat forces and support units would have no incentive to make long-term or durable investments in plant, equipment, or know-how, since the value of those investments would be drastically reduced if the relationship were prematurely terminated.

As we explained in Chapter Six, there are basically two ways to deal with the supplier-switching problem—through a long-term administered contract or through vertical integration to incorporate suppliers within a single organization. We also noted that vertical integration is often the best, or if not the best, the easiest way to safeguard the continuity of a valued relationship and thereby deal with problems of quality, availability, and reliability of supply and encourage investment in specific-purpose assets. Again, as we explained, this is because exclusive dealing gives rise to the monopoly problem and monopolies are very difficult to manage at arm's length.

Of course, theory tells us that a monopoly can be managed at arm's length by means of cost-based, two-part tariff mechanisms. The incentive-price mechanisms that are used to govern the behavior of prime contractors in the development and production of major weapons systems are an example of what we mean by a two-part tariff; the way one pays for telephone service is another. Similar arrangements could be designed that would permit combatant commanders to acquire fully equipped and well-trained combat and support units from the military departments. For example, the combatant command could pay one price to have a unit earmarked for

its use, which would be analogous to the hookup charge for telephone service, and a second price that would depend on the
intensity and location of the unit's activities, which would correspond to telephone usage charges. The problem is that two-part
tariffs must be very carefully calibrated to produce an efficient solution. Moreover, careful monitoring of accounts and, in some
cases, preaudit of expenses are needed to offset the seller's incentive
to cheat or to misreport.

   Given sufficiently extensive economies of scale or scope, asset
specificities or indivisibilities, and the like, it is sometimes easier to
internalize the relationship than to try to manage it at arm's length.
For example, unbalanced transfer prices can be used to manage the
relationship between customer and monopoly supplier within an
organization. They are often easier to administer to produce outcomes that are satisfactory for the organization as whole than are
cost-based two-part tariffs.

   Organizational and institutional design is largely concerned
with allocating property rights and accounting for the ownership
and use of assets. Where armed forces are concerned, the accounting
problem is doubly difficult, because efficient use of military force,
personnel, and materiel means one thing in peace and quite another
in war. For example, once a physical asset has been supplied, its use
should not in general affect decisions about operational intensity.
These decisions should reflect marginal costs; sunk costs should not
matter. Nevertheless, it is hard to imagine how ownership and use
of physical assets like ships, planes, or tanks could be transferred
from one independent organization to the next, at spot prices as
called for by Lerner, without biasing outcomes. Would a leasing
agency permit its assets to be taken into combat if it were liable for
their loss? Or, if losses in combat were charged to the combatant
command's account, would that not deter aggressive action on the
part of the commander? If so, captains would indeed have cause to
go down with their ships. The incentive here would seem to be
the reverse of that intended by the British Admiralty when they
executed Lord John Byng. "In this country it is found requisite,
now and then, to execute an admiral *pour encourager les autres*"
(chap. 23 of *Candide* by Voltaire; see Keegan, 1988, p. 45). Again,
this is a problem that is more easily handled within an organization

than between organizations, if only because it is much clearer to everyone concerned that the relevant accounts are merely numbers that can be moved around to produce the behaviors desired.

Decentralizing the Pentagon

In contrast to the difficulties and uncertainties that surround the Lerner proposal, the conceptual foundations of intraorganizational decentralization and their application to the Pentagon are fairly straightforward.

Align Strategy with Structure. An appreciation of the distinction between mission centers and support centers is central to a resolution of the Pentagon's strategy/structure mismatch. Mission centers contribute directly to the organization's objectives. They are the principal instruments of organizational policy. Support centers supply goods or services to other responsibility centers in the organization—that is, they perform functions for other support or mission centers.

According to contemporary military doctrine and strategy, the combatant commands are the principal instruments of U.S. defense policy. Contemporary doctrine and strategy assign supporting or service roles to the military departments. They are supposed to supply combat and support units to the combatant commands. The units they supply to the combatant commands are usually organized along functional lines, but the combatant commands are not. The Pentagon's mission structure does not follow functional lines. The Pentagon is a multimission, multifunction organization.

This fact is self-evident. For some reason, however, earlier analysts often failed to see that the Eisenhower reforms in combination with the doctrine of flexible response adopted during the McNamara era made the combatant commands the Pentagon's mission centers and assigned to the military departments the role of support centers.

Decentralize Where Possible. Fortunately, performance of the peacetime support role assigned to the military departments depends on the sequential performance of a series of tasks, as does the provision of these units to the combatant commands. The military departments are supposed to recruit, train, and equip combat-ready units and to supply those units to the combatant commands. Thus, the relationships between the responsibility centers and administrative units that comprise the Department of Defense are essentially bilateral rather than reciprocal in nature. As we have noted, where bilateral relationships are concerned, it is usually possible to set up some kind of transactional arrangement to eliminate or internalize spillovers. In most cases, these relationships can be governed satisfactorily via buyer-seller arrangements and, where they occur within the organization, by appropriate transfer prices. In many cases, support units can be made to compete within the context of a quasi-market dynamic with other units supplying similar services inside and outside the organization.

If these claims are accepted, then aligning the Pentagon's organizational structure with its strategy should be fairly straightforward, even easy: make the Department of Defense's basic organizational structure a matrix, with the Joint Chiefs of Staff at the top, the combatant commands or mission centers the rows, and the military departments or support centers the columns; issue budget guidance to the combatant commands and permit them to buy forces from the military departments, as shown in Figure 8.1.

Under this proposal, the military departments could be treated as quasi-investment centers. Evaluating the performance of their top officials in terms of the notational profit earned by their departments supplying services to the combatant commands would give those officials a powerful incentive to maximize the cost-effectiveness of the units they prepared for combat and the weapons they procured from the private sector. This would be one way to effect Stanford Business School professor David Baron's (1991, p. 14) suggestion to establish "an organization that can act as a residual claimant and procure major weapons systems from the private sector under performance and cost objectives specified by DOD."

Indeed, most of the service-providing Department of Defense agencies, the training commands, and the systems development commands, all of which are highly capital intensive, could probably be treated as investment centers. Most other entities within the Department of Defense would have to be treated either as cost or

**Figure 8.1. A Reorganized Management Control Structure
for the Department of Defense.**

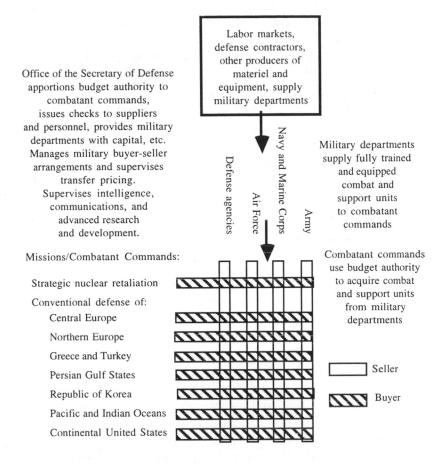

income centers (although in most cases their performance could be
evaluated in terms of quasi-profitability—that is, benchmark cost
less actual cost).

Like Lerner, we think the combatant commands should take
advantage of competition whenever possible. However, we do not
want them developing military technology or organizing and
equipping the military units assigned to them. Paradoxically, the
situation that led to centralization under McNamara—competition

among the military departments in the functional areas—is the chief prerequisite for decentralization to the combatant commands (Niskanen, 1967, p. 19; 1988). Many of America's existing weapons systems and logistical concepts are the products of interdepartmental competition.

Under organizational decentralization, each of the military departments would continue to be responsible for performing a variety of specialized functions, some partly complementary and some partly substitutable for those provided by the other departments. However, where the status quo discourages the development of capabilities outside of the military departments' assigned functional areas, we would encourage each department to develop new capabilities, weapons systems, formations, and tactical concepts designed to compete with those provided by the other military departments. As Martin J. Bailey (1967, p. 341) has explained,

> An important factor that tends to mitigate difficulties in monitoring the performance of the military services is that many of the activities and systems of one service are at least partly substitutable for those of another. Tactical air forces are operated by the Air Force, the Navy, and the Marine Corps, and even . . . the Army; and in some tasks these forces serve the same objective as does artillery. Deployment capability can be provided by air transport, operated by the Air Force, by sea transport, operated by the Navy, and by forward stockpiling in the theater of potential use, operated by the service whose equipment is stockpiled. . . . Because of the competition among substitutable systems, any temptation for a service to try to enlarge its budget by carrying performance requirements to expensive excess or by understating the capabilities of its systems will be tempered by the prospect that a reduction in its budget might result instead and that its systems might be partly replaced by those of another service.

J. A. Stockfisch (1973) also argues that this budgetary approach would provide a way to harness interdepartmental rivalry to a useful purpose. He reminds us that competition between the military departments to perform specialized functions will serve useful ends only if a higher authority clearly resolves mission requirements and objectives and if the combatant command has a rational basis on which to make choices: "Operational testing and objective evaluation procedures to treat combat readiness are critical if not necessary aids to perform this function. Thus if the Marine Corps shows that it can produce combat units of equal proficiency to the Army, it should get some of the Army's budget" (p. 263).

We interpret this to mean that the combatant commands must have satisfactory information on unit costs, as well as performance, if they are to choose wisely between forces supplied by the military departments. While it seems likely that, under decentralization, the Joint Chiefs of Staff and the combatant commands would want to maintain their own organizations for testing and evaluation, the real key to providing the information they need is the development of a sound cost-accounting system/transfer-pricing system within the Department of Defense.

Establish an Account Structure Based on Principles of Responsibility Budgeting. The Pentagon must impose common accounting standards and pricing policies on the military departments. This means implementing Business Operations Fund, unit-costing, the Defense Finance and Accounting system, and the Corporate Information Management system. Useful information for internal control purposes must be based on a common set of accounts. Furthermore, a unit would probably have to be created, perhaps in the Office of the Assistant Secretary of Defense (Comptroller), that would be concerned with establishing the internal pricing policies and cost-accounting procedures to be followed by mission and support centers within the Department of Defense. Its role would be similar to that played by a public utilities commission (see Barzelay, 1992). Of course, meaningful cost-accounting systems must be based on resources consumed rather than cash outlays or encumbrances.

Reconciling Mission with
Budgetary and Accounting Procedures

Decentralizing the Pentagon, implementing mission-driven, results-oriented budgets, and using market mechanisms to solve problems require two fundamental changes in the budgetary and accounting practices of the federal government. One of these changes would be dramatic, the other mundane, but both are critical. The dramatic change would be in the way Congress reviews and enacts the Pentagon's budget. This change is necessary to bring congressional review of the budget into line with mission budgeting. The mundane change would be in the federal government's basis of accounting. This change is necessary to bring federal accounting practices into line with the responsibility-accounting concept. Both changes are needed to bring budget accounting into line with responsibility accounting.

Existing Federal Budgetary and Accounting Procedures

While the executive's proposed budget focuses on outlays, the legislative budget has traditionally emphasized the provision of budget authority. Under procedures established by the Congressional Budget and Impoundment Control Act of 1974, Congress now also adopts comprehensive outlay targets for the federal government before it takes action on individual spending proposals. The Budget Enforcement Act sets ceilings (toplines) on both obligational authority and outlays.

Outlays in any given fiscal year flow in part from current-year budget authority and in part from the unexpended balances of prior-year budget authority. Estimating these flows—scorekeeping, in congressional budget lingo—and battling over the estimates have become congressional preoccupations, since the Budget Enforcement Act (Doyle and McCaffery, 1991).

This is actually quite remarkable, because outlays have little real economic significance. Most economists would accept the notion that the source of financing (for example, debt or taxes) used to acquire a publicly owned asset or the timing of payments has no discernible economic effects, except insofar as these choices influence long-term considerations arising from the level of savings or private-sector investment. For some reason, however, Congress has in recent years adopted the defunct Keynesian economics of the 1967 report of the President's Commission on Budget Concepts and now gives as much weight to outlays as to budget authority.

In any case, Table 8.1 shows the rates at which outlays have in the past liquidated obligations for various kinds of assets.

Table 8.1. Outlay Rates: Percentage of Budget Authority
Liquidated Each Year.

Category	Budget year	2nd year	3rd year	4th year	5th year
Procurement	14	27	28	18	8
Shipbuilding	4	12	28	21	15
Aircraft	12	36	29	12	5
Missiles	12	32	34	15	6
Tanks	8	32	34	13	6
Ammunition	34	11	33	6	10
Research, development, testing, and evaluation	48	37	10	3	
Operations and maintenance	74	20	3		
Military construction	18	40	21	7	4
Personnel	96	4			

Purchase is the penultimate step in the existing federal budget and accounting process. Purchases are measured when goods and services are actually delivered to the military. Deliveries may follow outlays, as they generally do in the acquisition of major weapons systems and military construction, where firms performing work for the military are paid when work is done rather than when the products produced by that work are delivered; they may occur in the same accounting period, or they may precede payment. The rates at which outlays for various kinds of goods and services are converted into deliveries to the military are shown in Table 8.2.

The last stage of the federal budget and accounting process is audit and evaluation to determine whether agency spending has complied with the provisions of the authorization and appropriations acts—to verify that operating managers in the Pentagon did what the appropriations act said they were supposed do and did not do what they were not authorized to do.

Reforming the Congressional Budgetary Process

That Congress should provide budget authority to mission centers—that is, combatant commands—rather than to the Departments of the

Table 8.2. Purchases: Deliveries as Percentage of Outlays.

Category	Budget and prior year	2nd year	3rd year	4th year	5th year
Procurement	25	30	30	10	5
Research, development, testing, and evaluation	50	40	10		
Operations and maintenance	55	40	5		
Military construction	30	55	10	5	
Personnel	80	20			

Army, Navy, and Air Force is the plain meaning of mission budgeting. Beyond this obvious point, however, there is also the matter of item-by-item budget approval. If mission budgeting means only that *existing* items will be grouped into new "mission" accounts rather than into military department or appropriation accounts, it is hard to see how this change would be more than cosmetic. To give the mission budget concept meaning and to make decentralization perform as intended, Congress must delegate to responsibility center managers some of its authority to acquire and use assets.

The question is, how much and what kind of authority is needed? This question is extremely important because Congress has not in recent years been willing to delegate much fiscal authority to the Pentagon.

Gansler (1989) answers this question by denying that detailed line-item approval serves any legitimate purpose whatsoever. He argues that Congress should get entirely out of the business of choosing among weapons systems, determining their rate of acquisition, providing for deployment of military units, setting reserve stocks, and so forth. He argues that Congress should concern itself with higher things—determining foreign policy objectives and constraints, making strategic choices that have major political implications, and allocating resources to the major military missions. "The answer, therefore, is to restructure the budget process so that Congress will be forced to vote on 'top line' (i.e., total budget) dollars for the various 'mission areas' rather than on the details of specific programs and projects that are clearly identified with districts and states. Such a move would restore Congress to a deliberative body acting in the national interest rather than a staff driven special-interest machine whose members see each budget action as a way to raise election funds and/or to obtain jobs for constituents" (p. 120). Although Gansler is ready to make radical changes in the scope and domain of congressional authority, he would leave the existing comprehensive, repetitive congressional budget process and its duplicative accounting procedures largely unchanged.

We think Gansler's proposal fundamentally misunderstands the role of Congress in the American system of government. Our point is not Harvey Brooks's (1989-90, p. 176), that Gansler is naive, that his proposal "would deprive members of Congress of one of their principal opportunities to visibly serve their constituents—the main basis for their continuation in office." Our point is, instead, that item-by-item budget approval is deeply rooted in the American constitutional order. It did not happen by accident or mistake.

The locus of Congress's power lies in its mastery of the purse and the details of administration, as exemplified by item-by-item approval (see Phaup, 1990, p. 9). More than any other institutional arrangement, item-by-item approval distinguishes congressional government from European-style parliamentary systems, in which the legislature's power is largely sham. In parliamentary systems, the budget documents handed down from cabinet to parliament are often cryptic, totally obscure, and largely uninformative. Parliament must vote the budget of each department as proposed by cabinet either up or down. Party discipline is rarely breached and the entire budget is usually enacted right on schedule, following perfunctory debate, just as it was handed down. (In contrast, the Department of Defense's fiscal year 1989 budget justification book ran 30,000 pages, individual line items are adjusted at at least fourteen points in the budget process, and the Defense budget has been enacted on time only once in the last ten years.) Is it really necessary to transform Congress from a decision-making body into a debating society to give meaning to the mission-budget concept?

We think not. Congress could allow enough flexibility to make mission budgeting work merely by adopting the *Gore Report* budget recommendations: by increasing the Pentagon's discretion to transfer budget authority between lines and forward through time, by treating budget authority as permissive (that is, permitting the obligation of funds, but not requiring it), and by restricting its propensity to fund long-term investment programs on a one-year-at-a-time basis (Gore, 1993, pp. 160–163). It might also be necessary to repeal the Anti-Deficiency Act.

Anthony would go a little further. He would divide the defense budget into an operating portion and a capital portion. The operating budget would be appropriated annually or biannually and would be expressed in terms of the amount of expenses authorized for the period in question. The capital budget would be directed to the acquisition of long-lived assets and would in essence be unchanged from existing provisions of obligational authority (Robert N. Anthony, personal communication, September 1990; see also Anthony, 1990, pp. 50–52; Anthony and Young, 1988, pp. 543–546).

Anthony recognizes that the combatant commands cannot possibly meet all of their needs using spot market transactions—that mission centers would frequently be required to enter into long-term, exclusive relationships with suppliers and that support centers within the Department of Defense will have to make long-term commitments, involving highly specific assets, to organize, train, and equip units for combat. Regardless of how the combatant command obtains the use of long-term assets, directly from a supplier or indirectly through one of the military departments, their employment and inventory depletion will give rise to discrepancies between obligations, outlays, and consumption. The depletion of long-term assets and inventories also gives rise to intertemporal spillovers from one budget period to the next and, therefore, to discrepancies between operating budget accounts and the Treasury's cash account. Reconciling these discrepancies under Anthony's proposal would necessitate the creation of an additional annual (or biannual) appropriation for changes in working capital (the mechanics of this process are explained in Anthony and Young, 1988, pp. 543–546). Presumably, too, Anthony would have Congress set up a capital fund to provide both the combatant commands and their suppliers with financing for the acquisition of long-term capital assets.

Our preference would be to go further still to make congressional budgeting even simpler, more comprehensible, and more coherent. We think congressional budgeting should be more like private sector capital budgeting (see Chapter Two).

Capital Budgeting the Way the Private Sector Does It

When we say that congressional budgeting should be more like private sector capital budgeting, we mean that it should be permissive, continuous, and selective. We also mean that it should focus on all of the cash flows that ensue from Congress's programmatic decisions, not just those that occur in their initial fiscal year. New obligational authority should be expressed in terms of the discounted present values of those cash flows.

If Congress wished to emulate private sector capital budgeting, it would deemphasize the budget resolution, with its unhealthy fixation on outlays, and reemphasize obligational authority. The core of congressional power lies in its authority to decide to go ahead with a program, activity, or acquisition, which is what the authorization/appropriations process has always been about. We think that Congress has more important things to worry about than scheduling cash flows. Congress had it right to begin with; it should go back to the way it used to do things.

Its next step would be to throw away the president's budget. Congress already treats the president's budget as little more than a policy statement and a summary report; it should in the future allow executive branch agencies to come forward at any time with proposals to change the scope, level, or timing of their operations. Congress should consider proposals to try something new as soon as they are ready to be considered, but consider them only once. Once a project has been approved by Congress, it should be reconsidered only if circumstances change or the project goes bad. This means that obligational authority should be granted for the life of the project and should reflect the discounted present value of the project's cash flows. Standing appropriations should be continuously adjusted to reflect these important decisions.

Congress currently takes about the right approach to providing budget authority for the acquisition of long-lived assets like weapons systems, although the system of one-year-at-a-time authorization and appropriation that Congress has adopted in recent years is inimical to sound management of acquisition projects. Nevertheless, where plant and equipment are concerned, current costs are present values. In contrast, where ongoing activities are concerned, current costs greatly understate government's actual obligations.

The third step would be to make defense budgeting more selective—more like the current process of authorization and appropriation for social security. Congressional budgeting should focus on significant changes in operations, activities, and equipment. Otherwise, congressional attention should not be necessary. It makes no sense for Congress to look at every purchase contemplated by the entire federal government every year.

To give meaning to mission budgeting, the combatant commands and some of the defense agencies should probably operate under permanent authority. The combatant commands would have to obtain budget authority from Congress to increase force structure and combat stocks or to renegotiate contractual relationships with the military departments, especially if the change increased the Treasury's liabilities. If Congress wanted to reduce military spending, it would have to enact programmatic changes that reduced permanent appropriations.

Under this approach to mission budgeting, the military departments would still probably be required to obtain congressional authorization to make major new investments in military hardware or changes in their corpus. And Congress would probably still want to reconsider funding levels for military research and development on an annual or biannual basis. Aside from these exceptions, however, all new obligational authority would be expressed in terms of discounted net cash flows—which, as we have noted, would dramatically change congressional authorizations and appropriations for operating purposes. Congress would probably also have to acknowledge formally that obligational authority is permissive rather than mandatory.

There is nothing new about any of these notions. Congressional budgeting has traditionally been permissive, continuous, and selective, rather than comprehensive and repetitive. In essence these changes would restore the congressional budget process that existed prior to the passage of the Budget Act in 1921, which established a comprehensive annual executive budget for the entire federal government, created what has become the Office of Management and Budget, and at the same time reduced congressional power. And, while the idea of providing budget authority to the Department of Defense in present-value terms may seem outlandish, it would not be totally unprecedented. Congress currently funds the federal government's loan-guarantee and insurance programs in precisely that manner (see Redburn, 1993; Meyers, 1990; Kennedy, 1992; Scott, Bushnell, and Sallee, 1990).

Fiscal control under this approach to congressional budgeting would remain more or less as it is now. Presumably, the Office of Management and Budget's monthly apportionments to the Pentagon and the combatant commands would remain at constant levels as long as Congress did not increase (or reduce) their budget authority. In addition, the Treasury should probably be authorized to buy and sell notes on behalf of the Pentagon to provide it with short-term liquidity and to match cash inflows with the actual pattern of cash outflows (see Blum, 1993, pp. 14–18).

Reporting

Finally, Congress should require the Pentagon to provide it with far better operational reports, including information on the performance of each mission center and on its current capabilities and readiness status. (Better—not more—reports. In fiscal year 1988, Congress required 719 studies, plans, reviews, certifications, and reports from the Department of Defense: "Every working day . . . entails an average of almost three new General Accounting Audits of the Department of Defense, an estimated 450 written queries and over 2,500 telephone inquiries from Capitol Hill, and nearly three separate reports to Congress, each of them averaging over 1,000 man-hours in preparation and approximately $50,000 in cost" [Morrow, 1989, p. 10].) The Pentagon should also provide comparative data on the cost effectiveness with which all of the military departments perform their functions as force suppliers.

We note in passing that measuring unit readiness is an issue that requires careful thought. The military departments now measure readiness in terms of hours flown and "steaming hours" or in terms of inputs: readiness equals the percentage of equipment, personnel, and spare parts that a unit has relative to what it is authorized to have under the military department's Table of Organization and Equipment. These are pretty good measures of combat readiness once military units have been trained, deployed, and committed to battle. But they are not good measures of peacetime readiness. According to Stockfisch (1973, p. 259), a better measure would "focus on outputs, or ability to perform mission-like tasks. How quickly can a ship get underway, how accurately and quickly can a reconnaissance unit locate and report back the location of a target, how well can a fighter-bomber unit shoot? These are measures that convey something about output performance. Units should be required to do these things on a no announcement basis." These readiness evaluations would obviously have to be performed by the Joint Chiefs of Staff or the combatant commands, rather than the military departments. They could serve as a basis for evaluating the relative performance of the commanders of combat units and, therefore, of implementing the *Gore Report* recommendations about decentralizing personnel policy. Evaluating military commanders, and not just the managers of support centers, on the basis of their unit's performance would, of course, be entirely consistent with the logic of responsibility budgeting, something that the Pentagon's existing system of personnel evaluation is not.

Indeed, decentralizing personnel policy, as recommended by the *Gore Report,* implies a drastically reduced emphasis on individual attributes and characteristics and increased emphasis on performance, especially unit effectiveness, in decisions about assignments and promotions. For military mission centers, this implies reduced attention to the bureaucratic personnel management and greater emphasis on unit cohesiveness. Both Stockfisch (1973) and Bassford (1988) argue that, in peacetime, evaluation of unit performance should focus entirely on the unit's readiness to perform its wartime mission. And, like Luttwak, they argue for an independent inspectorate to perform these evaluations.

While military organization per se is beyond the scope of this volume, we believe that the distinction between administrative and mission structures should be reflected in the military's system of promotion and career progression. One model for a system of promotion and career progression calls for a National Defense Staff to handle joint assignments, including all top combat commands, and to evaluate unit readiness, while the military departments would handle most combat assignments up to the regimental level, as well as intradepartmental administrative assignments (see Luttwak, 1984, pp. 272–296). The prototype for Luttwak's National Defense Staff is, of course, the German General Staff (see Dupuy, 1977; Van Creveld, 1982; Murray, 1992).

Reforming the Department of Defense's Basis of Accounting

Accrual accounting is also critical to effective responsibility budgeting. Accrued expenses measure the cost of the assets actually *consumed* in the production of a good or service and are, therefore, needed to provide accurate comparative data on cost-effectiveness. Full value from the application of the principles of modern managerial controls will be obtained only when the Pentagon adopts a meaningful form of accrual accounting. While Public Law 84-863 directs the Pentagon to do so as soon as possible, that law was enacted in 1955 and, although accrual accounting is at the top of the list of Department of Defense's current management initiatives, it has still not fully complied with the intent of the legislation.

Table 8.3 shows defense budgets or spending levels expressed in terms of obligations, outlays, purchases, and consumption. Note, however, that while the federal government accounts for purchases, outlays, and obligations, it does not account for expenses. Hence these estimates of expenses are statistical in nature—that is, they are not tied to the basic debit-and-credit accounting records of the Department of Defense. Without the discipline that debit and credit provide, cost information is likely to be so inaccurate as to be useless for anything but illustrative purposes.

Certainly these estimates cannot be used for purposes of budgeting, let alone managerial control—that is, responsibility accounting or standard-cost and variance analysis. Nevertheless, these figures illustrate an important point. Given that this rough consumption measure more accurately reflects the delivery of military

Table 8.3. Annual Defense Costs: Obligational Authority,
Outlays, Purchases, and Consumption
(in billions of constant fiscal year 1989 dollars).

Fiscal year	Obligational authority	Outlays	Purchases	Consumption[a]
1971	226.5	239	N.A.	254
1972	219.3	222	221	235
1973	208.7	203	212	233
1974	201.2	200	195	226
1975	194.6	196	192	232
1976	202.7	189	188	217
1977	212.7	192	189	218
1978	209.3	193	189	214
1979	208.9	200	192	212
1980	213.4	207	202	212
1981	241.1	217	212	220
1982	268.9	232	223	229
1983	290.8	250	242	231
1984	303.9	260	255	232
1985	325.5	277	276	236
1986	312.2	294	294	250
1987	301.6	296	309	249
1988 (est.)	292.8	287	301	256

Source: Office of the Assistant Secretary of Defense (Comptroller), 1988, pp. 53, 58–59, 68–70, 90–93, 102–106, 146–147 (Tables 5-7, 5-11, 6-2, 6-9, 6-12, 7-5); National Income and Product Accounts, 1988, p. 10 (Table 3-10).

[a]Estimated from sources (includes capital consumption from Table 8.4, plus purchases for salaries and operations).

services, or at least the effort to deliver military services, during the fiscal year than does budget authority, its significance can be seen in the contrast between the second column and the column on the far right (see Roll, 1978; U.S. Department of Commerce, 1987; Thompson, 1987). Even sophisticated analysts are frequently misled by federal financial information, reported as it usually is in terms of budget authority or outlays.

For example, critics of the Carter administration (see for example, Gray and Barlow, 1985) frequently identified the real dollar decrease in budget authority that occurred during the mid 1970s with a dramatic decline in American military power or capabilities.

What Table 8.3 shows, however, is either that there was in fact no great decline in American military capabilities during the 1970s or, more likely, that it was due not merely to insufficient resources, but to the management of these resources.

Another example: At the end of President Reagan's first term in office, many of his critics noted that his "huge military buildup" had so far failed to produce major increases in U.S. military capabilities (Niskanen, 1988; Wirls, 1992). While most of these critics acknowledged substantial improvements in personnel and training and some improvements in maintenance and unit readiness, they stressed that defense stocks continued to dwindle and that the average age of military hardware was still increasing, which was interpreted as evidence of the Reagan administration's mismanagement of the Department of Defense. Again, however, if the critics had attended to the last column of Table 8.3, they might have realized that such an assessment was wrong, or at least premature. This last point is demonstrated even more clearly by the information shown in Table 8.4.

Accrual accounting raises some difficult technical problems for the Department of Defense. Furthermore, we would acknowledge that many accounting principles and practices appropriate to business are not appropriate to government. This is due not simply to differences in terminology; neither is it a matter that can be resolved by adding or subtracting a few lines from financial statements. For example, most students of financial management recognize the contribution that fund accounting can make in evaluating a not-for-profit enterprise's maintenance of operating capital. Indeed, we applaud the Pentagon's use of this concept. Yet, where business is concerned, fund accounting never makes sense. It is also obvious that certain basic premises of business accounting are irrelevant to the needs of public entities (for example, the ongoing concern concept—a public entity may have substantial liquidation value, but in law it can have no value as an ongoing concern).

The biggest difference between what business needs and what government must have is in the area of asset valuation. In business accounting, assets are usually carried on the books at their historical cost (that is, what the entity paid to acquire them) and not their replacement cost, which is often a better measure of opportunity cost. This means that business does not measure the quantity of

**Table 8.4. Annual Investments in Plant and Equipment:
Obligational Authority, Outlays, Purchases, Consumption, and Stock
(in billions of constant fiscal year 1989 dollars).**

Fiscal year	Obligational authority	Outlays	Purchases	Consumption[a]	Stock[b]
1971	68	79	110	94	628
1972	71	72	83	94	611
1973	66	63	76	93	588
1974	62	64	70	90	560
1975	58	59	64	94	528
1976	66	56	61	82	503
1977	75	58	57	83	474
1978	72	58	57	78	452
1979	73	67	58	78	431
1980	74	69	66	78	412
1981	93	75	68	77	393
1982	114	82	72	73	387
1983	130	93	86	72	395
1984	139	100	95	72	412
1985	156	114	97	73	436
1986	148	126	107	82	472
1987	129	130	120	82	511
1988 (est.)	125	121	128	89	548
1989 (est.)	121	120	126	94	577

Source: Office of the Assistant Secretary of Defense (Comptroller), 1988, pp. 53, 58–59, 68–70, 90–93, 102–104, 146–147 (Tables 5-7, 5-11, 6-2, 6-9, 6-12, 7-5); National Income and Product Accounts, 1988, p. 10 (Table 3.10).

[a]Estimated from sources.

[b]Figures for fiscal years 1971–1977 from Roll, 1978, p. 24, adjusted using price indices from Table 5-7; figures for fiscal years 1978–1989 estimated from Roll's baseline using consumption estimates, investment purchases, and maintenance outlays.

capital resources actually consumed during an accounting period in a way that conforms to economic logic—or fact. However, where business is concerned, there are good reasons for this deviation from economic logic. First, historical cost information is easy to get; its use permits communication of clearly defined data based on well-understood rules to users on a caveat emptor basis. Second, no important information is lost through adherence to this principle; the economic value of the business entity as an ongoing concern is reflected far more accurately in the market price of its shares than it ever could be in any summation of alienable assets and liabilities. Third, since the firm's purpose is to make a profit on its owners' investment, historical cost valuation is consistent with the provision of appropriate incentives to operating managers—to buy cheap and sell dear, to avoid unnecessary tax liability, to combine resources so as to maximize net-revenue product, and so on—who are evaluated in terms of reported profit as well as share price. Obviously, these reasons for deviating from economic logic do not apply to the U.S. government.

Where the Pentagon uses historical cost to value long-term assets in its financial statements, it sacrifices valuable, perhaps critical information and actually distorts the incentives facing operating managers. Its distorting effect is greatest where capital consumption charges are at issue, but it also significantly distorts other elements of expense (for example, ground rents).

Our estimates of long-term capital consumption rates are based on Roll's data and, after 1977, his methodology. Roll estimated the replacement cost of all equipment (planes, trucks, tanks, typewriters, and so on) in the American inventory from 1956 to 1977. Consumption is defined to be equal to wastage plus depreciation. Depreciation is defined as wear and tear and obsolescence, adjusted for actual maintenance levels. It was calculated using half-life estimates. These factors were applied to the capital stock inventory to obtain constant dollar estimates of capital consumption. Based on Roll's technique, we recalculated his figures using 1989 prices and brought them up to date.

Hence, our approach differs in three ways from standard business practice: it uses current replacement cost, it adjusts the rate of depreciation for investments in maintenance, and it applies different depreciation rates to different kinds of military hardware. According to our figures, electronic systems and components currently comprise nearly half of America's military's capital stock, up from 30 percent fifteen years ago. Furthermore, with a half-life of about five years, this equipment is used up much faster than other military hardware—military aircraft engines have a half-life of about ten years on average, military airframes fifteen or more, and ships about twenty. As a result, we believe that real military capital consumption rates are on average higher than they were ten or twenty years ago. Nevertheless, our estimates are fundamentally as arbitrary as, say, the Department of Commerce's estimates of depreciation and the net military capital stock.

Whether real capital consumption rates are higher now than in the past is directly relevant to the level of investment required to maintain military capital stock levels and, therefore, to force structure planning. However, real rates of capital consumption cannot be known unless serious efforts are made to measure them. This means that where asset valuation and consumption levels are at issue, it is necessary for the Pentagon to go beyond standard business practice. Unfortunately, this fact has not been widely acknowledged by the accounting professionals in government, let alone accepted by the policy makers they serve.

Bookkeeping

Solving the conceptual problems that have frustrated the implementation of a meaningful form of accrual accounting in the Department of Defense will not automatically ensure accurate or useful cost measurement, however. Useful information for internal control purposes must be based on a common set of accounts. There are still scores of different accounting systems, payroll systems, and contract payment systems in use within the Department of Defense. The Department of Defense still does not even have a common ledger. The Department of Defense's basic bookkeeping systems must be standardized, computerized, and simplified if progress is to be made toward accurate responsibility costing.

A Question of Political and Administrative Feasibility

To implement the new public management, the Pentagon's leaders must have the time and will needed to overcome considerable bureaucratic resistance and organizational friction. As we have seen, Secretary Cheney tried to move in the right directions. He promised to streamline the weapons systems acquisition process and to consolidate all communications, data processing, and financial and accounting systems, contract management services, maintenance and supply activities, research and development, and intelligence operations. His staff tried to install a comprehensive cost-accounting and managerial control structure throughout the Pentagon and to establish a matrix structure for the Department of Defense, with its mission and support centers linked by transfer prices, responsibility budgets, and accrual accounts, using markets wherever possible to solve problems (Jones, 1992a, 1992b, 1993; see also Harr and Godfrey, 1991b). These well-intentioned initiatives were never fully implemented, however, in part because of administrative resistance from the military departments. Ultimately, Secretary Cheney and his staff ran out of time.

The Pentagon is still officially pledged to these reforms—indeed, they are at the heart of the Clinton administration's commitment to reinventing government. Furthermore, we have recently observed a great deal of grassroots enthusiasm throughout the Department of Defense for the administrative reforms proposed by the Gore Commission. What we have not observed is a great deal of action. We are inclined to attribute this inactivity to an absence of leadership at the top of the Department of Defense.

One of the most frequently quoted of Carl von Clausewitz's maxims is that "everything in war is simple, but friction makes even the simplest things difficult." In this case, what is true of war is largely true of administrative reform as well. The steps that must be taken are fairly straightforward, but bureaucratic resistance and organizational friction make implementing them difficult indeed. And, as in war, this friction can only be overcome by an "iron will," which "pulverizes every obstacle" (Clausewitz, 1984, p. 138). So far, this administration has shown more flexibility than resolve.

A second hurdle that must be overcome is congressional preoccupation with the details of administration. Virtually all of our proposals depend on reducing congressional supervision of the Pentagon's business. Is this realistic? Given that ours is a government of "separate institutions sharing powers," is it even desirable?

Barry Blechman (1990) speaks for the negative in a carefully argued history of Congress and defense policy after 1960. He claims that Congress will not back out of the Pentagon's business and probably should not. He observes that "Congress has been asserting a more intrusive role in the determination of U.S. defense policy for

twenty years now. . . . The notion that they should defer to the
executive branch is totally foreign [to its members]. For better or
worse, the congressional role in defense policy is a reality" (p. 206).
Furthermore, he maintains that Congress must control executive
abuse of its discretionary power: "Most Americans, the author included, believe that the . . . degree of congressional involvement
that existed prior to the 1970s was insufficient to insure that popular perspectives effectively bounded executive decisions" (p. 29).

Nevertheless, Blechman acknowledges the damage done by
congressional overextension, his term for congressional involvement in the details of administration, particularly detailed line-item
budgets and oversight of their execution. He claims that Congress
lacks the administrative information needed to exercise positive
leadership in the formulation of policy—that it is not organized in
such a way as to produce coherent policies of its own or of providing "continuous support for operational activities" (p. 28).

Of course, American legislatures were never intended to produce coherent, comprehensive blueprints for change in the government's responsibilities or its tactics. The founding fathers designed
Congress to retard, not to run, an active government. They designed
it to protect our lives, liberties, and property from the overweening
ambitions of a reckless and extravagant executive and the interests
of passionate minorities. The structure they established was intended to ensure that ours would be a government of law and that
the law would change slowly and incrementally and only when the
direction of change was endorsed by a large majority of the citi-
zenry. That Congress is driven by partisanship—rent by jealousy
between the two chambers and the particularities of committee interests—is no accident. The founding fathers relied on precisely
these antagonisms to check minority interests and to make Congress
an agent of negotiation and compromise that would reach its decisions through the discovery of the lowest common denominator
(Thompson, 1979).

Furthermore, Blechman believes that the incentives facing
members of Congress are largely inimical to the exercise of positive
leadership. Consequently, he concludes that "Congress has tended
to apply the powers seized in the 1970s with a heavy hand, sacrificing overall consistency and coherence of national policy for narrow

interests and short-term objectives. This is a natural consequence of the political calculus that inevitably dominates congressional decision making. If the Congress is to play a more farsighted role in defense policy, the form and boundaries of its new functions will have to be shaped in order to minimize opportunities for parochial political interests to dominate decision making" (p. 21).

If Blechman has accurately described the incentives facing members of Congress, there is little chance that they will reconsider their involvement in the details of administration. As our colleague Richard Doyle of the Naval Postgraduate School observes, the skillful use of budget detail "can deliver money and jobs as surely as writing a check." Terry M. Moe (1990, p. 140; see also 1989) of the Brookings Institution carries this argument even further. He argues that self-interest leads legislators to shun serious policy control and instead seek "particularized" control. Because they "want to be able to intervene quickly, inexpensively, and in ad hoc ways to protect or advance the interests of particular clients in particular matters," they prefer rules that impose rigid limits on an agency's discretion and its procedures. Hence, legislators favor administrative controls that are ineffective by design.

If this view is correct, little can be done to reduce congressional micromanagement, short of changing our political institutions. Why, after all, would Congress want to dismantle what it has so laboriously built if it serves the interests of its members so well? The clear implication of Blechman's assumptions about congressional motives is that current and future defense management reforms, especially those involving reductions in the level of congressional micromanagement, are destined to fail because they leave in place the congressional norms that guarantee failure. Of course, Blechman does not draw this conclusion. He does little explicit theorizing about Congress and pays even less attention to those who have. Because he does not really push his assumptions about congressional motives to their logical conclusions, he has little cause to question their validity.

Questioning the Assumptions

James Lindsay (1991) and Kenneth Mayer (1991) test the assumption that congressional behavior can be attributed primarily to parochial or partisan motives. The questions they raise and their methodology are similar, as are their conclusions. Both demonstrate that congressional decisions are best explained by the personal policy preferences of individual members—that is, by their conceptions of the public good and of the national interest.

That our legislators often try to promote the public welfare as they understand it should not surprise anyone who has carefully attended to the empirical literature on congressional voting (see, for examples, Kalt and Zupan, 1990; Peltzman, 1984, 1990) or even to case studies of highly visible measures such as trucking deregulation (Robyn, 1987) or tax reform (Birnbaum and Murray, 1987). Even casual observers can cite examples of Congress acting in a bipartisan fashion out of conviction rather than parochial interest. Enactment of the Goldwater-Nichols Department of Defense Reorganization Act in 1986, for example, reversed forty years of congressional (and Navy) opposition to the principle of unity of combat command and thereby greatly enhanced the ability of the United States to use its military forces in support of political objectives. Congressional promotion of fast sealift and special operations forces are additional examples. In these instances, Congress championed the needs of the regional commanders over the interests of the military departments and, in the case of special operations forces, pork had to be the furthest thing from its members' minds, since special operations forces have almost no budgetary consequences, depending as they do on small numbers of highly trained personnel and relatively low-tech equipment. Also, as we have observed, in 1988 Congress enacted a base closure procedure that drastically curbed its ability to interfere with base closings. By the time this was written, forty-seven major bases had been slated for shutdown and more were on the way (Koven, 1992).

Nevertheless, many of those who write about Congress and defense will find Lindsay's and Mayer's conclusions startling. For example, Mayer (1991, pp. 1–12) shows that:

- Members of Congress do not vote for weapons based on the economic benefit to their constituents.
- It is wrong to say that defense firms use their influence with Congress to obtain contracts; members of Congress cannot de-

mand that the Pentagon award contracts to pet firms in particular districts or states.

- The Pentagon does not use defense contracts as tools of persuasion by selectively awarding contracts to particular states or districts for political reasons.

Mayer's point is not that parochialism is completely irrelevant, but that it plays a distinctly subsidiary role in the legislative process. It is easy to cite evident instances of political log-rolling and pork-barreling—the buy-American provisions alluded to above are a good case in point—but there is plenty of evidence to suggest that, if naked redistribution were not somehow cloaked in the public interest, it would rarely be enacted or signed into law.

How then does one account for the conventional wisdom that ascribes congressional behavior to purely parochial motives? Mayer attributes much of it, correctly we think, to partisan criticism of the Democrat majority in Congress. Lindsay adds that colorful anecdotes that emphasize the more dramatic aspects of politics, such as log-rolling, pork-barreling, and strategic misrepresentation, are irresistible to newswriters and columnists and that their attention leads scholars to overestimate the importance of these phenomena. To this we would add the often mistaken assumption that there is a straightforward linear relation between government action, spending in a district for example, and its net effect on the distribution of income and wealth. Government action creates or preserves substantial rents for identifiable groups only where it produces above normal-wages or profits or where it safeguards the value of assets that cannot be profitably redeployed to other purposes. Some public policies have these consequences—protecting the steel-plate or jeweled-bearings industry, providing commodity price supports, or giving various protections to the coal-mining industry (see, for example, Higgs, 1990)—but for the most part, defense acquisition does not. The fixed assets of defense firms are usually either redeployable, as are the skills of their employees, or they are owned by the government. Consequently, the location-specific effects of military spending are often small and sometimes even negative.

Explaining Congressional Micromanagement

If parochial and partisan motives do not satisfactorily explain congressional micromanagement of the military, what does? When we raised this issue with defense expert Peter deLeon, he replied that we were asking the wrong question. He claimed that high levels of congressional attention to the details of administration are an inevitable consequence of the growth of federal spending. According to deLeon, Congress has always micromanaged federal spending—congressional preoccupation with the details of administration is ordained by the Constitution, which allocates to Congress the power of the purse, including the power to tax, to borrow, and to spend, and the power to raise and regulate armies. Indeed, the locus of these powers was the quintessential issue of the great Anglo-American battles of the seventeenth and eighteenth centuries. The prerogatives of the winners—Parliament, the colonial legislatures, and Congress—are unequivocally itemized in the Act of Settlement, the Bill of Rights, the Mutiny Acts, the Declaration of Independence, and especially the Constitution of 1789, with its separation of powers and system of checks and balances. These struggles also created the instruments American legislatures use to this day to effect their mastery of the details of administration.

DeLeon concluded that congressional micromanagement is a direct consequence of the exercise of government's substantive powers. He surmised that, if the absolute level of congressional micromanagement was lower before World War II, it was because the federal budget was so much smaller. The level of micromanagement is higher now because the federal budget is much larger. Before the war, a handful of members of Congress could look after the bases in their districts, others could worry about military construction, and the rest could focus on the remainder of the budget and still subject each item to exquisite scrutiny. For example, the following lines taken from a chapter entitled "Cessation of Mischievous Meddling by Congress: The First Need of the United States Navy," and written by J. W. Muller in 1915, have a distinctly contemporary ring:

The total naval appropriation act of . . . 1914 contains 14,000 words. Of these, just 270 words were used for appropriating money for ships. . . . The rest of the long Act was devoted to prescribing in detail exactly how the Navy Department might spend the other sums that are needed annually for its maintenance . . . ice, stationery, photographs and religious books. . . . It is this sort of legislation to which every Congress has given more time and attention than to an intelligent building of a great navy. It has not only tied the Navy . . . in a paralyzing web of red tape, causing immensely wasteful clerical systems, but it has prevented the experts who alone know how a navy should be made from using any money as their knowledge and experience might suggest. It is Congress . . . that runs the Navy, and after Congress adjourns, its dead hand remains heavily on the whole naval system in the form of these narrow Acts which no naval authority . . . may transgress under penalty of being punished for violation of the law. . . . Why . . . ? The answer is politics . . . logrolling extravagance [p. 134].

While deLeon's thesis has considerable validity on its face, it is not entirely consistent with the evidence. As Elias Huzar explained in his magisterial history of the military appropriation process, *The Purse and the Sword* (1950; see also Huzar, 1948), congressional attention to the details of administration periodically waxed and waned. Although Congress has zealously guarded its de jure authority to specify the purposes for which it authorizes and appropriates funds and its authority to regulate military procurement and personnel policies, de facto it has often chosen not to exercise its powers. Rather, it has often delegated a portion of its powers to the executive.

Indeed, according to Huzar, Congress has usually deferred to the executive about most issues of substantive military policy and their implementation through the budget. Moreover, Congress has usually relied on standing, open-ended authorizations covering the military departments' personnel levels and equipment—as it did during the 1945-1960 era. The only domain that has always commanded close and continuous scrutiny on the part of the congressional armed services committees is military construction, which includes oversight of military bases and arsenals. Furthermore, Congress often afforded the acquisition process a degree of benign neglect—providing fairly stable funding and refraining from second guessing the military departments' priorities, plans, and acquisition strategies (see also Dawson, 1963; Dexter, 1963; Kolodziej, 1966).

According to Huzar, Congress delegates a portion of its powers to the executive branch because its members understand that their distinctive competency is not management—that the proper function of Congress is the aggregation and articulation of interests and values, a function it performs best when it deals with broad national issues that demand the attention and scrutiny of the majority of its members. Besides, members of Congress recognize that the task of managing the Pentagon is overwhelming. Nowadays, despite huge increases in staff and a greater division of labor and jurisdiction—in 1960, twenty committees and subcommittees in both houses heard testimony on the military budget; in 1992, defense witnesses testified in hearings before thirty congressional committees, seventy-seven subcommittees, and four panels—and despite a twelvefold increase in budget line items and in witnesses called to testify in committee hearings on the defense budget, Congress still holds less than one hour of hearings for each $100 million it spends on defense.

The point is that, where Congress and the president agree on policy objectives, Congress often prefers to remove hard programmatic and budgetary choices from its agenda by delegating responsibility for them to the executive. As long as Congress is persuaded that the executive is willing and able to do what it would want done, it has often delegated authority to do those things to the executive. After World War II, and especially during the Eisenhower administration, that is precisely what Congress did.

Moreover, Huzar reminds us that Congress is especially eager to delegate responsibility for cutting budgets to the executive. Members of Congress understandably do not like retrenchment. Retrenchment means denying constituents tangible benefits or, even worse, taking them away. Most fully understand, however, that these hard choices must be made if government is to be fair, efficient, and fiscally responsible.

While Huzar does not use this language, it is reasonable to conclude from his survey that congressional micromanagement can in large part be attributed to distrust of the executive. In the past, mistrust has been inspired by a variety of causes: ideological and policy conflict, partisan dispute, and, perhaps most commonly, failures on the part of executive branch agencies. In their explanations of congressional micromanagement of the Pentagon, Blechman, Lindsay, and Mayer emphasize its past record of military, administrative, and political failure.

Other students of public administration believe that congressional indignation is a broader and deeper phenomenon. They stress the role played by the breakdown of the postwar foreign policy consensus in the rise of micromanagement in the 1960s and 1970s. As Allen Schick (1976, p. 296) explains, the discretion granted the Department of Defense during the postwar era by Congress reflected trust that "executive power would be applied benevolently in the national interest. . . . Viet Nam robbed nonpartisanship of its seductive hold on the loyalty of Congress. . . . Consequently, during the 1970s, Congress brought new controls into being and applied old controls more intensively." Aaron Wildavsky (1988, pp. 46–64) went further still, arguing that this breakdown reflected fundamental conflicts over deeply held values.

Despite the depth of congressional mistrust of the executive, and in contrast to explanations of micromanagement that begin and end with pork-seeking behavior, this explanation permits guarded optimism about the prospects for reform. It implies that Congress might grant the executive the authority it needs to run itself in a businesslike manner—if Congress can be persuaded that executive branch leaders will not abuse its trust.

A Tentatively Optimistic Prognosis

Three circumstances suggest that the time is ripe for a rapprochement between Congress and the executive branch. Foremost among these circumstances is the end of the Cold War, which has brought with it the possibility of renewed consensus as to the aims and purposes of American foreign policy and the role assigned to the military in support of these aims. A second is the inauguration of the Clinton administration. This has already reduced partisan conflict between the two branches of government and has gone far toward reassuring the Democratic leadership in Congress of the executive's fundamental trustworthiness—Congress has been far more receptive to the Gore Commission's proposals, for example, than it ever was to those of the Grace and Packard commissions. The third is the performance of the military in the Persian Gulf. Operation Desert Storm dramatically ended the Pentagon's string of operational failures and, in so doing, demonstrated the tactical, logistical, and technical excellence of American arms. If it did nothing else, Desert Storm should have demonstrated the Pentagon's competence to manage itself without quite so much help from Congress. We would also point out that in the coming era of retrenchment, Congress will have reason to want to disassociate itself as far as possible from decisions about raising and equipping the armed forces.

For those who would argue that the gulf between Congress and the executive branch is too deep and bitter to be bridged, we ask them to think about the half-century of executive-legislative conflict in Great Britain that produced the Puritan and the Glorious Revolutions and that unequivocally established Parliament's substantive powers (Ashley, 1961, pp. 309–381, 412–420; Smellie, 1962, pp. 19–40). This conflict was deeper and wider than anything most of us can imagine—in part, because it reflected fundamental religious differences and, in part, because, in that distant and nearly incomprehensible era, ruinous fines, the lash, and even the gibbet were commonplace tools of party politics.

Parliament was deeply suspicious of the Stuarts' foreign policy and was also repeatedly exasperated by the Crown's military incompetence. Because it mistrusted both the Stuarts' policies and their proficiency, Parliament refused to appropriate funds for the military. Mistrust also inspired Parliament to adopt a scheme of line-item encumbrance accounts to ensure that Crown spending was strictly limited to objects approved by Parliament. These before-the-fact controls are still the chief instrument through which legislatures control the behavior of executives and their officers.

However, once the religion issue had been firmly laid to rest by the Revolution of 1688–89 and a king was in place who was both militarily competent and committed to policies agreeable to Parliament, it freely provided the funds needed to carry the war to France and then left the military alone to get on with it. While the Act of Settlement of 1689 included provisions that could have totally subordinated administration of national security policy to Parliament, those provisions were not given force. Instead, Parliament wisely chose to exercise considerable self-restraint in the employment of its de jure powers.

To those who argue that reform is impossible, that continued micromanagement is inevitable, we would respond that what has happened once can happen again.

Notes

Chapter 1: Creating the Department of Defense

1. The combat version of this doctrine usually goes by the term *mission tactics,* an awkward but fundamentally sound translation of the German *Auftragstaktik* or *Auftragsbefehlgebung* (Van Creveld, 1982, 1985; see also Dupuy, 1977).
2. The distinction between before-the-fact and after-the-fact controls is discussed in greater detail in Chapters Three and Six.
3. One analysis of the relative military power of the United States and the Soviet Union estimates that the United States was sixteen times as powerful as the Soviet Union in 1950 and that Soviet forces did not achieve parity with those of the United States until the mid to late 1970s (Ward, 1984; see also Olvey, Golden, and Kelly, 1984, pp. 235–247).
4. Elihu Root was Secretary of War during the administrations of William McKinley and Theodore Roosevelt and became Secretary of State after the death of John Hay in 1905.

Chapter 2: Controlling the Military Departments

1. Anthony tells us that he no longer believes that it makes sense to include a charge for capital consumption in the cost of pro-

viding services, except perhaps where the fixed asset in question could be leased or rented (for example, an office building, but not the Washington Monument). He believes that it would be too difficult to measure capital consumption accurately and that basing the charge on an arbitrary depreciation standard (for instance, ten-year straight-line depreciation) would be worse than useless (Robert N. Anthony, letters to the authors, June 1990 and September 1990; Anthony, 1990). While we agree that there is no point to cascading an arbitrary depreciation charge forward, we do not believe it would be prohibitively expensive to measure capital consumption properly.

Chapter 3: Reengineering the Pentagon

1.   Some of the major laws are the Buy America Act, the Preference for U.S. Food, Clothing & Fibers Act, the Preference for Steel Plate Act, the Clean Air Act, the Equal Employment Act, the Fair Labor Standards Act of 1938, the Release of Product Information to Consumers Act, the Prohibition of Price Differentials Act, the Required Source for Jeweled Bearing Act (which requires military contractors to buy all their jeweled bearings from the government-owned Turtle Mountain Bearing Plant in Rolla, North Dakota), the Prison Made Supplies Act, the Required Source of Aluminum Ingot Act, the Small Business Act, the Labor Surplus Area Concerns Act, the Resource Conservation and Recovery Act, the Davis-Bacon Act, the National Women's Business Enterprise Policy Act, the Renegotiation Act, the Walsh-Healey Public Contract Acts, and many others.

2.   The information presented in this section reflects personal interviews with Deputy Secretary of Defense Donald Atwood, May 15, 1992; the Assistant Secretaries of Defense for Financial Management (Comptrollers) of the Departments of the Army, Navy, and Air Force, May 7–10, 1991; officials of the Office of the Department of Defense Comptroller, including Comptroller Sean O'Keefe, October 14–18, 1991, and February 10–14, 1992, and Donald Shycoff, Principal Deputy Comptroller and subsequently Acting Comptroller, March 13, 1992; and officials

of the Defense Finance and Accounting Service, including Director Al Conte, February 10–11, 1992.
3. The information presented in this section reflects interviews with some of the individuals involved—at this time many still wish to remain anonymous.

Chapter 4: Working with the Private Sector

1. Spinney, a civilian analyst with the Department of Defense, is known primarily for his briefing "Defense Facts of Life." Copies of the overheads used in this briefing are available from the Public Affairs Office, The Pentagon, Washington, D.C. 20301.

Chapter 6: Redesigning Control Systems

1. Several readers have objected to the term *management control*, reminding us that managing and controlling are definitely not the same activity (Landau and Stout, 1979). Consequently, we considered using other terms for the organizing concept of this chapter: *direction, governance,* and especially *accountability*. These seemed too broad for our purposes, however. For example, the entire discipline of accounting is concerned with the functioning of accountability relationships (Ijiri, 1975, p. ix); the branch of accounting that is concerned with influencing subordinate behavior is management (or administrative) control (Anthony and Young, 1988). The field of management control, like some main currents of public administration, traces its intellectual lineage through Chester I. Barnard (1938) back to Mary Parker Follett's (1927, 1937) rule of anticipated reactions. We align ourselves here with Follett's disciples, such as C. J. Friedrich (1940, p. 20), who believed that "no mere reliance on some traditional device . . . can be counted upon to render the vast public services of a modern government responsible . . . ; responsibility will remain fragmentary because of the indistinct voice of the principal whose [expert] agents the officials are supposed to be," and against those like Herman Finer (1941), who placed full confidence in rule-bound governance mechanisms. Our approach is consistent with the thrust of

Martin Landau's (1969, 1973) influential works, albeit not his terminology.

2. Normal goods have continuous and twice-differentiable supply schedules. In contrast, supply of a lumpy good is discrete, perhaps even a single point on the supply schedule. An appendectomy illustrates the concept of lumpiness. A second appendectomy would be useless, half an appendectomy worse than useless (Thompson, 1987).

Chapter 7: Cutting Overheads

1. In our view, this is an error. Pride of place should probably be awarded to the various buy-American mandates governing military procurement (see Higgs, 1990).
2. The following discussion reflects research studies carried out at the Naval Postgraduate School by G. A. Holk, N. J. Nelson, and R. M. Maholochic, under the supervision of L. R. Jones and Jerry McCaffery.
3. While the Department of Defense has successfully identified many properties with high alternative uses, it has been slow to transfer them to those uses.

   In 1988, one of the authors of this volume testified before the Defense Secretary's Base Closure and Realignment commission. His testimony stressed the importance of expeditiously transferring military bases, especially those hemmed in by urban encroachment, to better and higher civilian uses. Following his testimony, commissioner Louis Cabot sharply asked him if he proposed to privatize the entire domestic military base structure, leaving the military with the option of leasing back the bases it could economically bid away from alternative uses. The coauthor hastened to deny that he was proposing any such thing. Given the Pentagon's continued preoccupation with operating costs, however, and the difficulty it has had with divestiture, privatization does not really seem like such a bad idea after all. Privatization would give the military departments an incentive to use real property efficiently and ensure that land from unneeded bases and facilities was expeditiously transferred to higher-valued nonmilitary uses.

References

Ackerman, B. A., and Hassler, W. T. "Beyond the New Deal: Coal and the Clean Air Act." *Yale Law Journal*, 1980, *89*, 1466-1572.

Adelman, K., and Augustine, N. *The Defense Revolution*. San Francisco: ICS Press, 1990.

Alexander, T. "Making High-Tech Weapons for Less." *Fortune*, Feb. 4, 1985, pp. 20-25.

Allison, G. T., Jr. "Public and Private Management: Are They Fundamentally Alike in All Unimportant Particulars?" In R. T. Golembiewski and F. Gibson (eds.), *Readings in Public Administration*. (4th ed.) Boston: Houghton Mifflin, 1983.

Andrews, K. R. *The Concept of Corporate Strategy*. Homewood, Ill.: Dow Jones-Irwin, 1971.

Anthony, R. N. "New Frontiers in Defense Financial Management." *Federal Accountant*, 1962, *11*, 13-32.

Anthony, R. N. *Planning and Control Systems: A Framework for Analysis*. Boston: Graduate School of Business Administration, Harvard University, 1965.

Anthony, R. N. "The AICPA's Proposal for Federal Accounting Reform: It Should Focus on the Budget System, Not the Accounting System." *Management Accounting*, 1990, *72*(1), 48-52.

Anthony, R. N., and Young, D. *Management Control in Nonprofit Organizations*. (4th ed.) Homewood, Ill.: Irwin, 1988.

Anton, J. J., and Yao, D. A. "Measuring the Effectiveness of Competition in Defense Procurement." *Journal of Policy Analysis and Management,* 1990, *9,* 60–79.

Aronson, P., and Ordeshook, P. "The Political Bases of Public Sector Growth in a Representative Democracy." Paper presented at the Conference on the Causes and Consequences of Public Sector Growth, Dorado Beach, Puerto Rico, Dec. 1978.

Armacost, M. A. *The Politics of Weapons Innovation: The Thor-Jupiter Controversy.* New York: Columbia University Press, 1969.

Arnold, D. A. *Congress and the Bureaucracy.* Princeton, N.J.: Princeton University Press, 1979.

Art, R. J. *The TFX Decision: McNamara and the Military.* Boston: Little, Brown, 1968.

Art, R. J. "Congress and the Defense Budget: Enhancing Policy Oversight." *Political Science Quarterly,* 1985, *100*(2), 227–248.

Ashley, M. *Great Britain to 1688.* Ann Arbor: University of Michigan Press, 1961.

Aspin, L. *National Security in the Post–Cold War World.* Washington, D.C.: Office of the Secretary of Defense, Sept. 1993.

Augustine, N. *Augustine's Laws and Major Systems Development Programs.* New York: American Institute of Aeronautics and Astronautics, 1982.

Bailey, M. J. "Defense Decentralization Through Internal Prices." In S. Enke (ed.), *Defense Management.* Englewood Cliffs, N.J.: Prentice Hall, 1967.

Baldwin, H. "Slow-Down in the Pentagon." *Foreign Affairs,* 1965, *43*(2), 262–280.

Barnard, C. I. *The Functions of the Executive.* Cambridge, Mass.: Harvard University Press, 1938.

Baron, D. P. "Procurement Contracting: Efficiency, Renegotiation, and Performance Evaluation." *Information Economics and Policy,* 1988, *3*(1), 109–143.

Baron, D. P. "Defense Procurement: Politics, Management, and Incentives." Unpublished working paper, Stanford University, 1991.

Barro, R. J. *Macroeconomic Policy.* Cambridge, Mass.: Harvard University Press, 1990.

Barzelay, M., with Armajani, B. J. *Breaking Through Bureaucracy:*

A New Vision for Managing in Government. Berkeley: University of California Press, 1992.

Bassford, C. *The Spit-Shine Syndrome: Organizational Irrationality in the American Field Army.* Westport, Conn.: Greenwood Press, 1988.

Beach, C. P., Jr. *Memorandum for the Secretary of the Navy, Regarding the A-12 Administrative Inquiry.* Washington, D.C., Office of the Secretary of the Navy, Nov. 28, 1990.

Beard, J. *Developing the ICBM.* New York: Columbia University Press, 1976.

Becker, S. W., and Neuhauser, D. *The Efficient Organization.* Elsevier–North Holland Publishing Company, 1975.

Behar, R. "Gold Bricks?" *Forbes,* Apr. 22, 1985, p. 82.

Belkaoui, A. *Handbook of Management Control Systems.* New York: Quorum Books, 1986.

Bergerson, F. *The Army Gets an Air Force.* Baltimore, Md.: Johns Hopkins University Press, 1980.

Birnbaum, J. H., and Murray, A. S. *Showdown at Gucci Gulch: Lawmakers, Lobbyists, and the Unlikely Triumph of Tax Reform.* New York: Random House, 1987.

Blechman, B. M., with the assistance of Ellis, W. P. *The Politics of National Security: Congress and U.S. Defense Policy.* New York: Oxford University Press, 1990.

Blue Ribbon Commission on Defense Management [Packard Commission]. *A Quest for Excellence (Preliminary Report to the President).* Washington, D.C.: Department of Defense, Jan. 1986a.

Blue Ribbon Commission on Defense Management [Packard Commission]. *A Formula for Action (Interim Report to the President).* Washington, D.C.: Department of Defense, Apr. 1986b.

Blue Ribbon Commission on Defense Management [Packard Commission]. *A Quest for Excellence (Final Report to the President).* Washington, D.C.: Department of Defense, June 1986c.

Blum, B., and Lobaco, G. "Following the Money." *California Lawyer,* 1987, 7(5), 63–64, 71.

Blum, J. L. *Statement Before the Subcommittee on Readiness, Committee on Armed Services, House of Representatives.* Washington, D.C.: Congressional Budget Office, May 13, 1993.

Boo, K. "How Congress Won the War in the Gulf." *Washington Monthly*, 1991, *23*(10), 31–37.

Borcherding, T. E. "Some Revisionist Thoughts on the Theory of Public Bureaucracy." *European Journal of Political Economy*, 1988, *4*, 47–64.

Borowski, H. R. *A Hollow Threat: Strategic Air Power and Containment Before Korea.* Westport, Conn.: Greenwood Press, 1986.

Boskin, M. J. "New Estimates of the Value of Federal Mineral Rights and Land." *American Economic Review*, 1986, *75*(5), 931–934.

Bower, J. *The Resource Allocation Process.* Boston: Harvard Business School Division of Research, 1970.

Bracken, P. *The Command and Control of Nuclear Forces.* New Haven, Conn.: Yale University Press, 1980.

Breton, A., and Wintrobe, R. "The Equilibrium Size of a Budget-Maximizing Bureau." *Journal of Political Economy*, 1975, *83*, 195–207.

Breton, A., and Wintrobe, R. *The Logic of Bureaucratic Conduct.* New York: Cambridge University Press, 1982.

Brian-Bland, D., and Rasor, D. "Lies, Half-Truths, and Misrepresentations: How the Military Gets Its Money." Yale Law and Policy Review, 1986, *5*(1), 102–119.

Brooks, H. "U.S. Defense: Is Reform Possible?" *International Security*, 1989–90, *14*(3), 172–177.

Buchanan, J. M., Tollison, R. D., and Tullock, G. (eds.). *Toward a Theory of the Rent-Seeking Society.* Ann Arbor: University of Michigan Press, 1980.

Byron, J. L. "Reorganization of the U.S. Armed Forces." *U.S. Naval Institute Proceedings*, 1983, *109*(1), 68–75.

Caraley, D. *The Politics of Military Unification.* New York: Columbia University Press, 1966.

Carlton, D. W., and Perloff, J. M. *Modern Industrial Organization.* Glenview, Ill.: Scott, Foresman–Little, Brown Higher Education, 1990.

Carrick, P. M. "New Evidence on Government Efficiency." *Journal of Policy Analysis and Management*, 1988, *7*, 518–528.

Carter, G.A.C. *Should the Marine Corps Buy the M-1 Tank and, If*

So, How Many? Unpublished M.S. Thesis, Naval Postgraduate
School, Monterey, Calif., 1988.

Chalmers, M., and Unterseher, L. "Is There a Tank Gap?" *International Security*, 1988, *13*(1), 5–49.

Chandler, A. *Strategy and Structure: Chapters in the History of Industrial Enterprise*. Cambridge, Mass.: MIT Press, 1962.

Chapin, D. H. *Financial Management: Opportunities to Strengthen Management of the Defense Business Operations Fund*. Testimony before the Subcommittee on Readiness, Committee on Armed Services, U.S. House of Representatives. GAO-T-AFMD-93-4. Washington, D.C.: General Accounting Office, May 13, 1993.

Cheney, D. *Defense Management Report*. Washington, D.C.: Office of the Secretary of Defense, July 1989.

Church, G. J. "How Much Is Too Much?" *Time*, Feb. 12, 1990, pp. 19–26.

Clausewitz, C. von. *On War*. Edited and translated by Michael Howard and Peter Paret. Rev. ed. Princeton, N.J.: Princeton University Press, 1984.

Coakley, T. P. *Command and Control for War and Peace*. Washington, D.C.: National Defense University Press, 1992.

Cohen, E. A. "War as a Whole." *Public Interest*, 1982, *68*, 124–132.

Cohen, E. A., and Gooch, J. *Military Misfortune: The Anatomy of Failure in War*. New York: Free Press, 1990.

Committee on Armed Services, U.S. Senate. *Defense Organization: The Need for Change*. Staff report no. 99-86, Appendix B. Washington, D.C.: Committee on Armed Services, U.S. Senate, 1986.

Connor, P. E. *Organization Structure and Design*. Chicago: SRA Modules in Management, 1984.

Cooper, R. *Military Manpower and the All-Volunteer Force*. Santa Monica, Calif.: RAND Corporation, 1977.

Corum, J. S. *The Roots of Blitzkrieg: Hans von Seekt and German Military Reform*. Lawrence: University Press of Kansas, 1992.

Corvisier, A. *Armies and Societies in Europe, 1492–1789* (A. T. Siddall, trans.). Bloomington: Indiana University Press, 1979.

Coulam, R. F. *Illusions of Choice: The F-11 and the Problem of Weapons Acquisition Reform*. Princeton, N.J.: Princeton University Press, 1977.

Crecine, J. P. "Fiscal and Organizational Determinants of the Size and Shape of the U.S. Defense Budget." *Appendices: Commission on the Organization of the Government for the Conduct of Foreign Affairs.* Vol. 4. Washington, D.C.: U.S. Government Printing Office, 1975.

Crowley, J. J. *Program Manager's Course.* Washington, D.C.: Directorate of Science and Technology, Central Intelligence Agency, 1984.

Crozier, M. *The Bureaucratic Phenomenon.* Chicago: University of Chicago Press, 1964.

Cypher, J. M. "Military Spending, Technological Change, and Economic Growth." *Journal of Economic Issues,* 1987, *21*(1), 33–60.

Davis, V. "The Politics of Innovation: Patterns in Navy Cases." In R. G. Head and E. J. Rokke (eds.), *American Defense Policy.* (3rd ed.) Baltimore, Md.: Johns Hopkins University Press, 1973.

Dawson, R. H. "Innovation and Intervention in Defense Policy." In R. L. Peabody and N. W. Polsby (eds.), *New Perspectives on the House of Representatives.* Skokie, Ill.: Rand McNally, 1963.

Defense Finance and Accounting Service. *Implementation Plan.* Washington, D.C.: Office of the Assistant Secretary of Defense (Comptroller), Nov. 1990.

Demchak, C. C. *Military Organizations, Complex Machines: Modernization in the U.S. Armed Forces.* Ithaca, N.Y.: Cornell University Press, 1991.

Demski, J., and Feltham, G. *Cost Determination.* Ames: Iowa State University Press, 1976.

Department of the Navy. *Summary of Plans for Initial Implementation of the Defense Management Report.* Washington, D.C.: Office of the Secretary of the Navy, Oct. 1989.

Dexter, L. A. "Congressmen and the Making of Military Policy." In R. L. Peabody and N. W. Polsby (eds.), *New Perspectives on the House of Representatives.* Skokie, Ill.: Rand McNally, 1963.

Doughty, R. A. "The French Armed Forces, 1918–40." In A. R. Millett and W. Murray (eds.), *Military Effectiveness.* Vol. 2: *The Interwar Period.* Boston: Allen & Unwin, 1988.

Doyle, R., and McCaffery, J. "The Budget Enforcement Act of 1990: The Path to No Fault Budgeting." *Public Budgeting and Finance,* 1991, *11*(1), 25–40.

Drucker, P. *The Practice of Management.* New York: HarperCollins, 1953.

Drucker, P. "The Deadly Sins in Public Administration." In F. S. Lane (ed.), *Current Issues in Public Administration.* (2nd ed.) New York: St. Martin's Press, 1982.

Dunnigan, J., and Nofi, J. *Dirty Little Secrets.* New York: Morrow, 1990.

Dupuy, T. N. *A Genius for War: The German Army and the General Staff, 1807–1945.* Englewood Cliffs, N.J.: Prentice Hall, 1977.

Easterbrook, G. "The Real Lesson of the B-2: If You Want Better Weapons Systems, You Should Allow Competition to Work." *Newsweek,* Nov. 11, 1991, pp. 50–51.

Fallows, J. C. *National Defense.* New York: Random House, 1981.

Federal Property Reserve Services, General Services Administration. *How to Acquire Federal Property.* Washington, D.C.: General Services Administration, Apr. 21, 1980.

Ferris, J. M. and Graddy, E. "Production Costs, Transaction Costs, and Local Government Contractor Choice." *Economic Inquiry,* 1991, *19,* 541–554.

Field, J. L. *Facts and Figures on Defense Procurement.* Case no. 9-190-60: rev. Feb. 28, 1990. Boston: Harvard Business School, 1990.

Finer, H. "Administrative Responsibility in Democratic Government." *Public Administration Review,* 1941, *3,* 339–347.

Follett, M. P. "The Psychology of Control." In H. C. Metcalf (ed.), *Psychological Foundations of Business Administration.* New York: McGraw-Hill, 1927.

Follett, M. P. "Control as a Process." In L. Gulick and L. Urwick (eds.), *Papers on the Science of Administration.* New York: Institute of Public Administration, 1937.

Fox, J. R. *Arming America: How the U.S. Buys Weapons.* Boston: Harvard Business School Press, 1974.

Fox, J. R., with Field, J. L. *The Defense Management Challenge: Weapons Acquisition.* Boston: Harvard Business School Press, 1988.

France, S. "The Private War on Pentagon Fraud." *ABA Journal,* 1990, *76,* 46–49.

Frey, B., and Buhofer, H. "Prisoners and Property Rights." *Journal of Law and Economics,* 1988, *31*(1), 19–46.

Friedman, L. S. "Public Institutional Structure and Resource Allocation: The Analysis of Adjustment." *Research in Public Policy Analysis and Management,* 1981, *2,* 303–325.

Friedrich, C. J. "Public Policy and the Nature of Administrative Responsibility." *Public Policy,* 1940, *1,* 3–20.

Galbraith, J. R., and Nathanson, D. *Strategy Implementation: The Role of Structure and Process.* St. Paul, Minn.: West, 1978.

Gansler, J. S. *The Defense Industry.* Cambridge, Mass.: MIT Press, 1980.

Gansler, J. S. *Affording Defense.* Cambridge, Mass.: MIT Press, 1989.

General Accounting Office. *Detailed History of Real Property Owned by the United States and Used by the Department of Defense for Military Purposes Throughout the World as of September 30, 1982.* Washington, D.C.: General Accounting Office, May 1983.

General Accounting Office–Congressional Budget Office. *Analysis of the Grace Commission's Recommendations on Cost Control.* Washington, D.C.: General Accounting Office, Mar. 1984.

Gilroy, C. "The All-Volunteer Army: Fifteen Years Later." *Armed Forces and Society,* 1990, *16*(3), 329–350.

Goldberg, V. "Regulation and Administered Contracts." *Bell Journal of Economics,* 1976, 7(2), 426–448.

Goldman, F., and Brashares, E. "Performance and Accountability: Budget Reform in New Zealand." *Public Budgeting and Finance,* 1991, *11,* 75–85.

Goodman, G. W. "F-15E Simulator Designed for Complex Training." *Armed Forces Journal International,* Nov. 1988, p. 68.

Gore, A. *The Gore Report on Reinventing Government: From Red Tape to Results, Creating a Government That Works Better and Costs Less.* Report of the National Performance Review. New York: Times Books, 1993.

Gormley, W. T. *Taming the Bureaucracy: Muscles, Prayers, and Other Strategies.* Princeton, N.J.: Princeton University Press, 1989.

Gray, C. S., and Barlow, J. G. "Inexcusable Restraint: The Decline of American Military Power in the 1970s." *International Security*, 1985, *10*(2), 27–69.

Gregory, W. H. *The Defense Procurement Mess.* Lexington, Mass.: Lexington Books for the Twentieth Century Fund, 1989.

"A Guide to Better Buying." *Economist*, Oct. 18, 1986, p. 71.

Gunston, B., and Spick, M. *Modern Air Combat.* New York: Crescent Books, 1983.

Haedicke, J., and Feil, D. "In a DOD Environment Hughes Aircraft Sets the Standard for ABC." *Management Accounting*, 1991, *72*(8), 29–33.

Hahm, S.-D., Kamlet, M. S., and Mowery, D. C. "U.S. Defense Spending Under Gramm-Rudman-Hollings." *Public Administration Review*, 1992, *52*(1), 8–15.

Halperin, M. H., and Halperin, D. "The Key West Key." *Foreign Policy*, 1983–84, *53*(4), 114–130.

Hammer, M. "Reengineering Work: Don't Automate, Obliterate." *Harvard Business Review*, 1990, *68*(4), 104–112.

Hammond, P. Y. *Organizing for Defense: The American Military Establishment in the Twentieth Century.* Princeton: N.J.: Princeton University Press, 1961.

Hammond, P. Y. *Supercarriers and B-36 Bombers: Appropriations, Strategy, and Politics.* Inter-University Case Program no. 97. New York: Bobbs-Merrill, 1963.

Hammond, T. H. "Agenda Control, Organizational Structure, and Bureaucratic Politics." *American Journal of Political Science*, 1986, *30*, 379–420.

Harr, D. J. "Productive Unit Resourcing: A Business Perspective on Government Financial Management." *Government Accountants Journal*, 1989, *18*, 51–57.

Harr, D. J. "How Activity Accounting Works in Government." *Management Accounting*, 1990, *72*, 36–40.

Harr, D. J., and Godfrey, J. T. *Private Sector Financial Performance Measures and Their Applicability to Government Operations.* Montvale, N.J.: National Association of Accountants, 1991a.

Harr, D. J., and Godfrey, J. T. "The Total Unit Cost Approach to Government Financial Administration." Unpublished working paper, Department of Accounting, George Mason University, June 1991b.

Head, R. G. "Doctrinal Innovation and the A-7 Attack Aircraft Decisions." In R. G. Head and E. J. Rokke (eds.), *American Defense Policy*. (3rd ed.) Baltimore, Md.: Johns Hopkins University Press, 1973.

Hellman, H., and Wassall, G. H. "Estimating the Economic Impact of Military Base Closings: Loring Air Force Base, Maine." *New England Journal of Business and Economics*, 1982, *8*(2), 143–158.

Hemingway, A. W. "Cost Center Financial Management: Training OPTAR Managers." *Navy Comptroller*, 1993, *3*(3), 1–26.

Higgs, R. "Hard Coals Make Bad Law: Congressional Parochialism vs. National Defense." *Cato Journal*, 1990, *8*(1), 67–85.

Hirschleifer, J. "Transfer Pricing and Decentralized Decisions." In C. P. Bonini, R. Jaedicke, and H. M. Wagner (eds.), *Management Controls: New Directions for Basic Research*. New York: McGraw-Hill, 1964.

Hitch, C. J. *Decision Making for Defense*. Berkeley: University of California Press, 1965.

Hitch, C. J., and McKean, R. *The Economics of Defense in the Nuclear Age*. Cambridge, Mass.: Harvard University Press, 1960.

Hobkirk, M. *The Politics of Defense Budgeting*. Washington, D.C.: National Defense University Press, 1983.

Hofer, C., and Schendel, D. *Strategy Formulation: Analytical Concepts*. St. Paul, Minn.: West, 1976.

Hofstede, G. H. *The Game of Budget Control*. Amsterdam: Van Gorcum, 1967.

Holland, L. "Explaining Weapons Procurement: Matching Operational Performance and National Security Needs." *Armed Forces and Society*, 1993, *19*(3), 353–376.

Hone, T. "Spending Patterns of the U.S. Navy, 1921–1941." *Armed Forces and Society*, 1982, *8*(3), 86–95.

Hopwood, A. *Accounting and Human Behavior*. Englewood Cliffs, N.J.: Prentice Hall, 1976.

Horne, D. "The Impact of Soldier Quality on Army Performance." *Armed Forces and Society*, 1987, *13*(3), 43–55.

Huntington, S. E. *The Common Defense: Strategic Programs in National Politics*. New York: Columbia University Press, 1961.

Huntington, S. E. "Defense Organization and Military Strategy." *Public Interest*, 1984, *75*, 20–47.

Huzar, E. "Notes on the Unification Controversy." *Public Administration Review*, 1946, *6*(4), 297–314.

Huzar, E. "Security Without Militarism." *Public Administration Review*, 1948, *8*(4), 293–300.

Huzar, E. *The Purse and the Sword*. Ithaca, N.Y.: Cornell University Press, 1950.

Ijiri, Y. *Theory of Accounting Measurement*. Studies in Accounting Research, no. 10. Sarasota, Fla.: American Accounting Association, 1975.

Jacob, G. "The Legacy of the Pentagon: The Myth of the Peace Dividend." In A. Kirby (ed.), *The Pentagon and the Cities*. Urban Affairs Annual Reviews, no. 40. Newbury Park, Calif.: Sage, 1992.

"Japan's Defence Industry: At War with the Budget." *Economist*, Oct. 31, 1992, pp. 72–73.

John F. Kennedy School of Government. *The Multiple Launch Rocket System: On Time and Under Budget*. Report no. C16-87-773.0. Cambridge, Mass.: Case Program, John F. Kennedy School of Government, Harvard University, 1987.

Jones, L. R. "Minding the Pentagon's Business." *Government Executive*, Oct. 1992a, pp. 40–45.

Jones, L. R. "The Pentagon Squeeze." *Government Executive*, Feb. 1992b, pp. 19–28.

Jones, L. R. "Management of Budgetary Decline in the Department of Defense in Response to the End of the Cold War." *Armed Forces and Society*, 1993, *19*(4), 32–48.

Jones, L. R., and Bixler, G. C. *Mission Financing to Realign National Defense*. Greenwich, Conn.: JAI Press, 1992.

Jones, L. R., and Doyle, R. "Public Policy and Management Issues in Budgeting for Defense." *Defense Analysis*, 1992, *8*(1), 29–43.

Jones, L. R., and Thompson, F. "Taking Risks for Efficiency: The Political Economy of Uncertainty." *Academy of Management Review*, 1984, *9*(4), 746–756.

Jones, L. R., Thompson, F., and Zumeta, W. M. "The Logic of Budget Execution." *Economics of Education Review*, 1986, *6*, 44–53.

Joskow, P. "Asset Specificity and the Structure of Vertical Relationships: Empirical Evidence." *Journal of Law, Economics, and Organization,* 1988, *4*(1), 95–118.

Juola, P. "Unit Cost Resourcing: A Conceptual Framework for Financial Management." *Navy Comptroller,* 1993, *3*(3), 42–48.

Kahn, H. *On Thermonuclear War.* Princeton, N.J.: Princeton University Press, 1960.

Kaldor, M. *The Baroque Arsenal.* New York: Hill and Wang, 1981.

Kalt, J., and Zupan, M. "The Apparent Ideological Behavior of Legislators." *Journal of Law and Economics,* 1990, *33*(1), 103–132.

Kantor, A. *Defense Politics: A Budgetary Perspective.* Chicago: University of Chicago Press, 1979.

Kaufman, H. *Red Tape: Its Origins, Uses, and Abuses.* Washington, D.C.: Brookings Institution, 1972.

Kaufmann, W. W. *The McNamara Strategy.* New York: HarperCollins, 1964.

Kaufmann, W. W. *A Reasonable Defense.* Washington, D.C.: Brookings Institution, 1986.

Kaufmann, W. W. *Assessing the Base Force: How Much Is Too Much?* Washington, D.C.: Brookings Institution, 1992.

Keegan, J. *The Price of Admiralty.* New York: Penguin Books, 1988.

Kelman, S. *Procurement and Public Management: The Fear of Discretion and the Quality of Government Performance.* Washington, D.C.: AEI Press, 1990.

Kennedy, J. V. "Accrual Accounting and the President's Budget." *Budget and Economic Analysis,* 1992, *2*(3), 1–4.

Kettl, D. F. *Sharing Power: Public Governance and Private Markets.* Washington, D.C.: Brookings Institution, 1993.

Khandwalla, P. N. "Crisis Responses of Competing Versus Noncompeting Organizations." In C. Smart and W. T. Stanbury (eds.), *Studies on Crisis Management.* Montreal: Institute for Research on Public Policy, 1978.

Kinnard, D. *President Eisenhower and Strategy Management.* Lexington: University Press of Kentucky, 1977.

Kitfield, J. "Black Programs: Too Big to Hide?" *Military Forum,* 1989, *26*, 21–28.

Knott, J. H., and Miller, G. *Reforming Bureaucracy: The Politics of Institutional Choice.* Englewood Cliffs, N.J.: Prentice Hall, 1987.

Kolodziej, E. A. *The Uncommon Defense and Congress, 1945-1963.* Columbus: Ohio State University Press, 1966.

Korb, L. J. "The Budget Process in the Department of Defense, 1947-77: The Strengths and Weaknesses of Three Systems." *Public Administration Review,* 1977, *36*(4), 334-346.

Kovacic, W. E. "Blue Ribbon Defense Commissions." In R. Higgs (ed.), *Arms, Politics, and the Economy.* New York: Holmes & Meier, 1990a.

Kovacic, W. E. "The Sorcerer's Apprentice: Public Regulation of the Acquisitions Process." In R. Higgs (ed.), *Arms, Politics, and the Economy.* New York: Holmes & Meier, 1990b.

Koven, S. G. "Base Closings and the Politics-Administration Dichotomy Revisited." *Public Administration Review,* 1992, *52*(5), 526-531.

Kurth, J. "Why We Buy the Weapons We Do." *Foreign Policy,* 1973, *3*(2), 26-54.

Lamm, D. "Why Firms Refuse DOD Business." *National Contract Management Journal,* 1988, *21*, 45-55.

Landau, M. "Redundancy, Rationality, and the Problems of Duplication and Overlap." *Public Administration Review,* 1969, *29*, 346-358.

Landau, M. "On the Concept of a Self-Correcting Organization." *Public Administration Review,* 1973, *33*(6), 533-542.

Landau, M., and Stout, R. "To Manage Is Not to Control." *Public Administration Review,* 1979, *39*, 148-156.

Lerner, A. Ptachya, *The Economics of Control.* New York: Macmillan, 1944.

Levens, L. K., and Schemmer, B. "Army's $29.8-Billion LHX Competition Turns into an Absolute Horse Race." *Armed Forces Journal International,* Apr. 1991, pp. 58-59.

Lindsay, J. M. *Congress and Nuclear Weapons.* Baltimore, Md.: Johns Hopkins University Press, 1991.

Lorsch, J. W. *Organizations and Their Members: A Contingency Approach.* New York: HarperCollins, 1974.

Luttwak, E. *The Pentagon and the Art of War: The Question of Military Reform.* New York: Simon & Schuster, 1984.

Macmahon, A. W. "Congressional Oversight of Administration: The Power of the Purse." In R. L. Peabody and N. W. Polsby (eds.), *New Perspectives on the House of Representatives*. Skokie, Ill.: Rand McNally, 1963.

MacManus, S. A. "Why Businesses Are Reluctant to Sell to Governments." *Public Administration Review*, 1991, *51*(4), 328–344.

McNaugher, T. L. "Problems of Collaborative Weapons Development: The MBT-70." *Armed Forces and Society*, 1984, *10*(1), 123–145.

McNaugher, T. L. *New Weapons, Old Politics: America's Military Procurement Muddle*. Washington, D.C.: Brookings Institution, 1989.

Manchester, W. *American Caesar*. Boston: Little, Brown, 1978.

Marcus, A. A. "Responses to Externally Induced Innovation: Their Effects on Organizational Performance." *Strategic Management Journal*, 1988, *9*, 387–402.

Markusen, A., and Yudken, J. *Dismantling the Cold War Economy*. New York: Basic Books, 1992.

Marschak, T. *The Role of Project Histories in the Study of R&D*. Santa Monica, Calif.: RAND Corporation, 1965.

Marschak, T., Glennen, T. K., and Summers, R. (eds.). *Strategy for R&D: Studies in the Microeconomics of Development*. New York: Springer-Verlag, 1967.

Maser, S. M. "Transaction Costs in Public Administration." In D. Calista (ed.), *Bureaucratic and Governmental Reform*. Greenwich, Conn.: JAI Press, 1986.

Masten, S. E. "The Organization of Production." *Journal of Law and Economics*, 1984, *27*, 403–417.

Masten, S. E., Meehan, J. W., and Snyder, E. A. "The Costs of Organization." *Journal of Law, Economics, and Organization*, 1991, *7*(1), 1–25.

Mayer, A. C. "Base Closures: Law and Politics." *Armed Forces and Society*, 1982, *8*(3), 454–469.

Mayer, K. R. "Patterns of Congressional Influence in Defense Contracting." In R. Higgs (ed.), *Arms, Politics, and the Economy*. New York: Holmes & Meier, 1990.

Mayer, K. R. *The Political Economy of Defense Contracting*. New Haven, Conn.: Yale University Press, 1991.

Melman, S. "Economic Consequences of the Arms Race: The Second Rate Economy." *American Economic Review: Papers and Proceedings*, 1988, *78*(2), 55–59.

Merritt, J. N., and Sprey, P. "Negative Marginal Returns in Weapons Acquisition." In R. G. Head and E. J. Rokke (eds.), *American Defense Policy*. (3rd ed.) Baltimore, Md.: Johns Hopkins University Press, 1973.

Merton, R. *Social Theory and Social Structure*. New York: Free Press, 1957.

Messerschmidt, M. "German Military Effectiveness." In A. R. Millett and W. Murray (eds.), *Military Effectiveness*. Vol. 2: *The Interwar Period*. Boston: Allen & Unwin, 1988.

Meyers, R. T. *Pay-as-You-Go Budgeting*. Staff memorandum. Washington, D.C.: Congressional Budget Office, Mar. 1990.

"Military Bases: Not on My Toe." *Economist*, Apr. 20, 1991, p. 27.

Millis, W. *Arms and Men: A Study of American Military History*. New York: Putnam, 1956.

Minasian, J. "Land Utilization for Defense." In S. Enke (ed.), *Defense Management*. Englewood Cliffs, N.J.: Prentice Hall, 1967.

Moe, T. M. "The Politics of Bureaucratic Structure." In J. E. Chubb and P. E. Peterson (eds.), *Can the Government Govern?* Washington, D.C.: Brookings Institution, 1989.

Moe, T. M. "The Politics of Structural Choice: Toward a Theory of Public Bureaucracy." In O. E. Williamson (ed.), *Organization Theory: From Chester Barnard to the Present and Beyond*. New York: Oxford University Press, 1990.

Monteverde, K., and Teece, D. J. "Appropriable Rents and Quasi-Vertical Integration." *Journal of Law and Economics*, 1982, *25*, 403–418.

Morgan, J. "Bilateral Monopoly and the Competitive Output." *Quarterly Journal of Economics*, 1949, *63*, 370–381.

Morrison, D. C. "Pentagon's Top Secret 'Black' Budget Has Skyrocketed During Reagan Years." *National Journal*, Jan. 3, 1986, pp. 498–512.

Morrow, D. "DoD Is Preparing Presidential Report on Congress' Policy Gridlock, Due October 1." *Armed Forces Journal International*, July 1989, p. 10.

Mosher, F. C. *Program Budgeting: Theory and Practice with Par-*

ticular Reference to the U.S. Department of the Army. Chicago: Public Administration Service, 1954.

Mosher, F. C. "The Changing Responsibilities and Tactics of the Federal Government." *Public Administration Review*, 1980, *40*, 540–547.

Mowery, G. *The Republican Ascendancy*. New York: HarperCollins, 1958.

Muller, J. W. *The A-B-C of National Defense*. New York: Dutton, 1915.

Murphy, C. "Unfinished Business: Who's Holding Up Grace Commission Reform?" *Policy Review*, 1986, *12*(3), 62–66.

Murray, W. *German Military Effectiveness*. Baltimore, Md.: Nautical and Aviation Publishing Company of America, 1992.

Niskanen, W. A. "The Defense Resource Allocation Process." In S. Enke (ed.), *Defense Management*. Englewood Cliffs, N.J.: Prentice Hall, 1967.

Niskanen, W. A. *More Defense Spending for Smaller Forces: What Hath DOD Wrought?* Policy Analysis no. 110. Washington, D.C.: CATO Institute, July 29, 1988.

Noggle, B. *Teapot Dome: Oil and Politics in the 1920's*. Baton Rouge: Louisiana State University Press, 1962.

Novick, D. *Efficiency and Economy in Government Through New Budgeting and Accounting Procedures*. Report no. R-254. Santa Monica, Calif.: RAND Corporation, 1954.

Novick, D. *A New Approach to the Military Budget*. Report no. R-1759. Santa Monica, Calif.: RAND Corporation, 1956.

Office of the Assistant Secretary of Defense (Comptroller). *National Defense Budget Estimates for FY 1985*. Washington, D.C.: Office of the Secretary of Defense, Mar. 1984.

Office of the Assistant Secretary of Defense (Comptroller). *National Defense Budget Estimates for FY 1988–1989*. Washington, D.C.: Office of the Secretary of Defense, Apr. 1988.

Office of the Assistant Secretary of Defense (Comptroller). *National Defense Budget Estimates for FY 1992*. Washington, D.C: Office of the Secretary of Defense, Mar. 1991.

Office of the Assistant Secretary of Defense (Comptroller). *Implementation Plan Report: Department of Defense, Defense Business Operations Fund*. Report no. 102-311, prepared in response to requirement defined in the National Defense Authorization Act for FY 1992–93. Washington, D.C.: Office of the Secretary of Defense, Jan. 1992a.

Office of the Assistant Secretary of Defense (Comptroller). *Implementation of the Secretary of Defense's Defense Management Report to the President, Progress Report.* Washington, D.C.: Office of the Secretary of Defense, Feb. 1992b.

Office of the Assistant Secretary of Defense (Public Affairs). "Cheney Forwards Base Closing Recommendations to Commission." News release. Washington, D.C.: Apr. 12, 1991a.

Office of the Assistant Secretary of Defense (Public Affairs). *DOD News Briefing.* Washington, D.C.: Apr. 25, 1991b.

Office of Management and Budget. *Budget of the United States Government.* Washington, D.C.: Executive Office of the President, Office of Management and Budget, U.S. Government Printing Office, annual.

Office of the Secretary of Defense. *Department of Defense Justification of Estimates for Defense Management Report Initiatives.* Washington, D.C.: Office of the Secretary of Defense, Mar. 1990.

Office of the Secretary of Defense. *Base Closure and Realignment: Report.* Washington, D.C.: Office of the Secretary of Defense, Apr. 1991a.

Office of the Secretary of Defense. *Department of Defense Update of Justification of Estimates for FY 1991 Defense Management Report Initiatives.* Washington, D.C.: Office of the Secretary of Defense, Apr. 16, 1991b.

Olvey, L. D., Golden, J. R., and Kelly, R. C. *The Economics of National Security.* Wayne, N.J.: Avery, 1984.

Osborne, D., and Gaebler, T. *Reinventing Government: How the Entrepreneurial Spirit Is Transforming the Public Sector from Schoolhouse to Statehouse, City Hall to the Pentagon.* Reading, Mass.: Addison-Wesley, 1992.

Parker, T., and Lettes, T. "Is Accounting Standing in the Way of Flexible Computer-Integrated Manufacturing?" *Management Accounting,* 1991, 72(7), 34–38.

Parkinson, C. N. *Parkinson's Law, and Other Studies in Administration.* Boston: Houghton Mifflin, 1957.

Peltzman, S. "Constituent Interest and Congressional Voting." *Journal of Law and Economics,* 1984, *27*(1), 181-210.

Peltzman, S. "How Efficient Is the Voting Market?" *Journal of Law and Economics,* 1990, *33*(1), 27-63.

Perrow, C. A. "The Bureaucratic Paradox: The Efficient Organization Centralizes in Order to Decentralize," Organization Dynamics, Spring 1977, pp. 3-14.

Peters, R. "The Age of Fatal Visibility." *Military Review,* 1988, *68*(8), 50-54.

Peters, T. J., and Waterman, R. H. *In Search of Excellence: Lessons from America's Best-Run Companies.* New York: HarperCollins, 1982.

Phaup, M. *Some Conceptual Elements of Federal Budget Accounting: The Inconsistency of Budgeting and Depreciation.* Washington, D.C.: Congressional Budget Office, Mar. 6, 1990.

Phelps, C. *Is Offshore Procurement Such a Bad Thing?* Santa Monica, Calif.: RAND Corporation, 1983.

Pilling, D. L. *Competition in Procurement.* Washington, D.C.: Brookings Institution, 1989.

Pitsvada, B. T. "Flexibility in Federal Budget Execution." *Public Budgeting and Finance,* 1983, *3*, 17-26.

President's Committee on Administrative Management. *Report of the President's Committee on Administrative Management in the Government of the United States.* Washington, D.C.: U.S. Government Printing Office, 1937.

President's Private Sector Survey on Cost Control [Grace Commission]. *Task Force Report on the Office of the Secretary of Defense.* Arlington,Va.: President's Private Sector Survey on Cost Control, July 13, 1983.

Quinn-Judge, P. "Defense Experts Disappointed with Aspin." *Boston Globe,* Oct. 11, 1993, p. 4.

Radice, M. R. *The Defense Enterprise Program: A Managerial Assessment.* Unpublished M.S. Thesis, Naval Postgraduate School, Monterey, Calif., 1992.

Raffish, N. "How Much Does That Product Really Co$t? Finding Out May Be as Easy as ABC." *Management Accounting,* 1991, *72*(9), 36-39.

Redburn, F. S. "How Should the Government Measure Spending?

The Uses of Accrual Accounting." *Public Administration Review*, 1993, *53*(2), 213–221.

Rich, M., and Dews, E. *Improving the Military Acquisition Process: Lessons from RAND Research*. Report no. R-3373-AF/RC. Santa Monica, Calif.: RAND Corporation, 1986.

Ries, J. C. *The Management of Defense: Organization and Control of the U.S. Armed Services*. Baltimore, Md.: Johns Hopkins University Press, 1964.

Robyn, D. *Braking the Special Interests: Trucking Deregulation and the Politics of Reform*. Chicago: University of Chicago Press, 1987.

Roll, C. R. *Capital and Labor Shares in the Department of Defense*. Santa Monica, Calif.: RAND Corporation, 1978.

Roos, J. G. "Archive Would Bare Acquisitions Decisions." *Armed Forces Journal International*, June 1992, p. 4.

Roos, J. G., and Schemmer, B. F. "Revolution in NATO's Conventional Defense Looms from 'Competitive Strategies' Initiative." *Armed Forces Journal International*, Oct. 1988, pp. 114–121.

Roos, J. G., and Schemmer, B. F. "Desert Storm Bares 'Roundout' Flaw But Validates Army Modernization Goals." *Armed Forces Journal International*, Apr. 1991, p. 35.

Ropelewski, R. R. "Simulation Advances Permit New Training Opportunities." *Armed Forces Journal International*, Nov. 1988, p. 64.

Ropelewski, R. R. "Congress Stirs Pot, Air Force Simmers as Close Air Support Decision Nears." *Armed Forces Journal International*, Feb. 1990, pp. 22, 24.

Schemmer, B. F. "Panama and Just Cause: The Rebirth of Professional Soldiering." *Armed Forces Journal International*, Feb. 1990, p. 5.

Schick, A. "Control Patterns in State Budget Execution." *Public Administration Review*, 1964, *24*(2), 97–106.

Schick, A. "Congress and the Details of Administration." *Public Administration Review*, 1976, *36*(6), 516–528.

Schick, A. "Contemporary Problems in Financial Control." *Public Administration Review*, 1978, *38*(6), 513–519.

Schick, A. "Budgeting for Results: Recent Developments in Five

Industrialized Countries." *Public Administration Review*, 1990, *50*(1), 16–33.

Schlesinger, J. R. "The Changing Environment for Systems Analysis." In S. Enke (ed.), *Defense Management*. Englewood Cliffs, N.J.: Prentice Hall, 1967.

Schlesinger, J. R. "Systems Analysis and the Political Process." In F. S. Lane (ed.), *Current Issues in Public Administration*. (2nd ed.) New York: St. Martin's Press, 1982.

Scott, G., Bushnell, P., and Sallee, N. "Reform of the Core Public Sector: The New Zealand Experience." *Public Sector*, 1990, *13*(3), 11–24.

Scribner, B. L. "Are Smarter Tankers Better?" *Armed Forces and Society*, 1986, *12*(2), 193–206.

Seligman, D. "McNamara's Management Revolution." *Fortune*, 1965, *72*(1), 117–121, 244, 246, 248.

Shaw, G. B. *The Road to Equality*. Boston: Beacon Press, 1965.

Shiner, H. "The Air Force, the Navy, and Coast Defense: 1919–1941." *Military Affairs*, Oct. 1981, pp. 46–61.

Shycoff, D. B. *Unit Cost Resourcing Guidance*. Washington, D.C.: Office of the Assistant Secretary of Defense (Comptroller), Oct. 15, 1990.

"Slimming the General." *Economist*, Jan. 16, 1993, pp. 63–64.

Smellie, K. B. *Great Britain Since 1688*. Ann Arbor: University of Michigan Press, 1962.

Smelser, M. *The Congress Founds the Navy*. South Bend, Ind.: University of Notre Dame Press, 1959.

Smith, B.L.R. "Strategic Expertise and National Security Policy: A Case Study." *Public Policy*, 1964, *13*, 69–106.

Smith, D. "The Roots and Future of Modern-Day Military Reform." *Air University Review*, 1985, *16*(3), 33–40.

Smith, G. K., and others. *A Preliminary Perspective on Regulatory Activities and Effects in Weapons Acquisition*. Report no. R-3578-ACQ. Santa Monica, Calif.: RAND Corporation, Mar. 1988.

Smith, J. B., and Beck, M. E. "Representing Government Contractors Accused of Misconduct." *California Lawyer*, 1987, *7*(5), 55–58.

Smithies, A. *The Budgetary Process in the United States*. New York: McGraw-Hill, 1955.

"Software Engineering: Made to Measure." *Economist,* Jan. 23, 1993, p. 79.

Spector, R. *The Eagle Against the Sun.* New York: Free Press, 1984.

Spulber, N., and Horowitz, I. *Quantitative Economic Policy and Planning: Theory and Models of Economic Control.* New York: Norton, 1976.

Stalk, G., and Hout, T. M. *Competing Against Time: How Time-Based Competition Is Reshaping Global Markets.* New York: Free Press, 1990.

Stark, R., and Varley, T. "Bidding, Estimating, and Engineered Construction Contracting." In R. Engelbrecht-Wiggans, Martin Shubik, Robert M. Stark (eds.), *Auctions, Bidding, and Contracting.* New York: New York University Press, 1983.

Stedry, A. *Budget Control and Cost Behavior.* Englewood Cliffs, N.J.: Prentice Hall, 1960.

Stockfisch, J. A. *Plowshares into Swords.* New York: Mason and Lipscomb, 1973.

Stubbing, R. A., with Mendel, R. A. *The Defense Game.* New York: HarperCollins, 1986.

Swales, D. "The M-1 Tank." In F. Hampson (ed.), *Unguided Missiles: How America Buys Its Weapons.* New York: Norton, 1989.

Takeuchi, H., and Nonaka, I. "The New *New* Product Development Game." In *Managing Projects and Programs.* Boston: Harvard Business School Press, 1989.

Thompson, F. "American Legislative Decision Making and the Size Principle." *American Political Science Review,* 1979, *73*(4), 1100–1108.

Thompson, F. "Using Per-Unit Subsidies to Help Balance Budgets." *Journal of Policy Analysis and Management,* 1984, *4*(1), 72–76.

Thompson, F. "Reducing Barriers to Trade in Nontraded Goods and Services." *Canadian-American Law Journal,* 1985, *10*(2), 35–48.

Thompson, F. "Lumpy Goods and Cheap Riders." *Journal of Public Policy,* 1987, *7*(3), 427–445.

Thompson, F. "Management Control and the Pentagon: The Strategy-Structure Mismatch." *Public Administration Review,* 1991, *51*, 52–66.

Thompson, F., and Zumeta, W. M. "Control and Controls: A Reexamination of Control Patterns in Budget Execution." *Policy Sciences,* 1981, *13,* 25–50.

Thompson, J. D. *Organizations in Action.* New York: McGraw-Hill, 1967.

Thompson, M. "Stealth Law." *California Lawyer,* 1988, *8*(10), 33–37, 121.

Turcotte, W. A. "Control Systems, Performance, and Satisfaction in Two State Agencies." *Administrative Sciences Quarterly,* 1974, *19,* 60–73.

Twight, C. "Institutional Underpinning of Parochialism: The Case of Military Base Closures." *Cato Journal,* 1989, *9*(1), 74–101.

Twight, C. "Department of Defense Attempts to Close Military Bases: The Political Economy of Congressional Resistance." In R. Higgs (ed.), *Arms, Politics, and the Economy.* New York: Holmes & Meier, 1990.

Tyler, T. R. *Why People Obey the Law.* New Haven, Conn.: Yale University Press, 1990.

U.S. Department of Commerce. *Fixed Reproducible Tangible Wealth in the United States, 1925–85.* Washington, D.C.: U.S. Government Printing Office, June 1987.

U.S. Office of Technology Assessment. *Computerized Manufacturing Automation: Employment, Education, and the Workplace.* Washington, D.C.: U.S. Government Printing Office, 1984.

Vancil, R. *Decentralization: Management Ambiguity by Design.* Homewood, Ill.: Dow Jones–Irwin, 1979.

Van Creveld, M. *Fighting Power: German and U.S. Army Performance, 1939–1945.* Westport, Conn.: Greenwood Press, 1982.

Van Creveld, M. *Command in War.* Cambridge, Mass.: Harvard University Press, 1985.

Vining, A. R., and Weimer, D. "Government Supply and Government Production Failure: A Framework Based on Contestability." *Journal of Public Policy,* 1990, *10,* 54–90.

Wakefield, J. C., and Zoemer, R. C. "Federal Fiscal Programs." *Survey of Current Business,* 1984, *64,* pp. 29–35.

Ward, M. D. "Differential Paths to Parity: A Study of the Contemporary Arms Race." *American Political Science Review,* 1984, *78*(1), 297–311.

Weidenbaum, M. *Small Wars, Big Defense: Paying for the Military After the Cold War.* New York: Oxford University Press, 1992.

Weidenbaum, M., and DeFina, R. *The Cost of Federal Government Regulation of Economic Activity.* Washington, D.C.: American Enterprise Institute, 1978.

Weigley, R. *The American Way of War.* New York: Macmillan, 1983.

Wildavsky, A. *The Politics of the Budgetary Process.* Boston: Little, Brown, 1966a.

Wildavsky, A. "Toward a Radical Incrementalism." In A. De Grazia (ed.), *Congress: The First Branch of Government.* Washington, D.C.: American Enterprise Institute, 1966b.

Wildavsky, A. *The New Politics of the Budgetary Process.* Glenview Ill.: Scott, Foresman, 1988.

Wildavsky, A., and Hammond, A. "Comprehensive vs. Incremental Budgeting in the Department of Agriculture." *Administrative Sciences Quarterly,* 1965, *10,* 321-346.

Williamson, O. E. *The Economic Institutions of Capitalism.* New York: Free Press, 1985.

Wilson, J. Q. *Bureaucracy.* New York: Basic Books, 1989.

Wirls, D. *Buildup: The Politics of Defense in the Reagan Era.* Ithaca, N.Y.: Cornell University Press, 1992.

Yanarella, M. *The Missile Defense Controversy.* New York: Columbia University Press, 1969.

Zald, M. N. "Decentralization—Myth vs. Reality." *Personnel,* 1964, *41,* 19-26.

Zaloga, S. F. "Soviet Tank Development Revealed." *Armed Forces Journal International,* Dec. 1990, p. 24.

Name Index

Subject Index